HONECKER

HONECKER
and the New Politics of Europe

HEINZ LIPPMANN

Translated by Helen Sebba

The Macmillan Company · New York, New York

The Macmillan Company
866 Third Avenue, New York, N.Y. 10022
Collier-Macmillan Canada Ltd.,
Toronto, Ontario

Honecker and the New Politics of Europe was originally published in German by Verlag Wissenschaft und Politik under the title *Honecker: Porträt eines Nachfolgers* and this translation is published by permission.

Library of Congress Catalog Card Number: 72–83764

First Printing

Printed in the United States of America

Contents

ABBREVIATIONS USED IN THIS BOOK   ix

INTRODUCTION   xi

I. CHILDHOOD AND YOUTH

1. *Home and Childhood*   3

    SOCIAL AND POLITICAL CONDITIONS IN THE SAAR

    THE FAMILY

    CHILDHOOD IMPRESSIONS

    "REVOLUTION'S FUN"

    UNDER FRENCH OCCUPATION

    TEN YEARS OLD

    GROWTH OF THE KPD

    THE HUNDRED-DAY STRIKE

2. *The Young Communist*   17

    THE STALINIZATION PERIOD

    HONECKER THE ACTIVIST

    THE SPREAD OF COMMUNISM

    VISIT TO MOSCOW

    "AGITPROP"

    UNDERGROUND

3. *Imprisonment and Escape*   31

    A PRISONER AT BRANDENBURG-GÖRDEN

    WORK ON THE OUTSIDE AND ESCAPE

    FREEDOM IN HIDING

    A GAP IN HONECKER'S LIFE STORY

II. A PARTNER IN POWER

4. *On the Way Up*   41

    HONECKER BUILDS HIS OWN EMPIRE

    PIONEER CADRE WORK

    THE CENTRAL YOUTH COMMITTEE

    CONTROVERSIAL NONPARTISANSHIP

    PERSONNEL PROBLEMS

    PARTY DISCIPLINE AND MEMBERS OF THE HITLER YOUTH

5. *The Founding and Debut of the FDJ*   58

    THE ROAD TO UNITY

    PAUL VERNER IS OUTMANEUVERED

    THE FIRST FDJ CONGRESS

    FIGHT OVER THE STATUTES

6. *Building a Cadre Apparatus*   74

    TACTICAL DIFFICULTIES AND SUCCESSES

    UNITED YOUTH—UNITED GERMANY

    SECOND CONGRESS: MEISSEN, 1947

    PEACE FLIGHT TO THE EAST

    INTERNATIONAL ENDEAVORS

    THE ALL-GERMAN CONFERENCE

7. *The "New-Type" FDJ*   97

    WITHDRAWAL OF THE BOURGEOIS REPRESENTATIVES

    NO COMPETITION TOLERATED

    STRIVING FOR MONOPOLY

    "THE SAAR IS GERMAN"

8. *The FDJ and the Founding of the DDR*   109

    THE PLEDGE OF GERMAN YOUTH

WORKING STYLE AND STRUGGLES FOR POWER

THE "ALL-GERMANY" MEETING OF THE FDJ

SPONTANEITY AND "PUTSCHIST" TENDENCIES

STALIN'S TELEGRAM

9. *At the Power Center*   122

ULBRICHT'S AIDE

NATIONALIST EUPHORIA

THE WORLD FESTIVAL OF YOUTH IN BERLIN

10. *Honecker and the Building of Socialism*   132

SIGNS OF CRISIS

THE MILITARIZATION OF THE FDJ

DISTRUST IN THE POLITBURO

"SERVICE FOR GERMANY"

HONECKER AND THE SEVENTEENTH OF JUNE, 1953

THE ALL-GERMAN ELECTION SCARE

DECLINE AND PREPARATION FOR NEW TASKS

III. A FUNCTIONARY IN THE APPARATUS

11. *Preparation and Practice*   171

TRAINING IN MOSCOW

RETURN TO BERLIN

CONFLICT WITH THE SCHIRDEWAN GROUP

12. *From the Fifth Party Congress to the Building of the Wall*   182

MEMBER OF THE POLITBURO

HONECKER AND THE PEOPLE'S ARMY

MASTER-BUILDER OF THE "ANTI-FASCIST PROTECTIVE WALL"

13. *The Party Organizer*   190

ECONOMIC TASKS IN THE FOREGROUND

THE SIXTH CONGRESS

SIGNS OF LIBERALIZATION

HONECKER SLOWS DOWN THE LIBERALIZATION TREND

THE ELEVENTH SESSION OF THE CENTRAL COMMITTEE

(DECEMBER 15–18, 1965)

ALL-GERMAN ACTIVITY AND THE SEVENTH PARTY CONGRESS
(1966–67)

14. *The Great Test (1967–68)*   203
    DDR—SELF-CONFIDENT PARTNER
    HONECKER AND THE CZECH CRISIS
    ERFURT AND KASSEL
    THE CHANGE OF LEADERSHIP

15. *Leader of the Party*   217
    WHY HONECKER BECAME ULBRICHT'S SUCCESSOR
    THE TIMING OF THE CHANGE OF LEADERSHIP
    THE TEAM
    WORKING STYLE AND NEW DEPARTURES
    HONECKER'S STRENGTHS AND WEAKNESSES AS PARTY LEADER

APPENDIX

Extracts from the Verdict of the People's Court   241
against Erich Honecker

NOTES   253

INDEX   269

Abbreviations

BDM   *Bund Deutscher Mädchen*
League of German Girls

CDU   *Christlich-Demokratische Union*
Christian Democratic Union

CPSU   Communist Party of the Soviet Union

CSU   *Christlich-Soziale Union*
Christian Social Union

DDR   *Deutsche Demokratische Republik*
German Democratic Republic

EVD   *Europäische Verteidigungsgemeinschaft*
European Defense Community

FDGB   *Freier Deutscher Gewerkschaftsbund*
Free German Trade Union Federation

FDJ   *Freie Deutsche Jugend*
Free German Youth

KJI   *Kommunistische Jugendinternationale*
Communist Youth International

KJVD   *Kommunistischer Jugendverband Deutschlands*
Communist League of German Youth

KPD   *Kommunistische Partei Deutschlands*
Communist Party of Germany

KVP   *Kasernierte Volkspolizei*
"Police in Barracks"—paramilitary police

LDP   *Liberal-Demokratische Partei [Deutschlands]*
Liberal Democratic Party of Germany

MVD   *Ministerstvo Vnutrennikh Del*
Ministry of State Security of the Soviet Union (Secret Police)

NKVD   *Narodnii Kommissariat Vnutrennikh Del*
       People's Commissariat of Internal Affairs (the MVD before 1946)

NSDAP *Nationalsozialistische Deutsche Arbeiterpartei*
       National Socialist (Nazi) Party of Germany

NVA   *Nationale Volksarmee*
       National People's Army

SAP   *Sozialistische Arbeiterpartei Deutschlands*
       Socialist Workers' Party of Germany

SED   *Sozialistische Einheitspartei Deutschlands*
       Socialist Unity Party of Germany

SMAD   *Sowjetische Militäradministration in Deutschland*
       Soviet Military Administration of Germany

SPD   *Sozialdemokratische Partei Deutschlands*
       Social Democratic Party of Germany

SS   *Schutzstaffel*
       Storm Troopers

USPD   *Unabhängige Sozialistische Partei Deutschlands*
       Independent Socialist Party of Germany

VEB   *Volkseigener Betrieb*
       People's Enterprise

WBDJ   *Weltbund der Demokratischen Jugend*
       World Federation of Democratic Youth

ZPKK   *Zentrale Parteikontrollkommission*
       Central Party Control Commission

Introduction

THE BIOGRAPHY OF a prominent politician is not usually written within a few months of his coming to power. This is as true in the German Democratic Republic (DDR) as anywhere else. Friends of mine who asked booksellers and publishers in East Berlin whether a biography of Erich Honecker could be expected in the near future were always told that it was still much too soon, and that in any case Honecker himself, a very modest man, did not want a biography because he was opposed to any kind of personality cult.

Yet in spite of this I decided to write a biographical portrait of Honecker. There were several reasons for my decision. First, I believe that public opinion in West Germany and Western Europe as a whole should be fully informed about political and social developments in East Germany. This requires a thorough knowledge of the decision-makers: their background, interests, beliefs, concerns, and problems. Whether we like it or not, the DDR is one of the world's ten modern industrial nations. The West German policy of détente and orderly coexistence between the two German republics, which by no means precludes ideological controversy, demands balanced, factual information about the other Germany based on research into primary sources.

Erich Honecker has lived under three different regimes (not counting his five childhood years in imperial Germany): the Weimar Republic; Nazi Germany; and the Soviet Zone of Occupation, which later became the DDR. His political consciousness was shaped by parties and organizations which, while sharing a common ideological basis, have all followed their own historical course. This book will outline Erich Honecker's life. It is not a history of the Communist League of German Youth or the Free German Youth Party or the German Communist-Socialist Unity Party—or of the DDR. Nevertheless, Honecker's actions cannot be fully understood without a knowledge of his social and political background.

I had the opportunity of collaborating closely with Erich Honecker between 1946 and 1953. From 1946 until the third Free German Youth congress I was secretary of the party's state branch in Thuringia and in this capacity worked closely with the Central Council in Berlin. From 1949 until late 1953 I was a secretary of the Central Council, first as head of the department for Western affairs, later as second secretary and deputy to Honecker. But this political collaboration and the personal contact it involved have been no more than a helpful supplement in evaluating the biographical data and events of Honecker's life. Anyone hoping for sensational revelations about his private life will be disappointed. Before undertaking this "portrait of a successor," I set out to analyze all the available primary sources and documents and to question eyewitnesses. My task was made more difficult by the fact that often the only available source was published material. My book therefore does not claim to be definitive. Without the help I received from many different quarters it would not have been possible at all.

I owe especial thanks to the East German Anti-Fascist Resistance Committee, which on Honecker's instructions answered all queries submitted by my publishers and supplied important documents. This seems to indicate a change in the DDR's policy toward the news media.

I am also deeply indebted to the Archiv für Gesamtdeutsche Frage and particularly to its director, Dr. Werner Lambach; to the archives of the Gesamtdeutches Institut in West Berlin and its director, Herr Buch; to the university libraries of Cologne and Saarbrücken; to Frau Ilse Spittmann, Frau Gisela Helwig and Frau Irmgard Schaad, and to Frau Inge Bialek, widow of Robert Bialek, an official of the Free German Youth and an inspector in the People's Police. The detailed records kept by Robert Bialek and turned over to me by his wife have given me many important insights into Honecker.

I. Childhood and Youth

1. Home and Childhood

Social and Political Conditions in the Saar

IN MAY, 1971, when Erich Honecker became chairman of the SED, the national Socialist Unity Party of the DDR, little was known of him beyond the fact that he was a German Communist who would decisively influence the future of a country which is one of the world's leading industrial powers, although its international status as an independent nation is still challenged in the West. This book will investigate the formative forces that have made this man what he is today.

Erich Honecker was born in Neunkirchen in the Saar on August 25, 1912. Although most Germans did not realize it and those in power consciously or unconsciously chose to ignore it, the great clash predicted by Karl Marx in the *Communist Manifesto* of 1848 was already under way: "We speak of ideas that revolutionize a whole society. This is just another way of saying that within the old society the elements of a new one have already emerged, but the breakdown of the old ideas goes hand in hand with the breakdown of the old way of life."[1]

What was true of Europe in the first decade of the twentieth century—and the Russian revolution was an opening signal—was also true of Erich Honecker's homeland, the Saar, where industrial magnates like Baron Karl Friedrich von Stumm wielded such tyrannical power[2] that the region was commonly referred to as "the Kingdom of Stumm."[3] The mines were run in an authoritarian way; there was practically no provision for the review

3

of grievances. In 1913 the average day shift wage—Honecker's father was a miner—was still about 4.90 marks a day.[4] Beef or pork cost 1.40 a kilo, butter 2.40—almost half a day's pay.[5]

The miners were heavily fined for minor infractions. There was a penalty of one or two marks for returning to the cage five minutes early, which meant that nearly half a man's wages might be withheld for that alone.[6] And since most miners had a lot of children and their own parents usually lived with them, those wages often had to support a family of ten. This was the case in Honecker's family, where the household consisted of six children, their parents, and both grandparents.

During the period of rapid industrial expansion after the war of 1870–71, the Ruhr was a melting pot in which a heterogeneous labor force drawn from all the German provinces as well as foreign countries (notably Poland) was fused into an industrial proletariat. In the Saar, however, the miners came chiefly from the farms and often continued to work on the land in their spare time, living in rural communities rather than in huge tenements in dirty industrial towns. In 1905 the Saar mineworkers were distributed among 654 different communities.[7]

The Family

This was the background of the Honecker family. The father, Wilhelm Honecker, was born in the village of Wiebelskirchen on March 8, 1881. On December 9, 1905, he married Karoline Weidenhof, daughter of a metalworker in the Stumm factory, in her native village of Neunkirchen, not far from Wiebelskirchen. A year after the birth of their third child, Erich, Wilhelm Honecker bought a house in Wiebelskirchen (at 88 Neunkircher Strasse), where Erich and his three sisters and two brothers grew up. Erich's eldest sister, Katharina Honecker, born February 19, 1906, died of tuberculosis on December 29, 1925. Her death was directly attributable to the World War I famine and the inadequate medical care then available to working-class families.[8] Gertrud Honecker, now Gertrud Hoppstädter, born March 8, 1917, still lives in the family house in Wiebelskirchen.

Erich Honecker's brothers, Wilhelm, born September 22, 1907, and Karl-Robert, born February 12, 1923, are both dead. Wilhelm, a driver in the Nazi army, was killed on April 21, 1944, during the retreat from Romania.[9] Karl-Robert died on October 30, 1947, as a result of mistreatment suffered as a British prisoner-of-war in Egypt. He is reported to have spent several years lying under the open sky in a prisoner-of-war camp in the desert, without medical care of any kind.[10] Erich's mother died on April 22, 1963; his father on December 4, 1969.[11]

After World War I Wilhelm Honecker was a member of the Wiebelskirchen-Saar branch of the KPD, the German Communist Party, and served on the local executive committee. He was also a KPD member of the Wiebelskirchen municipal council. He worked at the Dechen pit until his retirement and served as an elected union representative.[12] As a young man he worked at the Kohl-wald pit (now shut down), where he was also a union representative and a member of the works council. In those days this called for courage and endurance, because any move toward the formation of a socialist party was rigorously suppressed by order of Karl Friedrich von Stumm. In 1877, even before the first national organization of labor unions was founded, a "Committee to Combat Social Democracy" was set up to represent all employers, including the national board of mines. Pro-socialist workers, or those suspected of being pro-socialist, were dismissed and never rehired in the Saar.[13] Members of the independent unions were treated in the same way, since management was as vigorously opposed to the unions as to socialism.

Union member Wilhelm Honecker played an active part in the Saar miners' strike of 1912–13. The strike, however, was unsuccessful because the powerful Catholic unions refused to participate—and in fact made strong propaganda against it.[14] To quote the *Kölnische Volkszeitung:* "Since the outbreak of the strike the conflict between the labor organizations in the Saar has flared up violently."[15] Even in those days Honecker's birthplace was known as a "red village," because in the Reichstag elections of 1912 the socialist candidate received the most votes.[16]

Childhood Impressions

Erich Honecker was born shortly before the outbreak of World War I among the soot-blackened walls of Neunkirchen in the Saar, an industrial town in the district of Ottweiler which, according to a local guidebook, "is anything but beautiful in the traditional sense of the word."[17] The dominant impressions of his childhood were hunger and revolution.

Before he was three, Germany had introduced food rationing; the first bread cards were issued on January 15, 1915.[18] Often, however, the cards were not honored. As Erich Honecker recalled after 1945, his mother frequently went hungry so that there might be a little more for his father and the children. The long hours his mother spent standing in line for food and her complaints about unbearable hardships left as deep a mark on Erich as talk within the family or with his father's fellow workers about the injustice of the mining bureaucracy which padded the payrolls with "dummy workers" who ran errands for the foreman, dug his potatoes, went out into the country black-marketing for him, yet still drew their share of the shift's pay—which ultimately came out of their fellow workers' pockets. There were also endless conversations with neighbors about the unfair distribution of food and the high black market prices, which the "high-ups" could afford but not the ordinary workingman.

After the war came talk of a different kind with comrades from the social-democratically oriented Independent Union to which Wilhelm Honecker belonged: discussion of the senselessness of war and of what would come next. Erich Honecker recalls that he first heard the names of Rosa Luxemburg and Karl Liebknecht soon after he started to school. In a private conversation during a rally held in January, 1950, to commemorate the anniversary of their murder, he said that he clearly remembers "coming into our living room—sneaking in really—because I was curious about the important matter my father was discussing with some of his fellow workers. He had told us that he didn't want to be disturbed. They were talking excitedly, so they didn't notice me. In front of them was a printed paper of some kind, and my father was reading from it. He told me later that it was a leaflet of Rosa Luxemburg's on the 'Crisis of Social Democracy.' Of course I didn't know anything about that at the time and couldn't have understood it anyhow, but the names Rosa and Karl and the constant repetition of the words 'Lenin' and 'revolution' had an unforgettable impact. Next day I asked my father: 'What does that mean—*Lenin* and *revolution*?' He looked at me in astonishment and tried to explain. I think what he said was: 'The workers in Russia—that's a country a long way off—have made a revolution.'

And when I still didn't understand, he took me by the hand and we went into the kitchen, where my mother was making soup. 'Look,' he said. 'You know we don't have much to eat, and things are hard for your mother. But other people—people I'm forced to work for—live on what I produce.' He pointed through the window. 'You see that apple tree. Suppose I climb up and pick the apples, and someone is standing there watching me. And when I've picked them all, he gives me a few and keeps the whole basketful for himself. They've changed all that in Russia. Now everybody gets what he earns. He can keep the apples he picks. They're for peace, too. And the coal mines don't belong just to a handful of people but to everybody who works in them. Lenin did all that. And Rosa and Karl want to do it here in Germany.' I remember it as if it happened yesterday—and I remember that when the German revolution came I asked my mother if we would now be allowed to keep all the apples."

"Revolution's Fun"

The Honecker household was a lively one in those days. Erich remembers that his father, who had served in the Imperial Navy at Kiel and Wilhelmshaven and toward the end of the war as a marine in Flanders, used to be out late nearly every night; otherwise he would bring friends home with him to talk into the early hours.[19] Erich found this very exciting because of the secrecy. Wilhelm Honecker belonged to the SPD, the Social Democratic Party of Germany, and to the Independent Union, and his house was a meeting place for members of both. One of these occasional visitors was Hermann Petri, union secretary for the so-called *Alter Verband* (Old Association) companies. After the collapse of the German empire, Petri served on the Neunkirchen Council of Workers and Soldiers[20] and, like Wilhelm Honecker, joined the SPD.

The aim of the Council was not to gain political and economic control of the Saar through the working class but simply to liberate the Saarlanders from the "patriarchal system" and give them the right of "democratic self-determination."[21] The Council was far from radical. Its members included a secretary of the Hirsch-Duncker unions, an ophthalmologist, a teacher, a businessman, a lawyer, and a judge.[22] At the age of six Erich did not of course understand the discussions that went on at home. Later his father told him that many of the Neunkirchen Social Democrats were very dissatisfied with the composition and performance of the Council of Workers and Soldiers and accused it of too much talk and too little action.

These childhood impressions certainly influenced Erich Honecker's attitude to power and may have strengthened his militant tendencies. In talking about this period in later years he constantly drew parallels with the situation in 1945–46 and with the merger of the Communist and Social Democratic parties in the SED. In discussions with opponents of the KPD's popular-front policy calling for the immediate establishment of socialism, he would regularly refer to the post-World War I period and to the Neunkirchen Council of Workers and Soldiers. His view, which he says he adopted from his father while he was still a child, is briefly that the mistake was not that they sought the collaboration of the bourgeois liberals but that "we failed to seize control right at the start and take over strategic power positions. That should be a lesson to us today." At that time, he says, the SPD had not clearly formulated its own aims. Basically, he thinks things have not changed much. Neither the bureaucracy nor the industrialists have been deprived of power. The Stumm company, for instance, survived both world wars. The Council's function was really no more than window-dressing. It was an impotent "bunch of generals without armies."

Under French Occupation

The Saar Council of Workers and Soldiers was short-lived. It was dissolved by the French occupation authorities on November 24, 1918, and the mines of the Saar were ceded to France.[23]

Erich Honecker was about to begin the third grade when the Saar mineworkers called their first postwar strike, demanding higher wages and an eight-hour day. The strike lasted from March 26 to April 10, 1919,[24] when the French military authorities ordered the resumption of work because maintenance of the mines was being endangered. When some miners refused to comply with the order, the French began to arrest strikers. Some four hundred miners, including fifty from the district of Ottweiler, where the Honeckers lived, were deported across the Rhine by trainloads. But the strike did achieve something. On April 12, 1919, the French military authorities announced that they were prepared to introduce the eight-hour day.[25]

Erich later proudly recalled, young as he was, helping his father to distribute leaflets. When he came home from school, his father would often send him off to deliver messages or invitations to fellow workers. On one of these errands he once had to watch French soldiers arresting a friend of his father's. Miners' children in those days had a remarkable sense of solidarity. Erich remembers that his mother would often put extra sandwiches in his school lunch so that he could share with children whose fathers had been deported by the French.

The terms of the Saar Statute drastically affected the lives of the Saarlanders. Although their rights and democratic freedoms were unconditionally guaranteed, and although the promise of a free plebiscite after fifteen years of occupation apparently assured their right to self-determination, most of the Saarlanders, whatever their political views, felt that they had been surrendered to the occupying power. Signs of passive resistance were to be seen everywhere—even in the schools. Erich remembers schoolmates of his taunting other boys as "Frog-lovers" because their parents had been unable to resist the tempting offers of the occupying power. Actually, the miners were better off than most other workers because they were paid in francs at a favorable rate of exchange. Erich remembers regular class warfare between miners' sons and boys whose fathers were harder hit by the manipulation of currency.

He says that even then he realized that management will always try to play off one group of workers against another, to split them in order to make them easier to control, and that the only effective means of fighting this is working-class unity. While the abstract formulation probably stems from later training, these childhood experiences must certainly have helped to make him receptive to the idea.

In the early 1920s a confrontation between the bourgeois parties and those of the left, the KPD and the Independent Socialist Party (USPD), was imminent. Wilhelm Honecker had been a member of the USPD since the end of the war.[26] Although in 1920 the Honecker household had been as anti-French as the rest of the Saarlanders, a year later it had reversed its position. Now the enemy was not the French but the bourgeois parties, the "old masters of the Saar" who, with the support of the German rightist militants, were determined to recapture their former positions of power.

The Communists—Erich's father had been a KPD member since 1919—remained aloof from the revival of nationalism of the early 1920s. When the first Saar delegation went to Geneva in September, 1921, the Communists and Independent Socialists denounced the League of Nations as a capitalist, nationalistic body and organized protest meetings. In a memorandum submitted to the League in December, 1921, the USPD, the KPD, and a number of union leaders stated that they had upheld the Treaty of Versailles from the outset and repudiated all radical opposition to it inspired by nationalistic motives. They therefore accepted (despite some reservations) the World Court's rulings establishing French administration of the mines and its definition of Saar residency. For economic reasons they also supported the introduction of the French franc.[27]

Young Erich Honecker, alert to all that was going on around him, was caught between two worlds. His dearest wish at that time was to join the Young Pioneers. His father would tell him: "What they're doing down there at Saarbrücken is no concern of ours. We Saarland proletarians are fed up with nationalistic talk. The new money [the franc] helps your mother keep the pot boiling. One side's no better than the other, but it may not be a bad thing that we belong to France now. After all, our French brothers and comrades have the same interests we do. And I'd rather have a French worker any day than Herr Stumm or Herr Röchling. They're just trying to impose their capitalistic exploitation on us again with their nationalistic slogans." But in the Wiebelskirchen Protestant elementary school Erich heard a different story. There they talked about the "occupation regime," told him that "the Frogs" were selling out the Saar with their foreign infiltration, that the Saar must always remain German, and so on.

Ten Years Old

The uncertainty and conflicts of the times were reflected in Wilhelm Honecker's political views. On the one hand, he felt himself to be German and, like all Saarlanders, regarded the French as an occupying power. He went along with the USPD and the KPD in censuring the attitude and bearing of the French troops in the Saar. One result of this was that on December 29, 1922, the KPD endorsed a joint memorandum of the liberal People's Party, the Social Democrats, and the German Democratic Party on the subject of "The French Forces in the Saar."[28] On the other hand, like all leftist socialists in the Saar, Honecker revered the revolutionary French traditions of 1789 and the Paris Commune of 1871 as inspiring models. To him the guarantee of freedom to establish unions and freedom of the press and the growing importance of the unions and labor parties were due to French influence. This was one of his reasons for leaving the SPD at the end of the war and joining first the USPD and then, in 1919, the KPD. He was becoming steadily more critical of the chauvinistic course the Social Democrats continued to pursue even after 1918.

He and his comrades were now convinced that in Germany and the Saar only a revolutionary solution on an international basis could improve the lot of the working class. In the Weimar Republic, however, the militant reactionary forces seemed to be on the rise. To Wilhelm Honecker the murder of Rosa Luxemburg and Karl Liebknecht, the use of army troops by order of Social Democratic Minister of the Interior Noske, and the brutal suppression of the Spartacus insurrection were irrefutable evidence of this.

Political developments—and especially their local aspects—were discussed in all their complexity in the Honecker household. Schoolmates and neighbors of Erich Honecker remember him as extraordinarily mature for a ten-year-old. He was interested in everything that went on around him; his favorite reading was history—especially the history of Germany. As a child whose earliest memories included grown-ups' stories of their terrible war experiences at Langemark or Verdun, he developed a curious combination of militancy and pacifism. He realized very early that the burden of wars always falls upon the little people, the workers and peasants. At the same time the Communists' militant strategy and their call to the final struggle that would assure peace forever made sense to him.

"I remember the First of May, 1922, when I was ten," he once said. "There was a parade with flags and posters. The people were happy that the hardships of the postwar years were over, but their happiness was premature, because the power still wasn't in the hands of the people."[29] It was then that Erich took his first step into political life—by joining the Young Pioneers, the Communist youth organization. The Wiebelskirchen chapter was a strong one, with over twenty members, mostly children of miners and metal-workers. Erich of course was more interested in recreation than political involvement, but precisely for that reason his years of membership were formative ones. In their own way the Young Pioneers promoted awareness of the class struggle: by reading working-class stories, organizing demonstrations of solidarity and projects to aid women and children, or just by listening to the reminiscences of Communists who had participated in the November Revolution in Kiel or Berlin.

Even before he joined the Young Pioneers, Erich used to help his mother or older brother deliver the Communist newspaper, the Saar *Arbeiterzeitung*. Neighbors got used to seeing the boy not just delivering "a grown-up newspaper" but reading it, too. The photograph albums of his Wiebelskirchen friends still contain pictures of Erich at the age of ten or twelve, with a dedicated expression on his face, guarding a red flag.

Growth of the KPD

The years 1922 and 1923 were decisive ones in the political life of the Saar—and in Erich Honecker's political development. In 1922 the Saar KPD began a radical political reorientation. The following year this *Schlageter-Kurs* (campaign for resistance to the French occupation) briefly dominated Communist Party policy in Germany, bringing it closer to the bourgeois nationalist groups.

On July 19, 1922, Helgsen, KPD spokesman at the inaugural session of the newly founded Saar legislature, denounced the Treaty of Versailles as coercive and the League of Nations as a representation of capitalist states. In the words of this programmatic statement, which amounted to the Communist Party's official declaration of war on the French Governing Commission for the Saar:

The function of the Commission as such is to protect the interests of the French bourgeoisie, which is authorized to exploit the Saar for fifteen years. In exercising this function, the Commission will inevitably contravene the interests of the working class, which comprises the majority of the inhabitants of the Saar.

The presence of French forces in the Saar violates the terms of the peace treaty and represents a constant threat to the working class. . . .

The Treaty of Versailles in its entirety is a treaty between capitalist states and as such a crime against labor all over the world.

The class-conscious workers of the Saar will be quick to join the united front of international labor against the coercive Treaty of Versailles.[30]

The eight-point KPD program included demands for legislation to check rising prices, profiteering, and the black market; the repeal of all regulations entailing wholesale dismissals; legalization of the eight-hour day; the expansion of social legislation and welfare; alleviation of the housing shortage; and the withdrawal of French troops. It also demanded that works councils in the Saar be granted rights at least equivalent to those enjoyed by such councils in Germany.

The Saar KPD's change of course was preceded by the expulsion of its chairman, Max Waltz who was accused of accepting large sums of money from the Saar government to influence party policy in accordance with its wishes.[31] The battle lines were now reversed. All the parties represented in the Saar legislature except the Communists now supported the Treaty of Versailles. The position of the KPD was undoubtedly influenced by the statement by Lenin and the Bolsheviks and the resolution of the second world congress of the Comintern in 1920 declaring Versailles to be a treaty between capitalist states and a crime against labor all over the world.

At that time the Saar KPD controlled key positions in the independent unions and among the shop stewards in the mines (one of whom was Wilhelm Honecker). It was much closer to the workers than the German Communist Party. This must have had its effect on the political development of Erich Honecker. The executive of the Saar KPD included far more workers than that of the German Communist Party. In the 1922 election for the Saar legislature, for instance, the thirty KPD candidates included ten miners, three foundry workers, two glassmakers, two housewives, several skilled and unskilled laborers, and just one union secretary.[32]

The Hundred-Day Strike

On December 30, 1922, the unions terminated the wage contract for the mining industry. The committee of shop stewards rejected the companies' compromise offer as insufficient. On February 5, 1923, the "hundred-day strike" began—the longest, hardest strike in the history of the Saar coal mines.[33]

The strike made a tremendous impression on Erich Honecker. As the FDJ (Free German Youth) newspaper *Junge Welt* wrote in 1954:

In the neighboring town of Neunkirchen the metalworkers came out on strike, too. They organized a demonstration, and Erich marched in the parade to Neunkirchen, with the group from the Communist Youth League, to take part in it. They sneaked past the police guards and joined in the strikers' demonstration. As it was beginning, the local police were incited to attack the workers. The children immediately moved to the front, and the police fell back. Some of them, however, were getting ready to attack the children. Then the women and the workers surged forward and pushed the police back, and the demonstration began.[34]

This bitter labor dispute was Erich Honecker's first political activity—though he participated only as a member of the Communist Youth organization. He had been no more than a young observer of the political controversy that preceded it. He had found it pleasantly exciting to listen to the mysterious speeches of his father's friends or help his mother and elder brother deliver the party newspaper. Now he was no longer just a passive onlooker; he was on his way to becoming politically active. And he was proud of it.

The strike had its effect on the activities of the Young Pioneers. It brought them new responsibilities. The children helped to distribute food to the strikers, many of whom suffered severe hardship. They served as messengers, kept an eye on the police and the French gendarmerie, distributed leaflets, and collected money for the miners. To quote Erich Honecker's own words: "We collected a lot of money for the relief of political prisoners, and we learned the Morse alphabet so that we could transmit news. We always took part in labor demonstrations."[35]

Erich Honecker never forgot these experiences: the bitter controversies with the French managers of the mines, the arrest of many of his father's friends, the lockout, the evictions from company-owned housing, all the hardships caused by the prolonged strike. In 1952, when, at his instigation, the West German FDJ proposed to establish committees of young miners and metalworkers in the Ruhr in order to gain more influence over union youth activity, he recalled the hundred-day strike of thirty years ago: "Although I was under eleven at the time," he said, "I was absolutely determined to grow up like those other comrades who risked their lives to fight exploitation and police brutality."

The strike was a success. Wages were increased. But the steady devaluation of the franc soon canceled out the gain. Three years later, in 1926, the miners again had to accept a wage cut spread over several months, and in 1927 temporary lay-offs were so frequent that most miners lost the equivalent of a month's pay.[36] Once again the miners' families suffered hunger and poverty.

Erich Honecker later described two important lessons he learned from the hundred-day strike:

1. Mass actions and strikes are always successful when labor is united. When the hundred-day strike began, it was disciplined and almost a hundred percent complete. The two union secretaries, Emil Becker and Karl Krämer, who resigned from the independent Union to organize a strike-breaking pro-French miners' league, failed dismally.[37]
2. However productive and successful strikes may be, in the long run they are effective only when one of their aims is to gain political power. If they are confined to the social and economic sphere, management will always find ways and means to offset the workers' gains by price increases.

He continued:

Thinking back to those days, I must say that the Pioneer organization can be enormously effective in developing class consciousness in young people. What you absorb at that age may not have much ideological basis but it makes such a deep impression that you never forget it. At least that's the way it was with me.

The Communist youth group that Honecker had joined in 1922 (which later became the Spartacus Youth League, whose members called themselves the Red Youth Pioneers) did indeed promote active social involvement. This could be seen, for example, in the Wiebelskirchen Protestant elementary school which Erich attended and where, according to his father, he was always at the top of his class. His favorite subjects were history, geography and arithmetic.[38] Speaking of the Young Pioneers' activities in school, Honecker says:

We were a strong group, including a lot of miners' children. We joined forces to support our parents' fight against exploitation by the mineowners. At school we fought physical punishment. When our singing teacher, a former army sergeant, was about to paddle one of us, the whole class would protest. The Pioneer paper, *Die Trommel,* gave us a lot of help in this campaign.[39]

2. The Young Communist

The Stalinization Period

WHEN ERICH HONECKER left school, he had a hard time finding a job. The mining industry was laying off and dismissing men, so he could not follow his father's trade. He tried unsuccessfully to become a railroad worker.[40] After he had spent two years in Neudorf in the district of Bublitz in Pomerania,[41] where he had once been sent by the "Children to the Country" fund while he was still at school, his uncle Ludwig Weidenhof finally took him on as an apprentice roofer.[42] He said later that he enjoyed this work because "standing on a roof and looking down on all the other houses gives you a feeling of freedom."

It has been said that Ulbricht and his successor both followed a similar course of development, that Honecker is an "Old Communist" of the same school and a member of the same generation as Ulbricht. This is not so. When Honecker joined the Spartacus Youth League in 1922, Ulbricht was already a member of the KPD executive. At the eighth party congress of 1923 he was elected to the Central Committee. He was responsible for reorganizing the central party apparatus to establish party cells in every branch. This earned him the nickname of "Comrade Cell." In this capacity he played a significant part in planning the organizational structure of the KPD—the same structure later adopted by the Communist League of German Youth (KJVD). Ulbricht took an active part in the numerous fights within the party and moved away from the left toward the central group. As a result the leftist-dominated ninth congress of April, 1924, did not reelect him to the Central Committee. His name was not even included in the list of candidates for the Reichstag election. Not until the eleventh congress, in 1927, when power had changed hands, was he reelected to the Central Committee.

Honecker's career has been much less dramatic. He did not go through the hard school of internal struggle within the KPD caucus in the Reichstag, because when he joined the KJVD in 1926 Stalin had already (in February, 1925) issued his twelve conditions for the bolshevization of the German Communist Party. Points 10 and 12 read as follows:

10. It is essential that the party systematically improve the social composition of its organization and purge itself of disruptive opportunistic elements. Its aim must always be maximum unity.
12. It is essential for the party to develop a rigorous proletarian discipline based upon ideological unity, clarity about the goals of the movement, unity in practical activities, and determined dedication to the party's tasks by the party masses.[43]

At the tenth KPD congress (July 12–17, 1925) the steps Stalin had outlined were included in the program of the bureau for party organization:

a. Establishment of order in the central party apparatus.
b. Creation of politically more reliable and organizationally stronger district leadership and strengthening of its authority.
c. Continuing close contact with the district branches.
d. Creation of a bolshevist corps of party functionaries.
e. Organizational preparation for and supervision of the carrying out of party campaigns.
f. Reorganization on the cell principle.[44]

In late 1925, after the deposition of the Communist leaders Ruth Fischer and Arkadi Maslow, both of whom belonged to the left wing of the KPD Reichstag caucus, the Comintern began to win out in Germany too. The party machine took over.

During this period a similar process occurred in relations between the Communist Youth International (KJI) and the KJVD. As the Comintern lost its original character as the world organization of international communism, the KJI lost its independence. World revolution was the primary aim of the policy of internationalism originally pursued by the Comintern and the KJI. Under

Lenin the national branches enjoyed a certain measure of equality, but as they became more and more dependent on the USSR, they were turned into foreign agencies of the Bolshevik Communist Party. Thus the Soviet-dominated policy of the Comintern had repercussions on the Communist Youth International, which obediently followed all its shifts.

The platform of the fifth session of the plenary executive of the KJI (April 7–13, 1925) includes this paragraph:

The rich experience of the Russian revolution, the Russian Communist Party and the struggle of the Russian youth movement is not being sufficiently studied and exploited by the national branches of the KJI. All units must familiarize themselves with the experiences and struggle of the Russian youth organization and master its generally important working methods. Mechanical application of the Russian experience to other units without regard to specific national conditions is, however, impossible.[45]

The KJVD very quickly accommodated itself to the Stalinization process within the German Communist Party. The executive of the Communist International sent an open letter to all units and members of the KPD censuring the Fischer-Maslow group in the party leadership and calling for concentration on work with the masses, especially in the trade unions.[46] At its ninth congress in Halle in October, 1925, the KJVD unconditionally endorsed this letter, which had been published in the official Communist paper *Rote Fahne* on September 1, 1925. At this congress the "overwhelming majority" of the KJVD (allegedly five-sixths of the delegates) "staunchly supported the Comintern."[47]

At the first party workers' convention of the KPD on November 1, 1925, a resolution was passed to give the youth group more support and tie it more closely to the party. The KJVD's numerical weakness was attributed to the fact that the party had done almost nothing to help the youth organization achieve a higher standing. "In order to make any headway in the field of youth work," all party organizations were required "to establish a KJVD cell in conjunction with every party cell, a local youth group in conjunction with every local branch of the party." All regional chairmen were required to take administrative steps to achieve this goal—such steps to include recruiting campaigns for the KJVD and the assignment of party cadres to youth work.[48]

Twenty-five years later, as chairman of the FDJ and a candidate-member of the Politburo (the Socialist Unity Party secretariat), Erich Honecker proposed that the SED pass similar resolutions in support of the FDJ.

When Honecker joined the Saar KJVD, its internal feuds were
more or less over and it was beginning a relatively sustained development, characterized by close ties to the KPD, loyalty to the
Communist Youth International and the Comintern (and hence
also to the Soviet Communist Party), and strict discipline. To
quote from the organizational statute of the KJVD adopted at the
Halle congress:

XII   League Discipline

Para. 46.   It is the duty of all League members and units to maintain the most rigorous discipline. The resolutions of the Communist
Youth International, the KJVD congress, the Central Committee, and
all other authorities are to be meticulously executed.[49]

This led to bureaucratization and militarization of the League's
activities. In the autumn of 1932 Ernst Thälmann made a tem-
peramental speech to the Central Committee of the KJVD criticizing this:

We need a more revolutionary team spirit in the work of the
League. Let's get rid of the authoritarian tone. The KJVD isn't
the army! Every trace of bureaucracy must be ruthlessly stamped
out. Am I right, comrades, in saying that a lot of high officials appear at cell or committee meetings with haughty and arrogant ex-
pressions and read out resolutions and recommendations in an impersonal, authoritarian tone? The all too prevalent flat, monotonous
language, the impersonal, cold, academic tone in discussions must
go.
    Why don't we assume the romantic revolutionary voice of the broad
masses of young workers? Why do we go about our work in such a dry,
sober spirit? We need more liveliness, more enthusiasm, more
verve, more dynamism, more passion! We must create magnets to attract young proletarians to the KJVD.[50]

Later, as chairman of the Free German Youth, Honecker often
made similar criticisms of the officials in charge of youth activities
—though without much effect, since the reasons for what he was
criticizing lie deeper: in the style of the movement's central planning and in the concept of its aims.

Honecker the Activist

One of the major tasks of the Communist League of German Youth at the time was to infiltrate the independent unions. At its first party workers' convention in November, 1925, the KPD had called upon members of the League and of the Red Youth Storm Troops, a paramilitary subsidiary of the KJVD, to join the unions.[51] As a disciplined young Communist, Honecker joined the woodworkers' union with which the roofers were affiliated.[52] He also joined the *Fichte* workers' gymnastic and sports association in Wiebelskirchen.[53]

Since he was not limited to any one place of work and was on very good terms with his uncle-employer, he was able to do all kinds of odd jobs for the KJVD group and soon became treasurer of the local branch.[54] He was one of the most active members of the Wiebelskirchen KJVD. He neither drank nor smoked. He was a drummer in the drum and fife band in which his father played the bass drum. By 1928 he was leader of the Wiebelskirchen branch of the KJVD and as such a member of the district leadership. At that time the Wiebelskirchen branch, with its eighty members, was the town's strongest youth group—as the KPD was its strongest party.[55] In December of that year[56] Honecker attended a week-long KJVD course in Marxist theory and practical youth work.[57] At Easter, 1928 and 1929, he participated in the League's third and fourth national youth rallies in Chemnitz and Düsseldorf. The fifth national youth rally was combined with the second national KJVD congress in which, as Honecker wrote later, a hundred thousand young workers, male and female, participated. They came from all over Germany and included many representatives of the Young Social Democratic Workers and Young Christian Workers[58] as well as young nonparty workers.

After 1945 Honecker continued the practice of combining the national youth rally with the national congress. The Federation of German Youth congress became the occasion for a mass rally (called, after 1945, the "Pentecost meeting" or the "national German meeting"). In 1950 a hundred thousand militant pacifists were scheduled to attend a rally in Dortmund.

The slogan of the national meeting of 1930 was "A United Front against Social Fascism and National Socialism," and the major enemy was the Social Democratic Party. At its second con-

gress (Berlin-Neukölln, September 26–29, 1929),[59] which Honecker attended as a delegate, the KJVD, citing the resolutions of
the twelfth KPD congress and of the tenth plenary session of the
Comintern, declared:

As the class struggle becomes more intense, social democracy,
inextricably linked with the capitalist government apparatus and involved with private enterprise, is steadily developing into social fascism. Its policy, geared to the needs of the bourgeoisie, is becoming
increasingly antilabor and counterrevolutionary.

The sharper the clash between the inner and outer contradictions
of capitalism and the more bitter the class struggle, the faster social
democracy turns into social fascism and the less room the Social Democratic Party has for face-saving maneuvers with the working class.
So it becomes ever more obvious that the party stands for the upper
bourgeoisie and the capitalist state. Its readiness to defend capitalist
interests is plainly revealed by the open endorsement by the SPD congress of dictatorship against the proletariat and the use of overtly
fascist terroristic methods.

Experience in Germany shows that social fascism is actually socialism in hypocritical name but fascism in fact. Social democracy's
development into social fascism is leading to an acute crisis within
the movement. It is depriving social democracy of its influence on the
working masses and creating a favorable climate for the Communist
Party's takeover of the majority of the working class.[60]

The welcoming address of the KPD Central Committee at the
Leipzig youth rally also pressed the attack:

Your resistance to capitalist attacks and your struggle against imperialism can only succeed if the young proletariat combines in a
united front against social fascism and national socialism.[61]

After 1945 Honecker dropped opposition to social democracy
(now considered to have been a mistake) as the movement's
principal goal. In an article written in 1952 commemorating the
fifth national youth rally in Leipzig, he said:

In 1930, inspired by the words of Ernst Thälmann, who pointed
the way, the members of the Communist League of Youth joined
members of the Young Social Democratic Workers and Young Christian Workers in a demonstration at the national youth rally in Leipzig under the banner of resistance to war and fascism.[62]

In 1929, the year of the worldwide economic crisis, Erich Honecker joined the German Communist Party.[63]

The Spread of Communism

At that time the Saar Communist Party had 1,200 members. Nonetheless, 16.7 percent of the Saarlanders voted Communist in April, 1928. Comparable figures show 10.3 percent in East Saxony, 7.2 percent in the district of Magdeburg-Anhalt, and 8.2 percent in Central Rhine.[64] In 1928 the Communists received a higher percentage of votes in the Saar than the Social Democrats (KPD: 16.7 percent; SPD: 15.6 percent).[65]

This success was chiefly due to the special character of the Communist Party in the Saar. Most of its leaders were drawn from the local working class.They were familiar with the workers' discontents and grievances and took them into account in formulating their demands.[66] Many of the workers regarded the KPD primarily as a protector of proletarian interests and only secondarily as a militant organization for gaining political power. In the industrial areas of the Saar the KPD was firmly anchored in the unions. It furnished many of the works council representatives and shop stewards. (Wilhelm Honecker served for many years on the works council of the Kohlwald pit.) The party was strongly represented on the town councils too. As Wilhelm Honecker—himself a KPD member of the Wiebelskirchen council —once said: "We hold eleven seats to the Socialists' three."[67]

The League of Red Front-Line Fighters and the Red Youth Storm Troops, both paramilitary subsidiaries of the Communist Party, did not become active in the Saar until after 1928, when confrontations with the Nazis were becoming more and more violent. By then Honecker already had some influence in the local KJVD. His entry into the Communist Party and his rise in its official hierarchy took place during the early days of the world depression, when young people and the unemployed were turning to the Communist youth organization and the KPD in ever greater numbers. (Between 1928 and 1932 the Communist vote rose by 6.4 percent.)[68]

The economic crisis made itself felt in the Saar a year before it became perceptible in Germany as a whole. Labor's limited control over its own political and economic situation and the relative impotence of the Saar legislature strengthened the Communists' influence. So far as the Saar legislature was concerned, their talk of "pseudo-parliaments" seemed appropriate enough.

Erich Honecker's closeness to the working class and his pride in his own background are partly rooted in this phase of the struggle in the Saar. We catch occasional glimpses of this today: for instance in his words to a works manager and his foundry workers in Karl Marx Stadt: "It's a fine thing to be manager of a factory where the working class is achieving such a magnificent performance."[69]

Visit to Moscow

In 1930 Honecker, together with other KJVD members from the districts of Hamburg, Lower Rhine, Württemberg, and Halle-Merseburg, was sent to the Communist Youth International school in Moscow for a year (ending in summer, 1931).[70] Later, as chairman of the Free German Youth, he would often talk, not without emotion, about his impressions on first crossing the Soviet frontier. When the train stopped at the Soviet frontier station, Soviet customs inspectors checked his passport and visa, and he saw the first banner with the words "Workers of the World, Unite!" He was firmly convinced that even the air he was breathing was different from the air at home. Later he liked to talk about how hard living conditions in the Soviet Union had been at that time, about the "heroic sacrifices" of a "revolutionary nation," which, despite its backwardness—its Czarist heritage—and the many deprivations resulting from its encirclement by its enemies, "had consistently followed the path of socialism." He liked to remind intellectuals and directors of student youth programs that his training at the Lenin Academy had included shooting, riding, and practical youth work as well as Marxism and Leninism. This "combination of revolutionary theory and practice," he said, was the most decisive factor in his education.

During his stay in the Soviet Union Honecker also served in one of the labor brigades that helped to build the Magnitogorsk steel works.[71] Forty years later, when it was already decided that he was to succeed Ulbricht as first secretary of the SED, he said at a meeting of the Vladimir Ilich Lenin metallurgical concern in Magnitogorsk:

Where Magnitogorsk stands today there was nothing but bare, barren steppe forty years ago. Building on the foundation of Soviet power and led by their Leninist party, the Soviet workers and Komsomols built the new factories and the new residential section at the cost of tremendous effort and sacrifice. I have vivid memories of their heroism in those days, of how they overcame extreme difficulties and of the unequaled achievement of our Soviet class-brothers. In summer, 1931, I was privileged to be one of a group of young German Communists that helped build Magnitogorsk. I shall never forget that time of heroic struggle with the pioneers of socialism.[72]

"Agitprop" (Agitation Propaganda)

On his return from Russia Honecker was made secretary for agitation and propaganda on the county secretariat of the KJVD and so became a full-time party functionary.[73] Erich Voltmer, now associate editor of the *Saarbrücker Zeitung,* knew him in those days; his father was foreman of the shift that Wilhelm Honecker worked on and represented on the works council. Voltmer himself comes out of the Catholic youth movement. This is how he remembers Erich Honecker:

My most notable memories of the young Communist Erich Honecker date back to the period of violent clashes between the Communists and the Nazis between 1930 and 1934. Our personal meetings (nearly all of them in the street) occurred during the same period. Erich Honecker was a typical example of the Communist Party functionary of those days. He didn't go in for physical confrontation of his political opponents in those tense times. He left that to his comrades, who regarded him as their unchallenged leader and spokesman— although most of them were a lot older than he was. In debate he wasn't just the equal of any of his political opponents: he was better. At the age of eighteen or twenty he was already an outstanding speaker. In Wiebelskirchen street-corner discussions he could outtalk anybody. But he didn't speak the typical Wiebelskirchen dialect. . . . He was a tough debater and wouldn't recognize any opinion but his own. And he got results, because in the November, 1932, election nine Communists, five Social Democrats, five Democrats, three representatives of the Center Party, and only two National Socialists were elected to the Wiebelskirchen town council.

Besides Erich Honecker there was one other outstanding Communist personality: Fritz Bäsel, later a member of the Saar legislature. But even in those days the present secretary of the SED was obviously not going to stop at the local or even the regional level.[74]

In autumn, 1931, Honecker became political director of the Saar branch of the KJVD.[75] In 1932, when the KPD and the KJVD finally called upon the Social Democrats to form a united front against fascism after years of denouncing them as social fascists, it was too late to change things in Germany. But the situation was different in the Saar. Even though the National Socialist Party (NSDAP) had been gaining influence ever since it emerged in 1925,[76] the Saar Statute still guaranteed free political organizations on a democratic basis. The Saar voters did not take the Nazis' nationalistic slogans as seriously as the voters in Germany did. In fact, the left and center parties received over 80 percent of the vote in the 1932 Saar elections. The KPD received 23.1 percent; and the Nazis only 6.7 percent. The National Socialist Party and the National People's Party together got only 8.3 percent.[77] In the Reich the reverse was true. There the Nazis were much stronger than the Communists. In this respect the situation in the Saar in 1932 was radically different from the internal political situation of the Weimar Republic. This was also true of the relative strength of the Social Democratic and Communist parties (KPD 23.1 percent; SPD 9.6 percent in 1932).[78] This local anomaly may have strengthened Erich Honecker's conviction that fascist and nationalistic movements stand no chance when the Communist Party is closely allied with the working class.

During the year 1933, however, after the Nazis took over in the Reich, the situation changed. Under Erich Honecker's leadership the KJVD did indeed organize another impressive demonstration in Saarbrücken on May 1, 1933 (although all parades had been prohibited by the governing commission), and the Young Social Democratic Workers participated in it.[79] But on that day it was already clear that many workers were following the Nazis' call for *fêtes d'intimidation* (intimidation demonstrations).[80]

In the Saar, too, the KPD reaped the fruits of its unrealistic policy of fighting the Social Democrats. During the first phase, from the Nazis' assumption of power in Germany until mid-1934, the Saar branch of the KPD steadily pursued its goal of overthrowing National Socialism and creating a "red Saar" within a German soviet union. It ignored the approaching plebiscite and continued to attack France and the League of Nations as servants of imperialism. Even after Hitler took over in the Reich, it kept up its fight against the Social Democrats, denouncing the leaders, including Braun, as "separatists" who were "paving the way for chauvinism and French annexation."[81]

The agreement between the KPD and the SPD for a joint plebiscite campaign, reached in June, 1932, also came too late. As Honecker saw it, though, the blame lay chiefly with the SPD. In 1954 he was still defending the Communists' disastrous antisocialist policy of twenty years before. In an article commemorating the fiftieth anniversary of the working-class youth movement in Germany, he said:

> When fascism took over as a result of rightist social democracy's treacherous policy and readiness to capitulate, hard times began for German youth, particularly working-class youth.[82]

Underground

By 1934 Saarbrücken, which was still free, had become the center of the illegal activity of the German Communist Party. Wilhelm Pieck and other party leaders had moved there. The plenary session of the KPD Central Committee was held there on February 3 and 4, 1934. The Saar branch of the KPD had been almost entirely taken over by German refugees from Berlin. Important units of the illegal German Communist Party known as the "transit center" and the "Reich technical training center" were located in Saarbrücken. Illegal Communist propaganda was printed there and smuggled across the frontier into Germany.[83]

At this time KPD policy was still dictated by the Comintern and was therefore quite unresponsive to the actual situation in the Saar. Moreover, the party was in a real dilemma. Its fight against the Saar Statute, the League of Nations, and French exploitation was bound to be unconvincing as long as the return of the Saar to Germany was ruled out as an alternative. Yet so long as the Nazis remained in power, the Communists could not support the return of the Saar to the Reich. The official Communist solution: to continue to demand a red Saar within a German soviet union, was utopian and inevitably created a split between the Communist Party and the working-class electorate. This was the Communists' major problem. Yet they failed to find—or seek —a satisfactory solution. Instead, in April, 1934, they called a congress to proclaim a "freedom campaign" against fascism in

Germany and fascist tendencies within the "German front." This campaign was also directed against the Social Democrats.

Honecker had already left the Saar by then, having been sent to Paris in the autumn of 1933 to head a Ruhr delegation to an international youth congress against fascism.[84] Many Communist refugees from the Reich were now living in Paris, the seat of the foreign headquarters of the KPD. Walter Ulbricht moved there early in October, 1933.[85]

Erich Honecker was not well known in the Reich and was not yet subject to police supervision there. He was therefore transferred from Paris to Essen to become political director of the Ruhr branch of the party—another indication of how little importance Communist Party headquarters attached to the Saar. Possibly it had already given up hope of achieving anything there. In Essen Honecker worked closely with Ewald Kaiser, secretary of the Ruhr branch of the KJVD. Kaiser was close to Chaplain Rossaint, who was working with young Catholics from Oberhausen and later from the congregation of St. Mary's in Düsseldorf. These groups gave the KPD valuable help when it had to go underground.[86] Using the cover name of Herbert Jung,[87] Honecker tried to mobilize these young people and some Social Democratic groups into an active united front. He even tried to work with certain members of the Hitler Youth who, because of their vaguely socialist views and working-class background, had become disenchanted with the Nazi policy after the party achieved power. He brought out a leaflet calling on all young workers to unite for action, including those who had made the mistake of joining the Hitler Youth. Its theme was: our generation has been sold out to the industrial magnates and the big landowners and robbed of its aspirations and hope by the Nazi Party.[88]

Little is known about Honecker's underground activity. The most extensive source of information is the findings of the "Peoples' Court," which, it should be noted, may also contain statements by "the accused" in his own defense. Honecker himself has said:

There [in the Ruhr] I was particularly interested in strengthening the influence of the youth groups in the factories and in mobilizing working-class youth to fight fascism. One of our chief aims was a joint antifascist movement by working-class youth and Communist, Social Democratic, and Christian youth organizations. Members of the

KJVD spoke at meetings and demonstrations of the Young Christians and Catholic youth groups.[89]

In fact Honecker tried to infiltrate KJVD agitators into the still-legal bourgeois youth groups. He organized apparently innocent sports and glee clubs and provided leaflets. But most of these groups did not survive long before they were suppressed by the Gestapo and their members arrested.

Honecker then received (via Amsterdam) new instructions from the refugee directorate in Paris. He was to return to the Saar to take part in the Communist plebiscite campaign. In the meantime the party's position in the Saar had worsened. The National Socialist Party was using methods of infiltration, terror, and blackmail. The civil servants, most of whom were dependent on the Reich, were alarmed by the "special powers act" and the "law to protect tenured government employees" passed by the German government. The Nazi Party sent circulars to communities, organizations, and various groups prescribing rules of conduct. It used overtly terroristic measures against Communists, Social Democrats, and Jews. Jewish shops and the Social Democratic newspaper *Volksstimme* were boycotted. Jews were forced out of cultural positions. Tavern and restaurant proprietors were prohibited (with terroristic threats) from renting their assembly rooms to groups opposing the return of the Saar to the German Reich. French and Jewish children were harassed at school or on their way to and from it. The first Gestapo and security officers were already arriving in the Saar, officially charged with keeping the Communist Party under observation and seeking out party printing presses and propaganda-distributing agencies. On one occasion, with the help of a Saar policeman, some Saarlanders were even taken across the frontier into Germany, where they were arrested.[90]

The Nazis also used demoralization tactics against the Communists. They would work on the national pride of certain Communists by inviting them on tours of the Reich to see National Socialist "achievements."[91]

The Saar plebiscite of January 3, 1935, resulted in an overwhelming victory for union with the Third Reich. Out of 539,541 registered voters, 528,105 went to the polls. Of these, 477,119 voted to return to Germany and only 46,613 for the status quo (the choice favored by the Communists). The latter figure was barely more than half the 84,000 votes the KPD alone had received in the 1932 election for the Saar legislature.[92]

Before the reincorporation of the Saar went into effect, Honecker returned once more to Essen. On February 18, 1935, he was arrested for the first time, outside the Lichtburg movie theater, while waiting for an underground contact. He was released after a check of his papers—which happened to be false.[93] (See court findings in Appendix.)

On February 27 Honecker left Germany. He went by way of Forbach to Paris, where he reported to the KPD refugee secretariat.[94] He was then appointed to the Central Committee of the KJVD and sent by way of Switzerland and Prague to Berlin,[95] where, under the name of Marten Tjaden of Amsterdam, he began his underground work as secretary of the KJVD for Greater Berlin.[96] The work was difficult and demanding. There were few comrades left to help him. They did manage to distribute a few antimilitarist leaflets during the fall army maneuvers of 1935 and to form three-men underground cells in a few factories, including the Siemens works, but these did not last long.

Honecker returned to Prague for discussions from November 9 to November 20, 1935. (See court findings in Appendix.) But his time had come. He was overtaken by the fate that awaited most of the Communists whom the refugee secretariat in Paris clandestinely sent back to Nazi Germany. On December 4, 1935, he was arrested, together with seven other KJVD officials. On June 7, 1937, after they had spent a year and a half in prison on remand, the trial of Bruno Baum, Erich Honecker, Sarah Fodorova, and Edwin Lautenbach began before the Second Senate of the People's Court. The charge was "conspiracy for high treason, with aggravating factors and gross forgery of documents." (See court verdict in Appendix.) The verdict was ten years of penal servitude, which Erich Honecker served in the Brandenburg-Görden prison until 1945.[97]

3. Imprisonment and Escape

A Prisoner at Brandenburg-Görden

LITTLE IS KNOWN about Erich Honecker's years in prison—and some of the available facts are contradictory. Insofar as the various sources of information coincide, the following picture emerges.

Honecker was admitted to Brandenburg-Görden in autumn, 1937. Unlike many other Communists imprisoned there, he spent only a short time in solitary confinement. Comrades admitted late in 1937 found him in a three-man cell in Building 2. At Brandenburg-Görden the usual prison atmosphere prevailed. In comparison with the concentration camps there was relatively little bullying, brutality, or torture. The personnel consisted chiefly of elderly police sergeants who performed their duties more or less correctly. Once a young Nazi guard began harassing some prisoners during a recreation period, ordering them to sing Nazi songs and march through deep snow wearing wooden clogs. The prisoners refused. The guard was furious, but before he could retaliate, an old Sergeant Meyer from the third floor of Building 2 took over the detachment, saving the prisoners from the over-zealous young Nazi's reprisals.

Probably because he was good with his hands, Honecker soon (before the end of 1937) became a trusty. He was put in charge of the feather-cleaning and oakum-picking detail under one of the most feared and corrupt guards in the whole prison. This man, Schilling by name, embezzled large quantities of raw materials and made the prisoners work overtime without entering the extra output in the records. He would then sell feather pillows and sisal on the side. Of course Honecker was not responsible for this criminal practice, since it was the guard who had selected him, not vice versa. A prisoner has no influence on his supervisor's business ethics.

Extensive research has failed to show whether or to what extent Honecker used his position to gain freedom of movement for underground political activity in Brandenburg-Görden or to make things easier for fellow Communists. On the contrary, many comrades describe him as a reserved, "snotty" character, who showed little spirit of solidarity, performed his duties as a trusty correctly, and was strict about quotas and careful work. He is said to have taken no part in the trading and illegal contacts that were a regular part of prison life and to have lived more or less in isolation. It is, however, entirely possible that this was all a clever front for illegal Communist activity within the prison. Party members, especially high-ranking ones, would normally keep away from other Communist prisoners, maintaining contact with one or at the most two other individuals.

Honecker was later promoted to serve as aide to Dr. Johannes Müller. Fellow prisoners admitted to the infirmary at that time say that there too he carried out his duties correctly but with reserve and had the reputation of being a loner.[98] Several former inmates all agree that Honecker did not participate in the illegal activity carried on by active Communists (including Professor Havemann) in Brandenburg-Görden.

As in most prisons and concentration camps, an underground party cell existed inside Brandenburg-Görden. Since there was apparently no serious conflict over policy, the various leftist groups were able to work together—and to collaborate with representatives of other political movements—on the underground committee. Here again Erich Honecker is said to have held aloof. Fellow prisoners say that he had no contact with this committee or with the underground party organization inside the prison.

Despite all this unanimous testimony, I personally consider it unlikely that Honecker was really isolated. At the time of his arrest, he was a member of the Central Committee of the KJVD, which would have made him one of the top Communist functionaries in the Brandenburg-Görden prison. It scarcely seems plausible that in this situation he should have remained outside the party organization. It is much more likely that because of his high rank his contacts were limited to one or two party comrades and that the other Communist prisoners interpreted this as isolation.

Honecker's own accounts after 1945 certainly suggest that he was involved in the work of the underground party group. He mentioned two fellow prisoners who could testify to this: Robert Menzel, now the East German Deputy Minister of Transport in charge of railways, and Alfred Neumann, member of the SED Politburo and First Deputy Chairman of the DDR Council of Ministers. Speaking of his confinement in Brandenburg-Görden, Menzel has said: "The comrades I got to know there included Alfred Neumann, Erich Honecker, and Waldemar Schmidt. It was from them that I acquired my first basic theoretical knowledge."[99]

How much of this is legend, how much fact, cannot be determined. It may indicate that there was more than one underground Communist cell at Brandenburg-Görden (as was the case in other prisons and concentration camps) and that because of Nazi terrorism they had to observe the utmost caution and avoid contact with one another. My query about Honecker's underground activity at Brandenburg-Görden was transmitted by my publishers to Erich Honecker himself. The Committee for Anti-Fascist Resistance in the DDR replied that it consisted in "meetings with comrades to discuss current problems; organization of mutual help; contact with the outside world (the Berlin KPD)."

Work on the Outside and Escape

When the air raids on Berlin became more intense and the bomb damage heavier, the prison board put Honecker in charge of an outside detail doing clean-up and repair work in Berlin. Most of the time he worked at his old trade: roofing. His parents were allowed to visit him once or twice a year, and he told them that he was in charge of a roofing detail, repairing bomb-damaged roofs in Berlin. "During the day Erich was outside. He only spent the nights in the prison."[100] He is said to have repaired damaged roofs at a penal institution in Lichtenberg used by the Russians as an MVD (secret police) prison after 1945. Many innocent Old Bolsheviks such as Kurt Müller, Deputy Chairman of the KPD, came to know this prison in the early 1950s, when they were arrested by state security officers and turned over to the Soviet secret police, which used brutal torture in its attempts to extort confessions.

Honecker's behavior while he was working on the outside has also been described as not particularly cooperative. Comrades who worked in the carpentry shop, where the party headquarters was located, say that he took no part in political work at that time. Professor Robert Havemann (who, with Erich Honecker's approval, was expelled from the SED in the 1960s and relieved of all his functions) was far more active. In Brandenburg-Görden in August, 1944, Havemann put together an effective shortwave receiver and published the news he picked up over the BBC, Radio Moscow, and several clandestine stations in a daily newspaper circulated in two copies among the various work details. This newspaper, written on both sides of one or two sheets of standard-size typewriter paper, helped to stiffen the prisoners' resistance and satisfy their hunger for news and also helped the party cell to prepare for possible Nazi liquidation measures. Only if it was accurately informed about events on the war fronts could the cell provide for the eventuality that the SS (storm troopers) might decide to liquidate all political prisoners before trying to escape.

But when the party cell took its final defensive measures (including plans to arm its active members)[101] on April 20, 1945—a day when thirty-three prisoners were executed—Erich Honecker was not there. He had escaped from his work detail on March 6, 1945—just fifty days before the liberation of the prison by the Red Army on April 27.[102] None of his fellow prisoners who were questioned could remember his having informed the party cell of his plan to escape.

While Honecker was escaping, the cell, in collaboration with other political prisoners, was making realistic plans for a revolt. To prevent their own liquidation, they planned to disarm their guards when the fighting came close. They began to make weapons in the prison workshops, particularly the locksmiths' shop. Robert Havemann got hold of some explosives and made thirty smoke bombs, to be used to get rid of the guards by creating panic among them.[103]

Honecker's escape seemed to jeopardize these extensive defensive measures, and for this reason his independent decision was censured by the party cell. In the last critical weeks before the generally expected collapse, underground party activity inside the prison was more dependent than ever on contact with the outside world. This contact was maintained by the outside work details. An escape from one of these details might have provoked incalculable reprisals. Honecker was chiefly criticized for not clearing his escape with the party cell in advance. This led to an internal party investigation (presided over by Grete Keilson) after the liberation in 1945. All high-ranking party functionaries who had been in prison or in a concentration camp had to make a report to the Central Committee on their own and their fellow Communists' behavior during their confinement. Relations with other prisoners and collaboration with the underground party cell were also investigated. Some fellow Communists from Brandenburg-Görden accused Honecker of undisciplined conduct because his escape had endangered the group's contact with the outside world and its plans for its own liberation. After Honecker had been interrogated, however, the inquiry was dropped, because his escape had in fact had no effect on the other prisoners.

Nevertheless, Erich Honecker has never liked to be reminded of this episode, because he was, to say the least, reproved for undisciplined conduct by the Central Committee. In a letter to young voters entitled "For the Happiness of Young People" written in 1954, he did not mention having escaped from the Brandenburg-Görden prison, but said: "I was carted off to Brandenburg-Görden, where soldiers of the glorious Soviet Army liberated me in 1945."[104] Or to quote the authorized biography issued by the Anti-Fascist Resistance Committee: ". . . he served eight years in Brandenburg-Görden, until the soldiers of the Soviet Army liberated him from the prison in April, 1945."

In fact, Honecker escaped at about 11 A.M. on March 6, 1945, from the Berlin-Lichtenberg girls' prison, where his detail was working.[105] Between then and May 8, when Germany surrendered, and for some time afterward, he lived with Comrade Klaus Küchenmeister and his family, becoming very friendly with Küchenmeister's sixteen-year-old daughter Vera. On May 4 he made contact with the Ulbricht Group.[106] An important phase of his life was over. His real political career was just beginning.

Freedom in Hiding

In April, 1945, Erich Honecker was taken in by the Küchenmeister family, who lived not far from the Alexanderplatz. He

was waiting for the Battle of Berlin to end. Vera Küchenmeister
has written an account of those days:

He spent that time at our home—or rather, in what was left of the
musty tenement, with its shored-up walls behind piles of smoke-
blackened rubble. I can see him now, sitting on the window ledge in
the kitchen, nailing a board across the broken window with his quick,
skillful hands. He looks thin—but then nearly everyone I know is
pretty skinny these days. His profile is clear-cut, his face open. His
eyes have a friendly, almost searching look.[107]

It was not easy for Erich Honecker to reestablish contact with
the party after his escape. How was he to get in touch with high-
ranking comrades in war-torn Berlin? Who and where were they?
At that time he knew nothing about the Ulbricht Group. How
could he have known that it had already begun work in Berlin on
May 2, 1945?[108]

Exactly how the first contact was made is not known. In her
short biography of Honecker, Vera Küchenmeister simply says:
"No one ever found him there [at the Küchenmeisters']—not even
the car the Central Committee sent for him, as he would later say
with amusement."[109] The Russian occupation authorities and the
members of the Ulbricht Group certainly had lists of names and
addresses of former Communists and antifascists,[110] and it is
possible that Klaus Küchenmeister's appeared on one of them, because he had done some writing for the KPD prior to 1933. It is
also possible that Honecker himself got in touch with the party
groups that were formed as soon as the fighting ceased to organize the supply of food, water, light, electric power, and gas to the
civilian population.[111]

Honecker himself has said virtually nothing about the period
between his escape from Brandenburg-Görden and his contact
with the Ulbricht Group. He once mentioned having made contact, when the fighting ended, with some Communists he knew
from his underground activities in Berlin in 1935 and learning
that a group of party activists had been formed. In mid-May the
first surviving KPD functionaries from Brandenburg-Görden established contact with the Ulbricht Group,[112] which was then
located at 80 Prinzenallee, Berlin-Lichtenberg. It therefore seems
likely that Honecker also worked with the group at that time.[113]

A Gap in Honecker's Life Story

It is curious that twenty years later, when Erich Honecker had long been one of the top party functionaries, the many published reminiscences of the early postwar period make no mention of him. In a series of articles in *Neues Deutschland* in 1965, in which most of the Ulbricht Group and the "veteran members" of the party administration gave an account of their experiences and activities, the only mention of Honecker's name is the following one in an article by Lieutenant-General Heinz Kessler entitled "We Have Faith in the Young Generation," commemorating the twentieth anniversary of the antifascist youth groups:

> The Central Youth Committee, which coordinated the work of all the youth groups, included outstanding antifascists such as the Communists Erich Honecker and Gerhard Rollack, the Social Democrats Edith Baumann and Theo Wiechert, the Catholic Vicar Lange, the Protestant Pastor Hanisch, and other personalities.[114]

The only explanation for this gap in Honecker's biography is that he may have been occupied in selecting the first cadres for the central and state youth committees. This, however, is not consistent with the official history of the Free German Youth, according to which young men of all political backgrounds spontaneously took the initiative in forming a nonparty youth organization. Reports that Honecker attended the Soviet *Antifa* (antifascist) school in Königswusterhausen during this period could not be substantiated.

One thing is certain: from May 4, 1945, when he made contact with the Ulbricht Group, until the reestablishment of the KPD and the formation of the Central Youth Committee in June and July, Honecker held no official position. On April 17, 1965, *Neues Deutschland* published a speech made by Walter Ulbricht on May 12, 1960, at a reception for the "veteran activists." Ulbricht expressly mentioned the "comrades from Brandenburg-Görden," some of them by name—but he made no reference to Erich Honecker.[115] The *Neues Deutschland* report of this reception describes many of the participants' activities in the early postwar period, but does not even mention Erich Honecker as having been present at the reception.[116]

Clearly the Ulbricht Group does not regard him as a member of

the "veteran activists." He himself has cast no light on the "ob-
scure" period between his escape from Brandenburg-Görden in
March, 1945, and the beginning of his activities in the Central
Party apparatus in July. He has never written about his experiences at Brandenburg-Görden, as Hermann Axen, for instance,
has about his own liberation from Buchenwald[117] or other Communists about their confinement in Sachsenhausen or Dachau.

II. A Partner in Power

4. On the Way Up

Honecker Builds His Own Empire

IN JULY, 1945, the Communist Party moved its headquarters from 80 Prinzenallee to a bigger building at 76–79 Wallstrasse.[1] Here Erich Honecker had his own office. He was responsible for youth work within the Communist Party and for preparations for the establishment of a central youth committee in Berlin. Time was short. The Soviet Military Administration (SMAD) was to recognize political parties at the end of July. By that time the Central Youth Committee had to be formally set up and ready to serve as the institutional basis for the central directorate of a youth organization still to be founded. The General Youth Committee of Berlin had met for the first time on June 20, 1945, in the education department of the Greater Berlin municipal council. Joint planning discussions had been held with the chairmen of the urban youth committees. The KPD had nominated its representative, Heinz Kessler, for the committee chairmanship. The Protestant, Catholic, "democratic," Jewish, Marxist, and nonparty youth movements each appointed two representatives. Under the direction of the Russian political advisers, Kessler made this committee into a model for the "nonpartisan youth work" it envisioned.

The first program the General Youth Committee of Berlin, adopted on June 20, 1945, was broad in scope and democratic in tone. This was the basis on which the various ideological groups were first to be brought to an agreement:

1. To bring together all antifascist youth for active collaboration.

41

2. To represent the interests of youth in vocational, professional, and public life.

3. To educate youth in a spirit of democracy, antifascism, humanity, and friendship toward all nations.

4. To involve youth in the great work of reconstruction and to raise its morale.[2]

The concept of a united front had already been adopted at the seventh world congress of the Comintern in Moscow in 1935. Germany and Italy were still under fascist control. The communist theory that fascism would quickly bankrupt itself had been refuted, and Stalin was seeking a new way out of the political impasse into which he had maneuvered international communism. The infiltration of liberal and social democratic parties under the "popular front" slogan was to extricate the Communists from their isolation. The real aims of the Comintern and the Communist Youth International were to be played down in favor of an emphatically national policy.

The KPD had already taken these resolutions under advisement at its congress in Brussels in October, 1935. To quote Heinz Kessler:

At the Brussels congress of October, 1935, the Communist Party of Germany, having already profited by the lessons of recent history, issued this call to youth: In the struggle against Hitlerism and after its inevitable defeat, the most important requirement is the unity of the labor movement and of all democrats. This is equally essential in the indispensable task of bringing working-class youth together as a *nucleus* for the union of all young people.[3]

Now, after Germany's collapse in 1945, this concept had to be put into practice. That is, a united youth organization must be created whose nucleus would consist of Communists but whose major function at first would be to get as many political groups as possible to collaborate with it. The formation of socialist and bourgeois youth groups was to be discouraged.

Five days after the first meeting of the General Youth Committee on Berlin on June 20, 1945, the first conference of Greater Berlin functionaries was held. Erich Honecker attended it. On this occasion Walter Ulbricht publicly stated for the first time: "We are forgoing a Communist youth organization because we wanted a united, free youth movement to rise."[4]

This was the official signal for the KPD to start youth work
without delay. There was no time to waste, because all kinds of
leftist-oriented youth activity was already under way. Once again
there were Communist League of German Youth groups, Socialist Youth groups, and *Antifa* committees, but also Free German
Youth groups, too, all reflecting the political views of their founders—most of whom were anything but young. If the founders
were former Communists or Social Democrats who had spent the
era of the Third Reich in the underground resistance, in the "inner emigration" (passive withdrawal), or in the total isolation of
prison, they would usually try to revive pre-1933 traditions and
would form local KJVD or Young Socialist units. Others, who had
learned of the popular front policy of the National Committee of
Free Germany through the underground in the concentration
camps of Buchenwald, Dachau, or Sachsenhausen, formed *Antifa* or youth committees. Groups of this kind were established
in the Rhineland, southern Germany, Thuringia, Saxony, and
other areas. Soon after the liberation, clashes inevitably began to
occur between the traditionalists, who founded KJVD groups, and
supporters of the Soviet popular-front line, who denounced the
others as leftist sectarians, extremists, or Trotskyites.

This conflict was a matter of concern to the party leadership,
which decided to put the following plan into effect as quickly as
possible:

1. Establishment of local youth committees as part of a broad nonpartisan program.
2. Establishment of a central youth committee, which would invite
the provincial committees to a joint conference.
3. Establishment of organizing committees to plan a united nonpartisan youth organization during this conference and subse-
quently to request Allied recognition of a "free German youth" organization.
4. Establishment of the Free German Youth.

These steps were to be completed by the end of 1945 so that the
Free German Youth could be founded on January 1, 1946. This
proved impossible, however, because some of the essential preliminaries could not be completed as quickly as the party administration had expected. One of these steps was the creation of the
organizational apparatus, the Central Youth Committee, which

was to be set up under the Central Administration for Education established on August 10, 1945. The Administration had made office space available to the Committee, but it proved extremely difficult to find workers who were ready and able to represent a nonparty policy. Honecker had been instructed to choose his staff on as broad a political basis as possible but to name reliable young Communists to the key positions of organization, personnel, finances, propaganda, and training.

Besides difficulties of organization and personnel, there were political obstacles too. The merger of the Communist and Social Democratic parties was taking longer than the KPD leadership had expected. In June, 1945, Max Fechner had proposed to Walter Ulbricht that "the previously discussed combined working-class organization be created,"[5] but the KPD had declined because it wished to complete all ideological and organizational preliminaries before setting its seal of approval on the merger. On June 19, 1945, Wilhelm Pieck said: "We know that there is a very strong desire for this merger, particularly in the working class. If the time has not yet come for the creation of this combined party, it is because a great spiritual transformation must first take place within the working class too to provide a firm basis for it."[6]

But the picture soon changed. The majority of the Social Democrats, who had at first reacted very favorably to the idea of a unified labor party, were forced to recognize that the KPD was not always sincere in its professed dedication to democracy and cooperation.[7] The stiffening of the opposition made it more difficult for Honecker to persuade a significant number of Social Democratic youth functionaries to join the Central Youth Committee. Nevertheless, in July the SPD leadership was still willing to appoint some. Among them was Edith Baumann, aged thirty-six.

Edith Baumann had been a member of the Young Social Democratic Workers and the Central Federation of Employees since 1925. In 1927 she joined the SPD, but resigned in 1931 to join the Socialist Workers Party (SAP). In 1930 she became a member of the Young Social Democratic Workers' secretariat. From 1933 to 1936 she was confined to the Barminstrasse women's prison in Berlin for attempted conspiracy for high treason.[8] In 1945 she rejoined the SPD and immediately became associated with its left wing. She later explained that she had become a member of the SPD instead of joining the KPD in the first instance, as she would have liked, because she wanted to work for the merger within the Social Democratic Party. In Edith Baumann, Erich Honecker found a good co-worker. He could trust her politically—and this was very important during the first few months, because as youth secretary of the KPD he had his office in the Wallstrasse, and Edith Baumann often had to be left in charge of the Central Youth Committee.

Since the Social Democratic Party was slightly suspicious of Edith Baumann because of her former membership in the SAP, its official representative on the Central Youth Committee was Theo Wiechert. He, however, was often ill (the result of his long imprisonment) and therefore had little influence. Another KPD representative was Paul Verner. Like Honecker, he had a double function: he was a KPD youth secretary and also a member of the Central Youth Committee. The son of a metalworker, born in Chemnitz on April 26, 1911, Verner is a year older than Honecker. His political career has followed a similar course. A member of the KJVD since 1922, he too joined the KPD in 1929 and worked in the German underground after 1933—as senior editor of the illegal KJVD paper *Junge Garde*. He later emigrated, fought in the Spanish civil war, and was interned in Sweden from 1939 to 1943. From Scandinavia he went to the Soviet Union, returning to Berlin in 1945.[9]

Honecker and Verner shared the work of the KPD youth secretariat, which at first consisted chiefly of making contact with representatives of other political youth groups and establishing the organizational apparatus of the Central Youth Committee: that is, appointing personnel and making practical administrative arrangements. They also kept in close touch with the youth officers of the political division of the Soviet Military Administration, with whom all activities had to be cleared and who had the last word on all appointments. This presented no problem to Verner, who, unlike Honecker, spoke fluent Russian.

A third KPD representative was Heinz Kessler. Although he was actually in charge of the General Youth Committee of Berlin, he had a voice in all important decisions of the KPD youth secretariat and the Central Youth Committee. At this time it had not yet been decided which of the top functionaries would continue to serve on the KPD youth secretariat and which would go over to the FDJ when it was founded. As chairman of the General Youth

Committee, Kessler had the most contact with non-Communist youth. He was the only one of the directorial staff regularly involved in practical youth work in Berlin, though Honecker took part in it sporadically.

Numerous youth groups and committees had been formed in the various sections of Greater Berlin, most of them on communist or socialist initiative. Despite the difficulties of the times and the catastrophic food shortages, these groups were extraordinarily active. Debates, lectures, organized games and dances were held, generally in private apartments or in schools. Party representatives held discussions with young people; former prisoners gave talks about atrocities in the Nazi concentration camps. In the artists' quarter of Wilmersdorf, the "Old Communist" Leo Dyk opened his apartment to young people of the neighborhood and even allowed it to be used for cultural events. Most of the young people were hesitant and suspicious at first; they had still not shaken off the Nazi ideology. Even the children of "Old Communists" were no exception, because their parents had usually been afraid to tell them about their own political past until the Nazi regime collapsed.

Naturally the Communists' primary aim was to gain influence over the young people. But in the confused months immediately after the war, when they still had to abide strictly by their proclaimed nonpartisanship, they also performed pioneer work in overcoming the fascist ideology and reorienting the young generation. Here Kessler and Honecker were in their element. Both of them were quick to make contact. They spoke the language of youth and soon became popular, especially Kessler, who was an old adopted Berliner, although his family came from Silesia.

Pioneer Cadre Work

At this point Honecker was still a functionary with an inferiority complex. He had a very unassuming manner and seemed receptive to other people's ideas and suggestions and always ready to learn. He worked mainly behind the scenes, and his particular field was political appointments. He carried on discussions with representatives of the Catholic and Protestant churches, with Vicar Robert Lange, diocesan youth chaplain, and with the Protestant youth pastor Oswald Hanisch, the representative of Protestant youth. But his principal activity was the selection of cadres for the Central Youth Committee and the establishment of a central organizational apparatus, which would then be incorporated in the Free German Youth. As the representative of the KPD youth secretariat and director of the Central Youth Committee, Honecker was a member of the cadre commission of the party executive, which welcomed back all Communists returning from emigration in the West or from concentration camps or prisons and decided where they should be used. Honecker would hold cadre talks with them, and he managed to recruit some of them for youth work. He was also a member of the commission that interviewed and assigned former prisoners-of-war returning from the *Antifa* schools in Russia.

At a cadre talk in the Rudersdorf *Antifa* camp, Honecker met Manfred Klein, a devout young Catholic, who gave the following account of their meeting:

I was told that I was qualified to set up a young people's radio station in Berlin. My first reaction was an absolutely wrong one. I indignantly challenged this assignment, because I had no experience in radio. Then and there I was taught an important lesson: a comrade does not ask questions about experience. He just accepts the party's orders if he has the proper basic attitude.

Perhaps it was chance or perhaps a human impulse that made Honecker ask me suddenly what experience I thought I had. What kind of experience can a twenty-year-old boy have who's been a soldier since he was seventeen? "In youth work," I retorted.

Honecker's face lit up. "You're right, Comrade. I should have thought of that myself. Yes, here we are: you were in the Catholic youth movement. The very man we need! You can represent Catholic youth on the Central Youth Committee. Report to me in the Wallstrasse on September 23."[10]

Although Honecker knew from the record that Manfred Klein had been in the Catholic youth movement, he never doubted that a six-week course in a Russian prisoner-of-war school was sufficient to make a comrade of him. This unconditional, unshakable trust in everything that came out of the Soviet Union was characteristic of his whole political attitude. Moreover, he believed firmly in the persuasive force of Marxism-Leninism. Anyone exposed to the teachings of Marxism for six weeks couldn't help being a Communist.

Basically Honecker had a strong aversion to bourgeois representatives with clerical affiliations. In a closed group of comrades
he made no secret of it. But since both the party and the Soviet
Union were stressing the common-front policy, he not only went
along with it but made a point of observing it meticulously. Nonetheless, it was hard for him to feign friendliness and tolerance
toward middle-class people. Also, he was insecure because of the
educational discrepancy, since most of these young men were
high school or university students. But they themselves were
often insecure too, and sometimes even obsequious, when talking to Honecker—at least that is how it appeared to outsiders. To
them he was the official representative of communism and of the
victorious Soviet military power, on whose decision their freedom
might depend. When Honecker met young people from this particular background for the first time and was trying to be affable,
he would assume an awkward kind of friendliness. Afterward he
was always "all in" and would ask the other comrades how he had
made out, or insist that he had "given the fellow a hard time." In
his accounts of these conversations he regularly exaggerated his
own role. But if he had several talks with the same person, his
cordiality would win out and his attitude would become more relaxed.

During the first phase of the Central Youth Committee and the
organizing of the FDJ, Honecker was willing to make many concessions. His main concern was to get representatives of other
political groups to serve. As the work was normalized and the
FDJ acquired a more rigid structure (after its second congress in
1947), he attached less and less importance to their collaboration,
which brought nothing but difficulties, especially the necessity of
getting the comrades together to lay down the party line in private before "the others" were called in. That point, however, had
not yet been reached. The important thing now was to create as
broad a basis as possible for the Central Youth Committee so that
the Western powers would recognize the Free German Youth as
the sole youth organization for all zones of occupation.

The Central Youth Committee

The exact date on which the Central Youth Committee began
its work is not easy to determine. KPD tactics at the time called

for the establishment of local youth groups everywhere the party had established itself. Especially in the *Länder* of the Soviet Zone (Saxony, Saxony-Anhalt, Thuringia, Mecklenburg, and Brandenburg) and in the Soviet zone of Berlin, state or general youth committees were to be founded and were to request the occupying power to recognize a central directorate. This was desirable because at the time only local organizations were recognized in the Western zones. So by arrangement with the Soviet youth officers of the state administrations—or more often on their instructions—comrades from the state youth committees sent resolutions and petitions to Berlin to this effect.

Youth committees above the local level followed their example, and on July 31 the Soviet Military Administration decided that the time had come to permit "the formation of antifascist youth committees."[11] Of course every official in the KPD state youth secretariats in Leipzig, Halle, Weimar, Schwerin, and Potsdam knew that the comrades in Berlin were busily setting up their apparatus. The KPD state committees untiringly established district, city, and village committees, so that in time a relatively solid youth organization was built up, though for the time being it stopped at the district level. Soviet tactics at the time were very cautious, because the Russians did not wish to jeopardize cooperation with the Western Allies. Meanwhile, the central apparatus in Berlin was steadily coalescing into a top leadership, although its link with the provisional committees was still weak.

Today Erich Honecker is often called an excellent organizer, but in those days he made a different impression. In fact, when representatives of the state committees came to Berlin, they always found that nothing functioned properly, that no one had an overall picture, that one official didn't know what the other was doing, and that countless conflicting orders were being issued. One of the reasons for this may have been that the composition of the Central Youth Committee was then extremely heterogeneous, and no one wanted to order other people around or issue directions. Also, the Communists withheld information from the bourgeois committee members.

To counteract this organizational chaos to some extent, and particularly to hasten the foundation of the FDJ, Honecker called the first business conference of the state youth committees in the Soviet Zone. It was scheduled for December 1–3 in Berlin. Then,

on December 4, also in Berlin, the first delegates' conference of
the antifascist youth organizations of Greater Berlin would meet
and request the establishment of the Free German Youth.[12] The
keynote speech at the business conference was given by Erich
Honecker. Its climax was an appeal to German youth to "become
heroes of the building of a new democratic Germany."[13] Heinz
Kessler spoke at the antifascist youth organizations' conference.

A major function of these first meetings was to unify the various forms of youth work in the individual states of the Soviet Zone
and bring them into line with the overall conception and timetable of the party leadership. But these matters were not discussed at the plenary session of the conference. Honecker and
Verner called in the leaders of the various delegations to inform
them of the party line. Here Honecker dropped the flowery language he had used at the conference in favor of blunt talk in the
old KJVD style. Without mincing his words, he told them that
anyone who did not abide by party decisions, tolerated other organizations in youth work—to say nothing of cooperating with
them—or failed to integrate them with regard to ideology and
organization must be prepared for serious consequences.

Controversial Nonpartisanship

What Honecker really thought about the nonpartisanship of
the youth committees and the future FDJ was expressed in something he said on this occasion to Robert Bialek, the party youth
secretary for Saxony. Bialek was advocating a working-class organization that would include both Communist and Social Democratic youth. Honecker rejected this conception outright:

Forget about that! Of course I'd prefer a socialist youth organization
too, but it wouldn't meet present needs. We're Communists, and un-
fortunately we have to accommodate our wishes to the requirements
of the political situation. A working-class organization would mean
that we'd have to recognize even more youth groups. Every bourgeois
party would demand its own youth organization—and the churches
too, of course. We can't afford that kind of fragmentation. We've got to
appeal to youth as a whole. We're not going to turn part of it over
to bourgeois groups. So we must build a nonpartisan, nondenomina-
tional youth organization that will embrace all parties and all religions.
We must make up our minds today how we're going to do this and
what measures we need to take to achieve this goal.[14]

When Bialek asked what the party intended to do about the
churches and whether it wanted to prohibit all church youth work,
Honecker continued:

At first we'll have to make very extensive compromises. We'll allow
church youth work so long as it's unstructured. We have no reason
to begin a *Kulturkampf* with the churches at any point. Above all, it's
up to us to get a lot of clergymen to support our plans. We must persuade the churches to give spontaneous approval to a unified youth
organization.

When Robert Bialek remarked that this youth movement might
be a "terrible mishmash," Honecker reassured him:

Don't make things look worse than they are, Robert. After all, the
bourgeois parties and the churches are both short of functionaries.
. . . We must do something about the training of youth officials without wasting any time. We must find something for the bourgeois and
church representatives to do in the future youth organization. How
shall we go about it? We'll give them so many seats on the executive
committees that they'll never be able to complain that we're discrim-
inating against them. As far as I'm concerned, they can have half of
all the board seats down to the district level. Our toughest comrades
sit on these boards. They'll hold out! Anyhow it's not there that the
practical youth work gets done. What we need to do is get control of
the work at the lowest level. In the places where young people work,
in the factories, in the neighborhoods, the group leaders must be our
men. They must gain the young people's trust through their activism
and their talent for youth leadership. If we succeed in this, it doesn't
matter how many representatives of the bourgeois parties and the
churches sit on the boards.[15]

It was decided that in January the youth groups in the *Länder*
of the Soviet Zone should begin a discussion campaign on the subject of the future youth organization. The youth committees and
groups were then to send resolutions to the Soviet Military Administration requesting or demanding the establishment of a nonpartisan, unified youth organization. Honecker continued:

Then the leaders of the bourgeois and church groups are in a bind.
They can't afford to vote against a unified youth organization, because that would mean opposing the majority of active youth. Only
by permitting a unified youth organization can the Soviet Military
Administration act in accordance with the will of youth. You can't be

any more democratic than that! You can't recognize a whole lot of youth organizations against the will of the overwhelming majority of antifascist youth!

In the big cities of all the states, rallies must be arranged immediately at which the question of the future youth organization must be brought up. Take a firm stand against recognizing a whole lot of youth organizations. Remember what the fragmentation of youth led to in the Weimar Republic—to the victory of fascism! Remember that Germany's need is so great that any fragmentation of youth is a crime against its future. Do what you like, but create an atmosphere in which no one from the bourgeois groups will dare to ask for multiple youth organizations unless he wants to lose all his influence on young people.[16]

Honecker reminded them that there was no time to waste. They must make the most of this time when the bourgeois parties were still occupied with building up their own organizations and would be happy to be left undisturbed. But for all their activism, they must be very cautious. Especially where the churches were concerned, they must tread very gently and think twice before they made any formal statements:

We can't afford any unfavorable comments by the churches right now. . . . One mistake and we'll spoil everything. We in the secretariat run less risk of making mistakes than you comrades who are constantly engaged in practical work or speaking at mass meetings.

Addressing himself to Robert Bialek in particular, he continued:

I know how much excitement you work up at these rallies and how carried away the young people get. But I know that you get carried away too! In that state of excitement you can make a lot of political mistakes when you're speaking completely impromptu. I want to remind you very strongly of this.[17]

This explicit warning was an indirect declaration of war on Bialek. Honecker, who lacked Bialek's rhetorical talent, saw him as a rival.[18]

At this December meeting between the state committees and the Central Youth Committee it was decided to complete the formulation of the principles and aims of the future youth organization by January. On this point Honecker said: "I suggest that we not discuss principles and aims in detail here. I will pre-

pare a draft based on the principles and aims of the Communist
Youth International—adapted to the present situation, of course
—and in a few weeks' time we'll go through it together, paragraph
by paragraph."

Here Honecker showed that he is quite able to develop ideas of
his own, provided he is pursuing a goal set by the party leadership. He went on:

I don't like the expression "principles and aims" as applied to the
new youth movement. It sounds too much like party jargon. I believe
that before setting social aims for young people you should let them
fight for their rights. I would therefore suggest that we call the organization's program "basic rights" or something like that.

In the subsequent debate the phrase "basic rights of the young
generation" was agreed upon. It was also decided that the future
organization should have a badge and a flag. No decision was
made about a uniform, but blue was adopted as its color and the
rising sun as its emblem.

Personnel Problems

Another problem was to strengthen the personnel of the Central Youth Committee. Since Saxony was the strongest *Land* organization, Honecker asked the Saxon comrades to assign one of
their officials to Berlin to help organize the Central Committee
and the future youth organization. Here he demonstrated his
tactical skill. He first offered the position to Robert Bialek, who
had done excellent work in Saxony, assuming—quite correctly—
that Bialek would not be interested in a desk job but would prefer
to be in constant direct touch with young people. Bialek demurred
that he was better suited to practical youth work and suggested
instead Hermann Axen, chairman of the state youth committee
of Saxony. Honecker needed no persuasion. It was agreed that
Axen should move to Berlin in February, 1946, to take over all
organizational preparations for the establishment of the FDJ.

Honecker's choice of Hermann Axen characterizes his concept
of political appointments. Here a short account of Axen's background and past is in order. He was born on March 6, 1916, and,
unlike Honecker and Verner, had a high school education. His
father, Rolf Axen, who was of Jewish origin, was regularly em-

ployed but was also a KPD functionary. Hermann joined the
KJVD in 1932. Like Honecker, he worked in the underground
after 1933 with Lena Fischer, who was expelled from the Central
Committee and the SED by resolution of the thirteenth conference
of the Central Committee held on May 14, 1953. The Central
Committee plenum based its decision on a report of the Central
Party Control Commission (ZPKK) on the interpretation of the
resolution of December 20, 1952: "On Lessons to Be Learned
from the Slansky Trial." The report stated:

> When she was arrested in 1935, Lena Fischer committed treason.
> She betrayed a number of KJVD members to the Gestapo and made
> extensive statements to the class enemy concerning the structure and
> activities of the illegal KJVD and the Communist Youth Inter-
> national. Lena Fischer withheld this fact from the party. The investi-
> gation further showed that Lena Fischer handled confidential party
> documents in a criminal manner and kept in her apartment hundreds
> of secretariat resolutions, cadre plans and documents, and confiden-
> tial reports.[19]

These findings are important because Lena's Fischer's expulsion resulted from charges made by Hermann Axen, who was
afraid of being caught himself in the morass of suspicion and
arrests of the 1950s. Like Honecker, Axen was arrested in 1935
and sentenced on October 19 by the first criminal division of the
Land superior court of Dresden to three years penal servitude,
which he served at the Zwickau prison. After his release, he managed to emigrate to France.[20] This in itself was unusual, since
most Communists of Jewish descent were automatically sent to
a concentration camp after completing their prison terms.

After the outbreak of World War II Axen was interned in
France and was later surrendered to Germany. He was sent to the
Auschwitz concentration camp, where he worked in the Javischo-
vitz coal mines. Axen once said something to Robert Bialek about
his refugee experiences in France. Bialek had told him that as
chairman of the state youth committee of Saxony he didn't need
to clear "every damned detail" with his superior. "Do you really
need to cover yourself like this?" he asked. Axen is said to have
replied: "I've had my experiences, my friend. The party left me
in the lurch for no reason at all, and I wound up in a concentration camp. I'm not going to give them any reason to mistrust me
a second time."[21]

It is true that Hermann Axen was deeply mistrusted at that time. Fritz Grosse, KPD cadre secretary in Saxony, warned Bialek:

Don't touch him! He's a shady character, and some things about his refugee years in France are still unexplained. He's supposed to have acted as an *agent provocateur* on two occasions. . . . A lot more comrades will be exposed when all the refugees get back. In Axen's case we still need statements from other comrades—some of them still in South America.[22]

Nevertheless, in December, 1945, Honecker appointed Axen to the Central Youth Committee and put him in charge of the important organization and cadre division. Axen had been shipped from Auschwitz to Buchenwald early in 1945, when the Red Army was advancing, and he returned to Saxony after the liberation. He now became in effect Honecker's second in command. He was responsible chiefly for building up the organization and staff of the central leadership apparatus of the committee and the future Central Council and linking it more closely with the individual state committees and the future state directorate of the FDJ. This organizational phase of the FDJ is intimately associated with the name of Hermann Axen, an extremely skillful tactician and an astute debater. A major reason for his uncompromising party discipline and his obvious desire to stay clear of all internal power struggles in the FDJ and the party leadership undoubtedly lies in his unfortunate experiences as a refugee and with the party leadership immediately after 1945.

Party Discipline and Members of the Hitler Youth

The December meetings also demonstrated Honecker's concept of party discipline. He admonished and criticized *Land* representatives who, he thought, had gone too far too fast in their political and organizational work. The Thuringian delegation, for instance, was strictly forbidden to refer to the first meeting of all *Land* youth committees, scheduled for December 27–29 in Gera, as the first *Land* conference of the Thuringian branch of the Free German Youth. The Thuringian group had to promise not to initiate anything that might be considered a youth organization but to wait for a starting signal from higher up.

Honecker's readiness to make independent decisions even in complicated and delicate matters was clearly demonstrated that first year in the controversy over the admission of former members and officers of the Hitler Youth to the work of the youth committees. When Marshal Zhukov recognized the work of these committees, youth officers in the various states of the Soviet Zone at first took the view that only young people who had never belonged to the Hitler Youth could serve on them. This was unfeasible in practice, because 95 percent of German youth had belonged to the Hitler Youth. Even children of underground antifascists had joined it for opportunistic or tactical reasons. The Soviet military administration later revised its ruling and permitted rank-and-file members to serve on the youth committees but not Hitler Youth or BDM (League of German Girls) leaders.

Emboldened by this partial success, Robert Bialek, KPD youth secretary of Saxony, undertook an experiment. On the assumption that much of German youth still recognized the authority of former Hitler Youth leaders of low and medium rank, he sought to attract those capable activist leadership elements that had been misused by the Nazis to the new antifascist youth movement. In September, 1945, he presented to the KPD *Land* secretariat of Saxony a plan to send some of the local Hitler Youth leaders written invitations to an open discussion as a way of initiating talks with them. He proposed to assign them specific jobs in the cleaning up and rebuilding of bombed cities and gradually to integrate them into the new youth work.

The secretariat considered this proposal too explosive for it to deal with. The *Land* party chairman, Hermann Matern, therefore suggested that Bialek submit it to Wilhelm Pieck. This could only be done through Erich Honecker, youth secretary in the party secretariat. Honecker should have been sympathetic to Bialek's plan, because he himself had tried, after 1933, to create in the Ruhr a common front of KJVD youth and Hitler Youth members with socialist leanings. However, he did not seem very enthusiastic.[23] He was obviously afraid that Pieck might ask him what he thought of the plan. If he supported it, he would be implicated if it failed. He therefore remained neutral and merely arranged a meeting between Pieck and Bialek, without mentioning its purpose.

After some hesitation, Pieck gave the plan a green light, and

Bialek began his difficult task, supported by the KPD in Saxony. After bitter, often tumultuous, controversies, many meetings, countless individual discussions, and some educational courses designed to fight the Nazi ideology with shock treatment, they did in fact succeed in overcoming the militant opposition of much of the Hitler Youth leadership and in recruiting a few suitable candidates for collaboration. Some of these, including Werner Tscheile and Dieter Schmotz, made sensational careers and by 1948 or 1949 had been promoted to top positions in the Central Council apparatus.

When this experiment proved a success, Erich Honecker made it appear that he had actively supported Robert Bialek's plan from the start and had personally taken part in the project. When Bialek later got into difficulties with the party for other reasons, Honecker continued to speak of the project as an example of the creative activism of the pioneer days—without even mentioning Bialek's name as its originator.

The year 1945 ended with recognition of the Free German Youth still not in sight. But a decision was made on the question of leadership. Erich Honecker became chairman of the Central Youth Committee, and Paul Verner remained on the KPD youth secretariat. Verner, however, was also to be director of the propaganda division of the Central Youth Committee. Honecker had taken a big step toward realizing his ambition of becoming chairman of the future unified youth organization.

5. The Founding and Debut of the FDJ

The Road to Unity

WHILE THE YEAR 1945 had been devoted to rallying all available antifascist and democratic forces and laying the first foundations of a new political order, 1946 saw the beginning of reconstruction and the creation of the essential preliminaries for a popular democratic order still to come.

One of Erich Honecker's principal tasks in 1946 was to familiarize the Central Youth Committee, with its many non-Communist, Social Democratic, and church members, with the important resolutions the Communists had passed at the meeting of the state youth committee executives in December, 1945. Above all, the non-Communists on the Committee had to be convinced of the necessity of supporting a unified youth organization to be called the Free German Youth.

Manfred Klein recalls that Honecker achieved this through a clever surprise maneuver. At one of the regular meetings of the Committee he told the unsuspecting bourgeois representatives that he thought the time had come to pave the way for the founding of a unified nonpartisan youth organization. He said that he had had preliminary talks with the Soviet Military Administration, which was prepared to recognize such an organization. He proposed that it should be called the Free German Youth and that the color of its flag should be blue. For the sake of smooth cooperation with the churches, he was not in favor of red. Blue, after all, was the color of the Protestant church, too. And no one could possibly raise any objection to the rising-sun emblem. Numerous youth committees from the Soviet Zone had petitioned the Central Youth Committee to recognize such an organization. As evidence of this, Axen produced laundry baskets full of petitions, resolutions, and letters from all over the Soviet Zone demanding the formation of a youth organization.[24] A delaying action by some church representatives was quickly defeated when Honecker promised them equal opportunity in building up the FDJ and minimized the significance of the actual founding of such an organization.

In practice the KPD representatives on the Committee had developed the following tactics. Honecker would propose a motion and argue the case for it. All the Communist members—and usually Edith Baumann too—would support it. Then they would wait for the reaction of the bourgeois representatives, who would generally try to delay a decision or make counterproposals. Then the whole Communist cast would run through the parts assigned to them. As a rule, Paul Verner or Heinz Kessler would reformulate Honecker's proposal even more drastically, while Honecker himself seemed prepared to compromise. This was to make the non-Communists think that the Communists were not a party bloc but represented diverse viewpoints. Then Edith Baumann would propose a compromise, which Kessler or Verner would criticize as not sufficiently far-reaching. Finally Honecker would take the floor, trying to look as if he were seeking a solution acceptable to all parties. This method often worked, because in the meantime the bourgeois representatives too had developed diverse viewpoints, and their front was "split wide open," as Honecker used to say. Finally there would be a resolution that conformed essentially to Honecker's original proposal but included a few minor concessions.

But the non-Communists, particularly the skilled tacticians who represented the churches, Diocesan Vicar Lange and Pastor Hanisch, saw through this play-acting and developed tactics of their own. They would rarely attack the substance of the Communist proposals but confined themselves to delaying decisions. They knew that the Communists wanted at all costs to keep them "in the fold." This offset their numerical inferiority, because the Communists' whole concept would have been exploded if they had withdrawn. Nevertheless, they were always at a disadvantage, because they were confronted with decisions only when all the details had already been worked out, and often when the *Länder* had already put them into practice.

The last trump of Erich Honecker and the Communist members of the Committee was always the Soviet Military Administration. When an agreement was at hand, Honecker would usually say that although a compromise solution might perhaps be worked out within the Central Youth Committee, even he could not go beyond a certain limit, because the Soviet occupying power had made its approval contingent upon one condition or another.

This was the case when Honecker announced that they could now prepare for the founding of a unified nonpartisan youth organization. The representatives of the church and the bourgeois parties were not opposed in principle to the establishment of a Free German Youth, but they wanted it to function as a parent organization under which the various youth groups disbanded during the Third Reich might be reconstituted. This Honecker categorically refused, saying that it would only fragmentize youth again. Besides, the church and bourgeois groups might then form their own FDJ leadership units.

The meeting ended with a statement by Honecker that the principles, aims, and statutes of such a youth organization would be worked out, and all questions could be fully discussed on the basis of this draft.[25] In fact, a first draft of the "basic rights of the young generation" had already been drawn up and was awaiting the KPD's decision. When the controversy with the non-Communists failed to produce a compromise, Honecker categorically announced that the Soviet Military Administration would recogcize either a unified youth organization or none at all.

On February 26, 1946, the Central Youth Committee resolved to request official recognition of the Free German Youth by the Soviet Military Administration and to set up an organizing committee to prepare for its establishment. This committee consisted of ten members, seven of whom belonged to the KPD or the SPD.[26]

In fact, a definite timetable had already been set up, although it was never officially discussed in the Central Youth Committee. The Free German Youth was to be officially founded throughout the Soviet Zone on March 7, 1946, and its first congress, the first "National Youth Day," was to be held at Pentecost (Whitsun). The selection of these dates was by no means a matter of chance. The

FDJ was to be founded before the unification congress of the Social Democratic and Communist parties, in order to present a *fait accompli* in the field of youth work. The first big meeting of the new youth organization, its first congress, at which its principles and aims would be determined, was not to be held until after the SPD–KPD unification congress, so that when it did take place Pieck and Grotewohl could represent the unified labor party as the leading force behind the youth organization.

Honecker later admitted that it had not been easy to get the party to accept this timetable, because there was some doubt whether the youth program would be far enough advanced to hold a national congress with elected delegates only three months after the foundation of the FDJ.

On February 26, 1946, when the Central Youth Committee met in the conference room of the Berlin City Council and passed a founding resolution, the timetable was not discussed. The resolution, a brief, sober document, states:

The members of the Central Youth Committee for the Soviet Zone of Occupation here present in the conference room of the City Council of Berlin, Parochialstrasse, on February 26, 1946, hereby announce their intention to make an application to the Soviet Military Administration of Germany for the purpose of founding a nonpartisan united democratic youth organization:

FREE GERMAN YOUTH

The basis of this appeal consists in the aims and bylaws of the Free German Youth, which are accepted by all the undersigned and appended to this document.
Berlin, 2.26.1946.[27]

The document was signed by thirteen members of the Central Youth Committee: Erich Honecker, Theo Wiechert, Edith Baumann, Gerhard Rollack, Paul Verner, Rudolf Miessner, Robert Lange (Diocesan Vicar), Oswald Hanisch (representing the Protestant Church), Heinz Külkens, Rudolf Böhm, Emil Amft, Fritz Klein (not to be confused with Manfred Klein), and Heinz Kessler.

This founding resolution poses some puzzling questions, which extensive research has failed to answer. In fact, the document of February 26, 1946, does bear these thirteen signatures, as the facsimile of 1951 clearly shows.[28] Five years later another facsimile of the same document was reproduced in the volume *Zur Geschichte der Arbeiterjugendbewegung in Deutschland* (On the History of the Working-Class Youth Movement in Germany), published in 1956. This reproduction shows only eleven signatures. The names of Emil Amft and Fritz Klein have been effaced.[29]

Falsification of photographs by the SED during this period was not unusual. In his book *Ulbricht Fälscht Geschichte* (Ulbricht Falsifies History) Hermann Weber shows through numerous photo-documents how names, figures, and faces have been effaced by retouching in order to conceal the fact that former top functionaries who have now been declared enemies of the people once ranked among the party's leading representatives.[30] But a falsification like the one on the FDJ founding resolution is unusual even by SED standards. There must have been some compelling reason for ordering two names to be removed from a key document in the history of the postwar German youth movement. An even more extraordinary note is that a picture book published in 1971 shows a facsimile of the founding resolution of 1946 with all thirteen names.[31]

Paul Verner Is Outmaneuvered

As the founding date drew nearer, excitement rose in the central organizing committee over who would be appointed president of the FDJ. Honecker was more "accepted" by young people, was a good mixer, and presented a convincing image of the youth functionary. Since Verner lacked these qualities, the SED leadership decided to make Honecker the head of the FDJ. Ulbricht, who at that time was only deputy party chairman (though nevertheless more powerful than Pieck), was probably already aware of Honecker's talents: his ability to make contact, his closeness to working-class youth, his wholehearted devotion to the party and the Soviet Union. The teacher-pupil relation between Ulbricht and Honecker dates back to this time, when the first ties were formed between these two quite dissimilar personalities—ties which would lead to a remarkable coalition. With the instinct of a well-trained functionary in the party apparatus, Honecker had quickly recognized that Walter Ulbricht, not Wilhelm Pieck, was the strong man in the party. Looking back, it is hard to say whether Paul Verner's lack of impact on working-class youth was the reason for Ulbricht's decision. Probably he preferred Honecker's character and manner, which made him seem open and frank and more uncomplicated and straightforward than the unquestionably more intelligent Verner. No one could ever have suspected Honecker of intrigue, but Verner's behavior was not so transparent. Be that as it may, Honecker had won the second power struggle of his post-1945 career.

After the third FDJ congress in Leipzig in 1949, he confessed that he had not been by any means sure of himself at the time. And indeed in this phase of his work, which lasted until the late 1950s, he had a pronounced inferiority complex—not least where Paul Verner was concerned. It sounded very plausible when he said in a private conversation in 1949:

I was surprised when the party made me president of the FDJ. Of course the party is the leading force, so that the party youth secretary is actually my superior. But I realized from the start that the FDJ would become so important that we would be the ones who would do the real work. And as you see, I was right. The party youth secretariat is really not in a position to do youth work any more; the party as a whole has to do it.

In fact, the rivalry between Honecker and Verner continued until 1950, when Honecker succeeded in persuading the central secretariat to abolish the youth secretariat.

On March 7, 1946, founding ceremonies and demonstrations were held in all state capitals. In Saxony and Thuringia the first groups paraded with blue flags. The FDJ immediately took over all property of the youth committees. Hostels for apprentices and trainees, vacation camps, sports fields and playgrounds, youth hostels, etc. were automatically affiliated with it, so that youth work outside the FDJ became almost impossible.

In the *Länder* the founding celebrations had been planned under the strict control of the youth officers of the Soviet Military Administration, who were guided by SMAD directives from Berlin-Karlshorst. The speeches of the future *Land* chairmen had to be worked out down to the last word and submitted to the youth officers for approval. Phrases like "Anglo-American imperialism" or "Anglo-American capitalism" and of course terms such as "class struggle" were totally prohibited.

Honecker and Verner worked in Berlin with the newly formed Komsomol group within the political division of the Soviet Military Administration. Its leader, Stepanov, was a member of the Komsomol central committee. The sons of two German "Old Communists" had been assigned to this group: Markus Johannes (Mischa) Wolf, son of the writer Friedrich Wolf and now head of the foreign intelligence service of the DDR, and Grischa Kurella, son of Alfred Kurella. At that time both of them wore the uniform of officers of the Soviet Army. They had received their school and university education in the Soviet Union.

Cooperation with the Soviet officers was very close. All resolutions prepared by the central organizing committee had to be submitted to the political division of SMAD in Karlshorst, including even those concerning the organizational development of the central apparatus and, of course, personnel. Honecker therefore talked to the youth officers in Karlshorst on the telephone nearly every day and met with them several times a week. If questions of principle were involved, the KPD or SED board and the appropriate divisions of SMAD had to be consulted. For example, Honecker's speech at the first FDJ congress, as well as the drafts of the "basic rights" and the FDJ statutes, were not only discussed in advance with Stepanov, Kurella, and Wolf but also were submitted to Colonel Tulpanov for approval.

The First FDJ Congress

Before the KPD–SPD unification congress Honecker was rarely to be found in the offices of the future Central Council of the FDJ at 30–31 Kronenstrasse, the Central Youth Committee's new address. He, Paul Verner, and Heinz Kessler were actively engaged in preparing for the fifteenth (and final) KPD congress to be held in East Berlin on April 19 and 20, 1946. They also participated in the unification congress on April 21 and 22. This time Verner scored over Honecker, because it was he, as party youth secretary, who reported to the congress on achievements in youth work. He informed it that 175,000 young people had already joined the FDJ.[32]

Verner, not Honecker, also had the say when it came to formulating those sections of the principles and aims of the Socialist Unity Party and of the manifesto of the unification congress that dealt with youth matters. In contrast to the FDJ's ostentatious insistence on its nonpartisanship, the point the SED stressed was that German youth was the hope of the party and that "our *Weltanschauung* must become the faith of the young generation."[33]

Nevertheless, only Erich Honecker and Edith Baumann were elected to the first SED party executive. Paul Verner did not make it until 1950. He did, however, take over the SED youth section. Edith Baumann, Erich Honecker, and Peter Nelken constituted a party youth commission which collectively discussed all questions before they were submitted to the FDJ.

After the unification congress, the FDJ began to look toward its first congress, scheduled for Pentecost, 1946, in Brandenburg on the Havel. The choice of location was another example of Honecker's tactical skill and ability to impress his opponents by making political capital out of his sentimentality. It had originally been intended to hold the congress in a city in Saxony—in Dresden or Leipzig—because the Saxon branch of the FDJ was the strongest in the Soviet Zone. The *Land* secretariat had already made concrete proposals to this effect. Nevertheless, after discussing it with the SED youth secretariat, Honecker decided on Brandenburg, although the FDJ organization there was much weaker. He explained this change of mind to the non-Communist members of the central organizing committee on the grounds that Brandenburg was the place where he had spent seven years of his life behind prison walls.[34] In fact, he had something quite different in mind. In Brandenburg, Catholic youth was much stronger than the FDJ, and this suited Honecker's purposes exactly, because it offered an opportunity—so important at this first congress—to demonstrate the organization's nonpartisanship. In Saxony, on the other hand, all the district chairmen were KPD members, and the state chairman, Robert Bialek, had the reputation of being a particularly radical and impulsive Communist. In Saxony the congress might have looked somewhat slanted, and this was just what they wanted to avoid.

Honecker's report to the first congress also showed considerable tactical skill, sensitivity to the situation of youth, and ability to set forth the party line in complicated situations without arousing the opposition of the churches or the bourgeois parties. He did a masterly job of reformulating the concept of the National

Unity Front for a generation still under the influence of the Hitler Youth and in using its language:

A nation's real interests have nothing to do with warmongering, chauvinistic plans of conquest. What we mean by national values is, after all, everything good that promotes the progress of one's own people and the well-being of mankind, too. It's time to nail the lie that the Krupps, Thyssens, Klöckners, and Flicks are national figures. Those men don't act in a national or German way, and we deny point-blank their claim to do so. They were—and in our eyes still are—men without a sense of country.[35]

This combination of patriotism and cleverly packaged class-struggle theory, together with the term "men without a sense of country," scored a great hit even within the party, which adopted it in its own argumentation.

Honecker did an equally good job of combining the German Communists' claim to the whole of Germany with a declaration of war on heavy industry and the popular demand for German unification. Recalling his youthful work with the KJVD in the Saar, when the KPD was fighting the annexation of the region by France, he said:

However deep you scratch a true-blue Saxon, Mecklenburger, Bavarian, Berliner, or Rhinelander, you'll always find a good German. But scratch a federalist or a separatist and you can bet your life you'll find a war criminal or someone who's ready to become one. Let's take a look at those people! They're *Junkers*, who are scared of land reform because they're afraid it will cut the ground for future military action from under their feet. They're the financial and industrial magnates of the Rhine and the Ruhr who are afraid—and for good reason—that a democratic Germany might interfere with their future war plans. So our fight to preserve Germany's unity is absolutely indispensable for the victory of democracy, peace, and progress. We of the Free German Youth have therefore made the preservation of German unity our first principle.[36]

Honecker's presentation was so skillfully thought out that neither the churches nor the bourgeois parties could oppose it. Here the foundation stone of the agitational technique still used by the SED was laid. Conditions in the Western zones were not attacked on ideological or socio-political grounds; instead, examples were cited to prove that fascist movements were reemerging there, that basic rights to employment, education, recreation, and leisure had better chances of being realized in the Soviet Zone than in the West, and so on.

Honecker told me that while he was still drafting his report he had revealed the "secret of our work" for the immediate future:

> It's all very simple really. Our demands must be formulated in such a way that they can always be understood by the majority or that they conform to the Potsdam Agreement. If we succeed in this, the others [primarily the churches] will have to go along or risk finding themselves isolated or in conflict with the occupying power.

Honecker's presidential address sounded completely plausible and convincing. Most delegates thought he was serious about nonpartisanship, strength through unity, and multiple interests. Only a few of the initiated knew that the Soviet Military Administration had made its approval of the congress contingent upon the demonstration's providing some visible signal. There was still hope that it might succeed, at least so far as youth was concerned, in creating a nonpartisan unified organization for Germany as a whole—something the party had failed to achieve.

Anyone who knew the pressure Honecker was under at this time, and how afraid he was that his concept might still be ruined by the churches or the leftist sectarians, had to respect his self-control. His optimistic front and outer calm clearly reflected his strength of will. When the first day of the congress ended without any untoward incident, he dropped his mask. According to Edith Baumann, it was almost impossible to talk to him that evening, and he reacted to everything with intense irritation.

Fight over the Statutes

The hardest part of the congress was still to come: the meetings of the committees, their reports, and the election of the new executive. Here it became clear that Honecker's choice of a chairman for the statutes commission had not been a fortunate one. Although he was aware that this particular commission was dynamite, he approved the nomination and election of Robert Bialek, *Land* secretary of the FDJ in Saxony, to its chairmanship. Honecker knew Bialek to be an avowed enemy of the church, who would have preferred a working-class youth organization to

the FDJ, which he had once called a "mishmash." He also knew
that the churches would raise objections when the statutes were
formulated. Even after the congress began, he had said to Bialek:

The basic rights of the young generation have been unanimously
approved by the secretariat, so it's possible that they may also be
adopted unanimously by the congress. But that's not the case with the
statutes. Here the church representatives have raised serious objections. . . . So I checked with the party, and they've decided that we can
make big concessions in the statutes. We've also decided that you
should head the statutes commission, because you helped draft them
and you know more about them than anyone else. But watch out! The
churches are sending their two strongest representatives to the commission.[37]

The most controversial question was how the church representatives should be integrated into the FDJ leadership. Some of
the SED functionaries, mostly Communists from the Western
zones, took the view that they should be elected like all other officials. After all, who would ever vote a "holy man" into office on
an FDJ board? The church representatives, however, thought
that they would serve as a liaison between the church and the
FDJ, and it was therefore the right of the appropriate church
councils to name their own delegates. In preliminary talks this
compromise formulation had been reached: "The directors of the
liaison agencies will be delegated by the respective churches after
consultation with the FDJ."[38]

But this formulation went too far for those FDJ representatives
who had not yet realized why the party leadership attached so
much importance to cooperation with the church, so it was foreseeable from the start that there might be trouble in the statutes
commission. It was therefore a serious tactical mistake on Honecker's part to entrust the chairmanship of this particular commission to the gifted but undisciplined Robert Bialek.

Honecker made another mistake at that time. He failed to give
the SED members from the *Länder* and the Communists from the
Western zones who had been elected to this commission advance
information of the party's decision and to subject them to party
discipline. He even neglected to tell Bialek which members of the
commission belonged to the SED and KPD and which were non-
Communists. Doubt has since been raised whether this was really

negligence—as Honecker himself self-critically declared. Edith Baumann was more inclined to think that it was an example of Honecker's characteristic way of dropping the reins at a certain point and evading difficulties.

An explosion did in fact occur—though its only significance in this context is that it showed Honecker acting in a typical manner. The facts can be quickly outlined. The stiffest opposition to compromise on the statutes came from the state secretary for Sachsen-Anhalt, Hans Gerats of the SED. Nevertheless, Bialek managed to persuade Gerats at least to abstain from voting. The argument between them continued after the session was over. Bialek argued:

In view of political necessities . . . the FDJ is the right policy. Precisely because we want gradually to free German youth from the influence of the churches and the bourgeois parties, we need the FDJ. As events take their course, we'll get the upper hand in the FDJ and eliminate the influence of the church and the bourgeois parties step by step. But you can't do that with a mallet. The only thing you can do with a mallet is smash china!

Gerats replied:

It's confoundedly dangerous—that policy. The damned priests will gain more and more influence over the young people. What can we do against them? As a result of all these concessions to the churches and the bourgeois parties, our hands are practically tied for any kind of action against the clergy in Saxony—and they're getting more presumptuous all the time. I hate the whole lot of them. All they do is cheat us.

Bialek went on:

Do you think I'm particularly fond of them myself? But that's not the point. Speaking practically, we're using the policy of the carrot and the stick. Right now we're dangling the carrots, and you'd rather be wielding the stick. But your policy wants to do things backwards. Whoever performs the most active and the best work in the FDJ will come out on top. Give your damned priests . . . more work so that they can't pay so much attention to the young people. Put them on your state and district boards and keep them busy. Then they won't have so much time to bother with practical youth work.[39]

This conversation, which was carried on in loud tones, was

overheard by Kurt Woituczek, a Catholic delegate from the Eischs-feld in Thuringia and a co-member of the commission. Neither Bialek nor Gerats noticed him.[40] Woituczek alerted Diocesan Vicar Lange and Pastor Hanisch, who in turn notified their church councils. They decided to withdraw from the congress unless it dissociated itself from Bialek's remark the next day.

That is how matters stood when the third day of the congress began. Honecker's reaction showed that even then he was not fazed by complicated situations. Manfred Klein, Catholic dele-gate to the congress, says in his book *Jugend Zwischen den Dik-taturen* (Youth between Dictatorships):

When we arrived, somewhat late, at the conference building after church, Honecker and Major Bodin were waiting for us at the door. They told us quite openly that they were afraid something had hap-pened to mar the admirable harmony of the congress. From Bodin's explanations we gathered that he was afraid we were deeply upset about the interruption of the prayer. Pastor Hanisch repaid frankness with frankness. That was of no account, he said, but if a top official such as Robert Bialek, state secretary of the FDJ in Saxony, was going to wring the churches' necks, there wouldn't be any basis for future cooperation. The congress must be informed of this. We intended to tell the plenum what had happened and then leave the congress. Honecker's dismay was genuine and profound. He implored us not to carry out our intentions and to clear the matter up before entering the conference hall.[41]

Honecker's "genuine dismay" was actually feigned, because he was already fully informed about the church representatives' reaction and the reason for it. That morning there had been a private meeting of all *Land* executives at which they had been told to avoid all provocation, to instruct their delegations to exercise discipline, and to respond to every attempt by the church repre-sentatives to cause a breach with assurances of the unity and nonpartisanship of the FDJ. Paul Verner had already forbidden Bialek to speak and ordered him not to allow himself to be pro-voked in any circumstances. Gerhard Heidenreich's motion to submit the incident to a commission to be elected from within the congress also originated higher up; it had been formulated in collaboration with Captain Yerochin, youth officer of the Soviet Military Administration in Saxony.[42]

What Honecker really thought about the affair came out during a break in the conference, when it had been more or less disposed of. He said to Robert Bialek:

That was really something, Robert! We almost blew the whole congress. The FDJ's future was hanging by a thread. It just shows that you can't be too careful when you say something not meant for other people's ears. You're right, of course, but today there are some things one simply can't say out loud. Oh well, we'll straighten it out somehow or other.

When the contrite Bialek protested that he ought to submit to party punishment and be relieved of his position, Honecker replied:

Are you crazy? We need functionaries everywhere, but we need them most in youth work. . . . To sacrifice our best youth official just because of these firecrackers is out of the question. We'll pacify them somehow. Time will tell. We'll set up an investigating committee, and make Paul Verner chairman of it. You don't know Paul. He's smart, cooperative and obliging—and up to all the tricks. He'll tame them down all right. He's a genius at obstructionism. He'll argue them blue in the face until they don't know which end is up any more. After a few months they themselves will be anxious to bury the whole thing. Our nerves are stronger than theirs.[43]

Nevertheless, Bialek later paid the price for the incident. In November, 1946, when he had long forgotten it, the secretariat of the SED executive decided, in response to a motion by Honecker and Verner, that Bialek should relinquish his position as *Land* chairman of the FDJ in Saxony to Gerhard Heidenreich (now party secretary in the Ministry for State Security) and become *Land* youth secretary of the SED in Saxony.[44] In this way they hoped to remove him from active youth work without officially disciplining him. Since the party was considered the leading force and the party youth secretary was the formal head of the FDJ, this did not represent a demotion. In fact, however, it tied Bialek's hands, and his dynamic activism was considerably restricted, because the work of an SED youth secretary consisted essentially of bureaucratic party duties, while the field work with young people was the responsibility of the FDJ.

The importance Honecker and Verner attached to Bialek's transfer is shown by the fact that they both rushed off to Dresden when they learned that the Soviet Military Administration in

Saxony opposed the party executive's decision and was reluctant
to release Bialek from the FDJ. The arguments between Honecker
and Verner on the one side, and the SMAD officers on the other,
typify Honecker's behavior in those days. Although he was just as
interested as Verner, if not more so, in settling the Bialek case, he
left the negotiations largely to Verner. He did not want to become
involved in a conflict with SMAD. His reasoning was probably
this: if Verner succeeded in deposing Bialek as FDJ chairman
and making him youth secretary, he (Honecker) would be rid of
one of his most dangerous rivals in the FDJ. If he failed, however, Verner would have exposed himself and weakened his position in the party.

Bialek later recalled Honecker's saying triumphantly when they
met: "You see, Robert, there's no sense in opposing us. We have
all kinds of ways of achieving what we want." When Bialek reminded him that he had hardly shown his face during the whole
episode, he replied with a knowing smile: "That's exactly the
point. A good functionary is not one who does everything himself
but one who delegates the work to others while keeping an eye on
the overall picture. That affair was Paul's baby!"

The thing that disturbed Honecker most was that Bishop Dibelius had not come to Brandenburg. He is said to have been on his
way to the congress when he was intercepted by a messenger
from the church representatives and informed of the incident.
He decided to cancel his welcoming speech and returned home.
Honecker made the following comment:

> It's a pity of course that Bishop Dibelius didn't make an appearance
> at the conference. It would have helped our future work with Chris-
> tian youth considerably and strengthened our international reputation
> immediately. But it can't be helped. We'll pull through even without
> the divine blessing from Dibelius.[45]

In spite of everything, the elections to the first Central Council
went more or less according to plan. Altogether the first congress
was a milestone in Erich Honecker's career. Except for this one
incident, he had accomplished all the tasks entrusted to him. The
church representatives had remained "in the fold." The SED had
a safe majority in the first Central Council if only because the
newly elected *Land* secretaries were all SED members. On the
Central Council secretariat, however, there were eight SED offi-

cials to seven representatives of the churches and bourgeois parties—which maintained the outward appearance of a nonpartisan organization.

The participation of large numbers of young people from the Western zones created the image of an all-German organization, and the presence of seventeen foreign groups, some of which made welcoming addresses, struck an international note—considering Germany's isolation at the time—even though they represented exclusively Communist or pro-Communist organizations.

The first congress brought to an end in the Soviet Zone the vital opening phase in the founding of the first youth organization since the collapse of Germany.

6. Building a Cadre Apparatus

Tactical Difficulties and Successes

AFTER ITS FIRST CONGRESS, the Free German Youth began a period of hectic activity. By order of the party, the principal goal it was to pursue was to make itself the "cadre-building apparatus" and "cadre reservoir" of the party and the governmental machine. This task was of major importance for Honecker's career. The Soviet Union and the German Communists were following a different course toward reconstruction from the occupying powers and political forces in the Western zones. There, aided by the beginning of the cold war, the old higher strata were being reintegrated into the economy, administration, judiciary, police, and educational system, no matter how compromised they might be by their relations with the National Socialist dictatorship. The Russians, on the other hand, invoking the authority of the Potsdam agreement, completely demolished the former power structure and gradually replaced it by a new one.

In 1945 and 1946, however, the Communist and Social Democratic parties had very few leadership cadres at their disposal and very few medium and low-level functionaries. The old cadre of Communists who had survived the Third Reich consisted almost entirely of functionaries who had returned to Germany from emigration in the Soviet Union or the West or had spent the years of the Nazi regime in the underground or in prisons or concentration camps. The SPD did have a large number of experienced administrative officials, especially on the local level, but neither

the Russian occupation authorities nor the KPD trusted them—
not even after the compulsory merger of the Communist and
Social Democratic parties in the Socialist Unity Party. Most of
the KPD's functionaries had perished in Hitler's concentration
camps, and many of its members, especially those of the generation born between 1912 and 1920 who had been among the most
active in the Communist children's and youth organizations, had
been killed in the Spanish civil war or in World War II. One section of the pre-1933 party membership and KPD electorate had
more or less come to terms with National Socialism.

The remnants of the KPD that fought on in the resistance, still
loyal to communism, were prevented by the Nazi party's terrorism
and espionage system from immunizing their children against
fascism, if only by considerations of safety. The Russians and the
KPD emigrants who had returned from the Soviet Union regarded
the German "Old Communists" who had survived the Third Reich
or returned from emigration in the West as intrinsically unreliable. They considered the Communists who had remained in
Germany guilty of complicity and the emigrants returning from
capitalist countries as unreliable. For this reason the Soviet administration was particularly interested in the education and
ideological training of youth. At numerous meetings I attended
as an FDJ official, Colonel Tulpanov and, later, High Commis-
sioner Semyonov declared that the hope of the Soviet Union lay in
winning over German youth.

Directly or indirectly, then, Stalin's slogan about the youth
organization being the place where the party cadres would be
forged became the watchword of the FDJ's work as a whole.
Within a few years, hundreds and thousands of political and technical cadres in all fields were to be built up, on a scale hitherto
unknown even in the Soviet Union, into an elite whose essential
loyalty the party need never question.

Here lies the basis of Honecker's special position at that time,
his subsequent career, and his present position of power. In those
days he was responsible to the party for supplying new teachers
and judges, young police officers, future army cadres for the KVP
(paramilitary police), and so on. Today he has the backing of
these forces, which in the meantime have become decision-
makers.

After its first congress in 1946, the FDJ had more than 200,000 members. This, however, was not nearly enough to meet the countless demands for political appointees without endangering the so recently completed structure of the youth organization. The FDJ was therefore faced with three central tasks, which had to be accomplished virtually simultaneously:

1. Recruitment of new young members for the FDJ in conjunction with the buildup of new basic organizations and the expansion and training of leadership units.
2. Training of new members and functionaries through participation in mass activities and the establishment of large numbers of schools.
3. Meeting the permanent need for activist FDJ forces in the special fields of education, administration, justice, and police work—as well as in the party itself.

Without the rapid training of young, reliable forces of this sort, the planned transition to a people's democracy could not be achieved. So immediately after the first congress, in the summer of 1946, the Youth Training College was founded on the Bogensee in Berlin. State youth schools had been started in Saxony and Thuringia even before the congress. Now the state branches of the FDJ began to establish large numbers of district schools, where at first weekend courses were held and later longer ones.

All this had to be done very cautiously and without attracting attention, because the party leadership thought the time was not yet ripe to divorce itself from the bourgeois elements in the FDJ Central Council. The first step was to extend to the SED the strong position the KPD had achieved in the Soviet Zone with the help of the occupying power and to reinforce it by election results. At a meeting of state secretaries which I attended, Honecker re-defined the role of the FDJ so that he could mobilize its consider-able power behind the party. The FDJ, he said, was indeed a non-partisan organization but not a nonpolitical one. It therefore supported any activities that promoted an antifascist, democratic order. To win over youth "for the great ideals of freedom, human-ism, and a militant democracy" (Principles and Aims of the FDJ: Point 2) meant first to crush the Nazi ideology and to educate youth to recognize the roots of fascism, race-hatred, and wars of conquest, which were to be sought primarily among trust mag-nates, stockholders in heavy industry, *Junkers,* and Prussianism in general.

During this phase Honecker developed considerable tactical skill, which stood him in good stead later in dealing with the representatives of the West German bourgeoisie and nationalist groups. In 1946 and 1947 he succeeded in neutralizing the non-SED members of the Central Secretariat to the point where, despite their obvious misgivings, they were not prepared to precipitate a split. At the same time he led the FDJ into the first "all-out battles" of its history. First came participation in the campaign for a plebiscite in Saxony on the proposed law for the punishment of war criminals and Nazi activists and the elimination of the power of the industrial trusts (June 30, 1946) and active support of land reform. In both cases the FDJ directly or indirectly supported the activity of the SED and acted as its auxiliary. The plebiscite was limited to the *Land* of Saxony, but the FDJ passed its first big test in the Soviet Zone as a whole in the local, district, and county elections for the *Land* legislature held in September and October, 1946.

To maintain the nonpartisan façade of the FDJ while giving the SED active help in the election, Honecker, Verner, and Axen devised a special technique, which probably originated in the Soviet Military Administration. (At that time the *Land* FDJ boards received their instructions as to which candidates they should support in the first instance from the SMAD *Land* organizations.) The FDJ did not actively come out for the SED but called upon young voters to elect the one party that "represented the interests of the young generation" and would support "the basic rights of the young generation," especially political rights: the lowering of the voting age to eighteen.[46] That meant, of course, the SED, with which an agreement on the FDJ's demands had been reached in advance.

In fact, the FDJ was the only winner in the first and last relatively free elections held in the Soviet Zone. As a result, its authority was considerably strengthened, as was Erich Honecker's authority within the party. Despite the disappointing showing of the SED, the FDJ had succeeded in electing more than two thousand young people to the local councils, 225 youth representatives to the district ones, and thirteen FDJ members to the *Land* legislatures.[47]

The elected *Land* legislatures presented a front of democratic legitimacy behind which the party could complete the transition to a people's democracy. So after the elections even the FDJ no longer had any great interest in keeping the church and bourgeois representatives in the central leadership at any price. Honecker was instructed to shift the emphasis of the FDJ's work without delay to tightening up its organization, recruiting new members, and strengthening ideological training to the maximum. At the regular internal session with SED members from the states that preceded one of the first meetings of the Central Council in 1947, he told me with relief that the "tightrope walking" would soon be over. What had to be done now was turn the FDJ into an aggressive, disciplined, tightly organized youth movement. It would be better if the bourgeois elements would cooperate, but if they resisted they would be replaced by delegates from the other parties whose grounding in socialism would ensure better cooperation. "We won't do anything to provoke a break. But we won't go down on our knees to keep them either."

Another conclusion was drawn from the SED's disappointing showing in the election. Representatives of the Soviet Military Administration and the SED agreed that the FDJ must stress the nationalist angle more strongly. Many young people had not voted for the Socialist Unity Party because of the persisting influence of Nazi propaganda, which made it easy for the SED's opponents in the West Berlin and the Western zones to vilify it. In addition, the Soviet Union's German policy for 1947 envisaged a propaganda campaign for unification, with the object of leaving the Western powers holding the bag when the inevitable partition came. To supplement this line, which was put forward at the meeting of the premiers of all four zones of occupation in May, 1947, the FDJ was to try to establish closer ties with the youth organizations that had in the meantime been set up in the West.

So the fourth session of the Central Council (November 28–30, 1946) saw Erich Honecker beating the nationalist drum. Quoting extensively from Gottfried Keller, Ludwig Uhland, and Goethe, he called upon youth to fight for peace, freedom, and progress and proclaimed a "realistic humanism" whose essence would be "a new will for humanity."

The goal of our association is the free man aware of his organic ties to family, nation and the human race. . . . We want to arouse their sense of truth, justice, helpfulness, progress, and self-respect. . . . We

want ultimately to give them a world view which will rest upon rever-
ence for those noble laws of human communal life that stem from the
reason and the heart.[48]

This speech is important in evaluating Honecker because it
shows his ability to translate Ulbricht's broad political directives
into a language young people would respond to.

United Youth—United Germany

The year 1947 was Erich Honecker's nationalist year. The
steady intensification of the cold war and the alignment of the
zones of occupation with the corresponding power blocs were
deepening the division of Germany. Structural changes in the
Soviet Zone in 1945 and 1946 had created a new social climate
which impeded efforts toward unification. Despite this, or perhaps precisely because of it, the Soviet Union was demonstrating
its readiness to make concessions by scrupulously observing the
Potsdam agreement.[49]

Here Honecker showed his talent for negotiation. At the February meeting of the Central Council, the church representatives
had attempted a minor palace revolution. They introduced a motion which they hoped would force the SED majority in the Council to take a position on the question of force.[50] Honecker had no
way of informing the party, but he quickly called in the most
reliable *Land* delegation leaders and informed himself of the facts.
He instructed them not to react to provocation and ordered several good speakers to respond to the expected motion quite objectively. Whatever happened, they must avoid "giving those people a chance to precipitate a split. On the other hand, we can't
compromise to the point of supporting the motion." The first
thing to remember was: keep calm. Act as if nothing were wrong.
Bring up pertinent arguments and delay a decision. The time was
not far off when these "professional disturbance-makers" would
have to be replaced by other, more cooperative representatives of
the bourgeois camp. But so long as adequate preparations for this
had not been made, a break must be avoided at all cost.

This was done. The motion, introduced by Manfred Klein, was
hotly debated, and the minority quickly realized that it had no
chance of passing. But since the whole debate was carried on ac-

cording to democratic rules of order, the minority could not find any plausible excuse for an official rupture. In the end, it seemed relieved when a motion was made to postpone the discussion to an appropriate future date.

Shortly after this came an exchange of letters between the German Catholic Youth and the FDJ, which led to a meeting in November, 1947, between Honecker and Josef Rommerskirchen, president of the German Catholic Youth. In a letter signed by Ludgera Kersholt and Josef Rommerskirchen, the lay leaders of the German Catholic Youth stated their position with regard to the "basic rights of the young generation," which had been distributed, with an accompanying letter, to all youth groups in the Western zones by the first FDJ congress in Brandenburg. The Catholic youth leaders recognized with pleasure "the FDJ's desire to extricate youth from its passivity and misery and to lead it toward active collaboration in the great public tasks for the life and future of German youth." Their reaction to the efforts of the Brandenburg youth congress was "in this sense very positive." Nevertheless, they denied the FDJ's claim to represent "German youth as a whole." They also objected to its demand that the voting age be lowered to eighteen and that "German youth as a whole be organized within the FDJ."

In spite of these differences of opinion, the Catholic youth leadership corps stressed that it would welcome "genuine cooperation of youth organizations, whatever their political views, in democratically structured youth committees" and declared itself essentially in agreement with the social demands of the Brandenburg youth congress. "We recognize with pleasure the positive elements in the work of the Brandenburg youth congress and gladly participate in it as part of German youth."[51]

After the clash in the Central Council in February, this letter came as a godsend to Honecker. In Thuringia shortly afterward, Edith Baumann said that it had been a real bombshell in Berlin and that Honecker had used it as a trump card against all those members of the SED executive who thought that the FDJ was in too much of a hurry to become a cadre organization. Honecker waved the letter about like a trophy and rushed over to the party executive in the Wallstrasse to show it to Walter Ulbricht. He came back beaming and said the letter had been a great help in taking the wind out of the sails of those who thought the FDJ should proceed more cautiously and guard against the risk of a premature withdrawal of the bourgeois representatives. This letter was the best proof that the FDJ was not acting too hastily.

The reply to Catholic youth, signed by Honecker but composed by Horst Brasch and Kessler, was conciliatory and cooperative. The FDJ's readiness to collaborate "in youth groups and committees" was particularly stressed, although "in certain questions" differences of opinion prevailed. The FDJ denied ever having claimed to be "sole representative of all German youth" and recalled its invitation to all youth organizations to attend the world youth conference in Prague in 1947.[52]

Second Congress: Meissen, 1947

When the second FDJ congress was held at Pentecost, 1947, the major structural changes in the Soviet Zone were more or less complete. But the time had still not come to move on to the "new-type party" and force the former Social Democrats out of office once and for all. This placed the Communists in the curious situation of seeing the Free German Youth leading the political vanguard, while the party—according to Leninist theory, the leading force—followed along behind. This tactic, which was also used against the Western occupying powers and the political forces in the Western zones, strengthened Honecker's position. Bypassing the secretariat of the party executive, on which eight Social Democrats still sat opposite eight Communists, Ulbricht, together with Honecker, laid down the line their youth policy would follow. Honecker and Verner were then to work out a draft, which would be submitted to the secretariat. Honecker meticulously followed Ulbricht's instructions, which included keeping the drafts for the secretariat as general as possible so that there should not be too much discussion in the party leadership.

Later, when the "new-type party" had long been a reality, Honecker remarked how simple everything is today. At that time, between 1945 and 1946, he had had to walk a tightrope between the bourgeois representatives in the FDJ secretariat, on the one side, and the SED secretariat, on the other. "And even then you had to watch what you said. If it hadn't been for Comrade Ulbricht! . . . He always gave me fresh courage. He backed me to the hilt all the way."

In 1947 Ulbricht ordered Honecker to use the second FDJ congress to launch the national "Campaign for German Unity," which
the SED's Second Congress would then adopt as its primary objective. A demonstration for German unification was important,
because a plan to develop the governmental basis for the future
DDR had already been conceived, and the more strongly the FDJ
supported the unification campaign at its congress, the more effectively these preparations could be concealed. But it was not
just a matter of camouflage. The Russians realized that they
would have no say in the reshaping of Germany as a whole once
the individual administrations were firmly established in the
Western zones and in their own area of occupation. They hoped
still to impede this process by mobilizing all German forces prepared to cooperate.

For the USSR the FDJ's second congress also had another purpose: to impress the Western powers with "youth's desire for
unity." It was supposed to create the impression that the wishes of
vast segments of the German population coincided with Soviet
policy and that the Western powers alone were resisting this kind
of development. The Russians had then no way of knowing how
strong an influence they would retain over Germany as a whole.
They still hoped to oblige the Western powers to enforce land reform, some expropriation of heavy industry, and higher repara-
tions payments. Also, it was not yet clear what effect the merger
of the Communist and Social Democratic parties in the SED
would have in the West. The Russians therefore developed a mul-
titrack policy, pressing ahead with the foundations for a separate
state, while at the same time keeping the door open for negotiations. In addition, all the political potential in the West was to be
activated in support of reunification.

In this situation Honecker was extraordinarily successful in
speaking to youth in language it could understand. After numerous conversations with representatives of the Soviet Military Administration and with Ulbricht, he, Verner, and Edith Baumann
drafted a speech, which, after countless changes, additions, and
revisions, was approved by Ulbricht and Pieck. Honecker had indeed succeeded in translating the policy of the SED into the language of youth. Most of the delegates, including the bourgeois
ones, could find little to object to. Nonetheless, his speech was
forceful and far more aggressive than the one he had delivered

at the first congress. He countered his opponents' argument that the FDJ was communistic:

If any one of them has the nerve to find anything communistic in wage increases for 1,800,000 young people, the 42-hour week for juveniles up to the age of sixteen, the admission of sons and daughters of the people to educational institutions, the take-over of *Junkerland* by free peasants and of its castles by young people, the right to participate, the youth franchise in Saxony—in brief, in our struggle, on behalf of over half a million young people, to give youth a bigger role in society, then we say quite openly: all right, we prefer that kind of communism to the world of the men from whom those hacks take their orders.[53]

At the second congress Honecker proceeded to outline the Communist interpretation of the role of the Weimar Republic and the reasons for its downfall. This was the official starting signal for partisan interpretations within the FDJ. For the first time, he used the expression "monopoly capitalism" in this connection— an expression which at the first congress in 1946 had still been prohibited by the Soviet representatives. His 1947 definition is interesting because in 1971 he used essentially the same arguments in demanding the separation of the DDR from the Federal Republic.

As we see it, Weimar fell because it lacked orientation. Out of its soil grew the fascist tyranny. It proved that to combine democracy and monopoly capital under one roof is as impossible as to combine fire and water. It is impossible if only because, as we see it, monopoly capitalism would try to rebuild its positions. It would again try to influence public opinion through all available channels. It would try to recapture its position in the world market through a war of aggression.[54]

He gave a clever explanation of the FDJ's rejection of parliamentary democracy:

We hate fascism and its tyranny. But we despise Weimar for its weakness in dealing with the two or three hundred families who ruled heaven and earth there. We despise it for its weakness toward the terrorism of the Nazi storm troops. Last but not least, we despise it because the misery of our own times has its roots in the weakness of Weimar.

We have no ties—no ties at all—to the formal democracy of the old, pre-1933 days. We are unshakably aware that fascist barbarism, with its suppression of all liberal order, its extermination cars and shots in the back of the head, is abominable. Not for nothing have we gone through the hell of war and the agony of the collapse of our fatherland—for which Hitler was to blame.[55]

In the matter of German unity Honecker played a major political role at the second congress. After rigorous discussion with Ulbricht, this section of his speech had been separately checked and considerably supplemented by the Soviet Military Administration. Honecker was still working on it when the congress opened. He told me and Ernst Horn, FDJ secretary for Thuringia, that he still had to revise the section on policy for Germany because the Russian comrades had expressed some further "wishes." He was very proud that it should fall to him to announce the Soviet Union's plan for Germany and the SED's German policy before such an assembly.

He began by deploring the differences of opinion among the victorious powers that had developed during the foreign ministers' conference held in Moscow in March and April, 1947, and expressing the hope that they might be overcome. Then he said that it was the wish of the young generation that Germany should get a peace treaty that would enable the German people "to deal ruthlessly with those primarily responsible for Germany's predicament." Another item he mentioned was "the complete elimination of economic power positions in the hands of monopoly capitalists and big landowners." This, he suggested, would be more effective than "simply sentencing a few of the culprits to eight to ten years of forced labor."

He dealt in considerable detail with the subject of German unity, provided for in the Potsdam agreement. Opposing all separatist plans, he declared that the young generation, "on whose shoulders democratic Germany will some day rest, can never accept a division of Germany based on coercion." In accordance with the Russians' wish that pressure be brought to bear on the Western occupying powers, he said that it was a mistake to suppose that "we, the German people," could do nothing "to preserve a peace which to a great extent serves German interests too."

We must therefore emphatically insist that such notions are mistaken and quite uncalled for. On the contrary, the attitude of the

German people and its youth has a decisive bearing on the Allies' approach to the handling of the German question.[56]

He then discussed with unusual frankness the problem of German economic unity. The Russians had apparently asked that this section of the speech in particular be expanded. They obviously already knew that a few days after the congress, on May 29, 1947, in Frankfurt on the Main, General Clay and General Robertson would announce the formation of the Bizonal Economic Council. The fact that this section of Honecker's speech had been cleared with SMAD gives added significance to his statement that in the matter of Germany's economic unity the American and Russian viewpoints largely coincided:

America favors economic rehabilitation and joint exploitation of German resources. The Soviet Union favors the execution of the Potsdam agreement, that is to say, the economic unity of Germany. To attain this economic unity, I recommend that the Bizonal agreement between the British and American zones, which is an obstacle to it, be terminated and that steel production in Germany be raised to ten to twelve million tons a year.[57]

Honecker stressed that "the Ruhr and the Saar must unquestionably remain German," but took a less positive stand on the question of the eastern frontier, merely expressing the hope that it would not become a source of chauvinistic agitation. "We strongly favor the fostering of friendly relations between the German and the Polish people."[58]

He then turned from high-level policy to the social, economic, and public-health problems of youth and to vocational training. He spoke openly and critically about how few rights apprentices enjoyed, about widespread ill health and unemployment among young people, and about the lack of training programs.[59] He advocated the elimination of youthful unemployment and recommended that the FDJ help to place the more than 180,000 boys and girls about to leave school in training programs. He was especially outspoken about young people's precarious state of health.[60] This state of affairs made it questionable "whether in some areas of Germany a love of democracy can be aroused in youth unless at the same time everything possible is done to change things."[61]

Honecker's efforts to improve the situation of young people were genuine. Naturally he attacked social shortcomings in the Western zones much more sharply in order to accentuate the contrast between the Soviet Zone and the areas administered by the Western powers. But this tactic also gave him an opportunity to defend the interests of youth in the Soviet Zone more openly.

Years later, when we were alone in the secretariat, he told me that it had been necessary then to "give them a prod" ("them" being both the Russians and the SED leadership). It was true that he had concentrated on the negative aspect of things in the Western zones, but this had enabled him to point out problems in the Soviet Zone. "The quickest way to where you want to go isn't always a straight line," he said with a smile. "With the magic words: 'If you don't put anything in, you don't get anything out' we got them moving very nicely."

The belief commonly held in the West that the SED did so much for youth only in order to win it over for its own purposes is certainly true; on the other hand, we should not forget that in those days it was not always easy to gain the support of the party functionaries, particularly on the medium and lower levels. In the early years, the efforts of the party and FDJ leadership to support youth met with considerable resistance in the SED and in the administration. It was an undeniable triumph on Honecker's part to eliminate many of these obstacles through skillful tactics. No doubt he did it partly to further his career, but I often got the impression that he was also prompted by his social conscience.

The point of his speech at the second congress was not lost on the SMAD representatives. I remember a conversation with Captain Komin, youth officer for Thuringia and, one might almost say, a co-founder of the FDJ, who over the years came to feel closer to that organization than to his Komsomol unit. After Honecker's speech he came up to me with a grin and said in his harsh German: "Comrade Honecker really went after us this time!"

Honecker's speech to the second congress was an unqualified success. His statements on German policy raised him overnight from the status of a youth official to one of the leading decision-makers in the Soviet Zone, head of his own governmental empire. Edith Baumann proudly announced to the congress that 454,231 young people had joined the FDJ in the first year of its existence.

Its total membership, including the units in the Western zones, was over half a million.[62] This gave added significance to what Honecker had to say.

Peace Flight to the East

One important duty the Soviet Military Administration and the party required of the FDJ in 1947 was to make an international appearance before the other youth organizations in the Western zones could do so. This was to prove to world opinion that the Free German Youth was accepted by a large number of foreign organizations as a nonpartisan, unified organization of German youth. Groups of foreign observers had in fact attended its second congress in Meissen, including delegations from the Yugoslavian People's Youth, the Komsomol, and the World Federation of Democratic Youth (WBDJ). These contacts needed to be developed in preparation for the FDJ's admission to the Federation. To break down the resistance to German youth that still existed even within the pro-Communist foreign youth movement, some visible gesture was necessary. A visit to the USSR by a delegation of leading FDJ officials would, it was hoped, do a lot to overcome the lack of acceptance. Besides, the FDJ favored such a visit for reasons of its own. Within the framework of the transition to a people's democracy, and handicapped by its nonpartisan status, it had to give the Soviet Union a leading role in its vocational-training system without at first being able to justify this ideologically on Communist grounds. The first visit of an FDJ delegation to the country that had been worst devastated by Hitler's troops offered a good opportunity for propaganda.

At one of the first meetings of the Central Council after the second congress, Pastor Hanisch, of all people, expressed the wish that some young Germans might be invited to visit the Soviet Union.[63] Honecker told me later that the pastor's initiative resulted from a conversation with SMAD political officers, who had encouraged him to make the proposal. He did so on the assumption that he and Diocesan Vicar Lange would accompany the delegation. His innocent suggestion gave Honecker the occasion to send to SMAD the official letter already agreed upon between them. Shortly afterward, on July 17, 1947, the answer was received: the Anti-Fascist Committee of the Soviet Union had invited eleven members of the Free German Youth to Moscow for the sports parade.[64]

The selection of the delegation raised great problems, because all the political groups still represented in the FDJ wanted to be included. Then SMAD abruptly decided that the delegation must be limited to five people and that there was no time for lengthy deliberations, because the flight was leaving the next night, July 18. So Honecker arranged that in addition to himself only Edith Baumann, Heinz Kessler, Robert Menzel, and Herbert Geisler should go. Geisler was the only non-SED member; he belonged to the Liberal Democratic Party. He had been extremely loyal to the FDJ from the start and was one of the bourgeois representatives whom Honecker expected to retain in the organization. He kept the diary of the delegation, which was published under his name by the Neues Leben publishing company, with a political introduction by Erich Honecker.

Nevertheless Geisler later resigned from the FDJ, and as a result was the victim of a typical falsification of his photograph. Twenty years after this visit, the periodical *Junge Welt* commemorated that "historic event" by publishing a photograph showing Robert Menzel, Edith Baumann, Erich Honecker, and Heinz Kessler. The same picture had been published on page 47 of *Friedensflug Nach Osten* (Peace Flight to the East), except that there Herbert Geisler appears next to Robert Menzel. On the photograph reproduced twenty years later, his figure has been cut out. The caption says only: "Twenty years ago . . . five representatives of the FDJ, led by its chairman, Erich Honecker, flew to the Soviet Union for the first time."[65]

The delegation, which took part in the traditional sports rally of Soviet Youth in Moscow, also went to Stalingrad and Leningrad, visited a Pioneer camp and innumerable factories, and gathered information on educational questions. In his report on the visit, Honecker discussed principally whether foreigners enjoy freedom of movement in the Soviet Union, whether Soviet citizens can voice open criticism, and why there is only one political party. He commented that in the Soviet Union socialism did not imply a mass society, but that Russian society centered on man as a human being.[66]

This first visit to the Soviet Union was indeed an unforgettable experience for Honecker and the other members of the delegation. They were the first to see Russia since the war. The terrible devastation in Stalingrad and Leningrad was still plainly visible and came as a great shock to Honecker. He was not putting on an act or playing a political role when he gave us his impressions in a private talk after the special session of the Central Council. He spoke enthusiastically about how different Moscow looked from the way he remembered it in 1930. He was particularly impressed by the many new buildings. He estimated that more than half of them had been erected since 1930 and suggested that this tremendous building program proved the invincibility of the Soviet system. When one considered the circumstances in which the Russian comrades had begun in 1917, surrounded by a hostile world, with a backward, illiterate people, weakened by foreign intervention, civil war, poverty, famine, internal terrorism, and sabotage, when one recalled the size of this gigantic empire, and above all when one remembered that it had had only ten or twelve years between the chaos of civil war and foreign intervention and World War II to devote to internal development, then one realized what gigantic pioneering feats communism could perform.

This was the first time I heard Honecker state his view of Germany's future plausibly and convincingly:

I can only say, Comrades, that in 1930 I was delighted by the Soviet comrades' faith in the future. I was less impressed by what they had built than by the Russian people's own dynamism and strength. They were always talking about what things would be like tomorrow, and it took a lot of imagination for me to see it. But now I've seen what they've accomplished in those ten years. And now I'm a hundred percent sure that nothing can stop them on their way to communism.

And I'll tell you something else. If we in Germany want to reach our goal of building a modern socialist Germany out of the rubble of Hitlerist fascism, the one and only way we can do it is side by side with our Soviet comrades and with their support. It's true that the Nazi occupiers inflicted deep wounds on the land of the Soviets, but now that I've seen what they achieved between 1930 and 1940, I have no doubts. In a few years those wounds will be healed, and the Soviet Union will be a strong country. No, it will be the strongest country in the world! If we remain the ally of the Soviet Union, all Germany will soon belong to us, and then nothing can stop socialism in Europe.

Although this conversation took place more than twenty years ago, I remember it vividly because Honecker presented his con-

fession of faith in the Soviet Union with such fervor and provoca-
tive impact. Looking back, I am convinced that this first visit to
Russia marked a milestone in his development. In later years
when doubt or criticism of the Soviet Union was voiced among
the top FDJ decision-makers, Honecker would not content himself with a reference to party orders or Russian sacrifices in
World War II. He would always recall his 1947 visit and empha-
size that no matter what had happened, it was only at the side of
the Soviet Union that the SED could pursue an effective policy.

During the trip, various incidents revealed some bourgeois
traits in Honecker's character. The other members of the delegation were not the only ones to notice them; to the Russian youth
officers, too, they came as an unexpected sidelight. Herbert Geisler
says with some amusement in his diary that Honecker took a deck
of *skat* cards with him: "Customs inspection. Our suitcases are
checked. Everything in order. Only Erich's *skat* cards raise a
smile."[67]

Or to quote another passage from Geisler's diary:

> We keep seeing men carrying children in their arms, looking as
> proud as peacocks. Edith can't get over it. "That will give the Berlin
> Women's League something to talk about!" she says.
> "Just so long as they don't try to introduce it!" Erich retorts.[68]

Much as he admired the Soviet Union, there were certain things
he would not have accepted for himself or for Germany. Recalling his impressions of Stalingrad, where many people were still
living in holes in the ground, he said with a glance at Edith Baumann: "We simply couldn't imagine it. For us it would mean the
end of the world if we had to do without flush toilets and baths."
For all his admiration of Russian frugality, this remark indicated
to me that Honecker was truly aware of the civilization gap between Russia and Germany, deriving from their different history.

Something else also became clear. Honecker was already quite
at home in the bureaucratic status system. He told us with apparently genuine emotion that as a German he had felt ashamed
when he saw the devastation in Stalingrad and Leningrad, yet he
took it as a matter of course that the delegation should be luxuri-
ously housed and fed, while the inhabitants of those cities were
living in foxholes and had to make do with the bare necessities.

It never occurred to him to ask his Russian hosts to cut out the luxury and give the German group the same food as the Russian people. I think it was Otto Funke of Thuringia who confronted him with this question. Honecker looked at him in bewilderment. He seemed embarrassed and said that in fact they had expected to sleep in tents in Stalingrad. But after they had seen the city's wonderful rebuilding achievements, they could not possibly have thought, as a delegation of German youth, of offending the Russian comrades. He added that such criticism almost amounted to egalitarianism and was nothing but bourgeois nonsense.

So Honecker's visit to Russia had a personal significance besides its official political one. After ten years imprisonment and many ideological uncertainties connected with complicated popular-front tactics within the nonpartisan youth organization, he had firm ground under his feet again. Although he never said so, we all felt that after this trip he was more self-confident and more authoritative in his bearing.

International Endeavors

After the Russian trip, Honecker was to attend the world youth conference in Prague from August 21 to August 30. The World Federation of Democratic Youth had originally invited a group of a hundred German guests to the first world youth festival in Prague, but they had been refused entry visas.[69] Honecker was accompanied only by Horst Brasch, the one German observer who had been allowed to attend the world youth meeting in London in 1945.[70] Honecker was to report to the WBDJ council on the situation of German youth and try to arrange for the FDJ to be admitted to the League.

Here Honecker and the Russians did not see eye to eye. While Honecker believed that immediate admission of the FDJ would help it to gain prestige in the Western zones, the vice-president of the WBDJ, Nicolai Michailov, who was also president of the Komsomol, and the Soviet Military Administration in Karlshorst took the view that the League must abide by one of its own by-laws which restricted membership to national organizations. Moreover, it would be better for the FDJ to concentrate for the time being on building up an all-German youth fellowship. Long after the FDJ had joined the World Federation, Honecker re-

vealed that in 1947 he had been very reluctant to go to Prague,
because he didn't relish being "lectured." But he went just the
same.

Although Honecker always professed to be an internationalist,
he drew a fine distinction between foreign Communist representatives whose parties were in power and those from capitalist
countries. The president of the WBDJ at that time was Guy de
Bouisson, a French aristocrat and student in whom Honecker saw
a descendant of the Frenchmen who had occupied and exploited
his homeland, the Saar, after World War I. Whenever he encountered de Bouisson, he was courteous but extremely reserved.
He had no wish to appeal "to people of that sort" to admit the
FDJ to membership.

His attitude toward the WBDJ later became even more critical.
As the FDJ grew more powerful, he treated representatives of the
Federation condescendingly and more than once remarked that
they were, after all, dependent on the FDJ for financial contributions and other help. He made this very clear not only to the bourgeois representatives but also to the Communists from the West.
So far as contributions were concerned, he was always very gen-
erous to them, but a certain arrogance went along with the gener-
osity. By the early 1950s for instance, the FDJ was already fur-
nishing tents, flags, and special equipment for nearly all the
Federation's European meetings, printing its numerous brochures,
and even providing it with special cars fitted with cages from
which the obligatory flock of peace doves could be released. These
contributions, in addition to considerable financial ones, sometimes prompted Honecker to observe that FDJ wasn't just a cow
to be milked indefinitely, but that the time had now come to
grant it appropriate functions in the secretariat and on the executive committee.

In 1947, however, this was still a long way off. In Prague
Honecker spoke for forty-five minutes on the political and economic situation of Germany and the different course developments were taking in the various zones. He stressed emphatically
that certain successes were already visible in the Soviet Zone,
while in the West power was back in the hands of the old gang.
He formulated the FDJ's request for admittance to the World
Federation of Democratic Youth very skillfully by representing the
Free German Youth as the one organization in which all progres-

sive youth forces had come together. He hoped in this way to get around the bylaw that restricted Federation membership to national youth organizations.

After a lengthy debate, in which even some Communist representatives expressed resentment of Germany—which angered Honecker—the Federation Council passed a resolution on German youth. The FDJ's application was refused, on the grounds of the bylaw. Erich Honecker was instructed to take measures for the formation of an all-German youth committee to include all the major democratic youth groups. The WBDJ council advised further cooperation with all democratic youth organizations in Germany and recommended that the Free German Youth strengthen its effort to educate German youth "in the spirit of democracy."[71]

Years later Erich Honecker and Horst Brasch were still laughing at the arrogant formulation of the Federation Council's resolution. When a strong FDJ delegation (of which I was a member) went to the world youth festival in Budapest in 1949, Honecker said sarcastically: "Now we'll tell the Federation a thing or two about our successes in education." He himself did not take the episode too seriously. As he said later, he had already realized that international recognition would come in direct proportion to the FDJ's achievements and successes "on the home front."

The All-German Conference

A success of this kind "on the home front" was exactly what Erich Honecker was looking for in November, 1947, when he met with representatives of the major youth groups of the Western zones in Altenberg, the traditional headquarters of Catholic youth. The starting point of this meeting was the correspondence of spring, 1947, between the German Catholic Youth and the FDJ, and also Honecker's speech at the second FDJ congress in Meissen and the letter the congress had addressed to all democratic youth organizations and youth groups in Germany. This letter had suggested getting together a team of German youth groups to work toward a fellowship of German youth in which the individual units would enjoy full independence. The FDJ's purpose was to put into practice the SED's plan to create all-German committees that would bring influence to bear on the

Allied foreign ministers' discussions and decisions with regard to Germany's political and economic unity.[72]

So in November, 1947, at Altenberg House, Josef Rommerskirchen and Willi Weiskirch representing Catholic youth, Heinz Westphal and Erich Lindstädt representing the Falcons, Perrey representing Youth Sport from the British Zone, Dr. Jordan and Dr. Gruber representing Confederate Youth, and Klaus von Bismarck representing Protestant youth[73] met with the FDJ delegation led by Honecker. Edith Baumann and Heinz Kessler were the other two FDJ representatives.[74]

Preliminary talks had been held at the Youth Training College on the Bogensee shortly before the second FBJ congress, and in his congressional speech Honecker had spoken very optimistically about their results:

Although there is still a conflict of opinion on a number of questions, as, for instance, in the matter of cooperation with the World Federation for Democratic Youth, we do not see this as an obstacle to cooperation within the national framework of Germany.[75]

There were some sharp clashes in Altenberg, because other youth organizations in the Soviet Zone had not been able to participate. Here again Honecker revealed his skill in negotiating. Although the attacks of the Western youth representatives could not be refuted or argued out of existence, he is said to have succeeded in soothing ruffled feelings, minimizing divisiveness and focusing the spotlight on "the great national tasks" that could only be accomplished jointly.[76] At any rate the conference was certainly not as unproductive as Willi Weiskirch suggested in 1971.[77]

On some questions at least agreement was reached. "It was decided to recommend all groups to address a resolution to the foreign ministers' conference in London urging the creation of a unified, democratic Germany." And cooperation was to be strengthened "by the exchange of information derived from practical experience." It was further agreed that there should be another meeting at Sudelfeld House in Bavaria in February, 1948, when the "basic rights of the young generation" adopted at the first FDJ conference in Brandenburg would be discussed, with the object of expanding them into a working basis for all organizations.[78]

So Honecker brought back at least a partial success, even though he had not achieved his primary goal of establishing a fellowship of German youth. The Sudelfeld meeting, it is true, never took place, and attempts to integrate at least the West German FDJ into the youth fellowship that was later formed came to nothing. Nevertheless the party leadership in East Berlin was very satisfied with the partial success of Altenberg, and this again strengthened Honecker's position.

The year 1947, then, was an important one in his career. At the second congress he had succeeded in interpreting SED policy without letting the bourgeois representatives precipitate a break. In his visit to Russia and his appearances in Prague and Altenberg, he had shown himself to be a politician of stature. His authority in the SED leadership had grown.

In his private life too his status had been reinforced by his marriage to Edith Baumann, a fellow member of the SED executive, who was widely esteemed by her many confidants and friends. A daughter, Erica, was born to them in 1948. This marriage marked the end of Honecker's bachelor existence; he began to live as regular a life as circumstances permitted. They moved into a spacious apartment in an old building at 12 Puderstrasse, Berlin-Treptow, where Honecker, still good with his hands, did much of the interior decorating himself. Edith Baumann's influence on him was positive in every respect. He looked better groomed and had more poise than before. Decisions concerning his staff—especially those involving the disciplining of other officials—were often made less harsh or obviated altogether by Edith Baumann.

At that time Honecker made the impression of a very unassuming man who lived quite unostentatiously. In this respect he was agreeably different from many Communists who had spent their best years in prison or concentration camps and now wanted to make up for all they had missed. Such time as his official duties allowed for private life he would spend playing his beloved *skat*. He also enjoyed movies and the theater and going out to dinner with friends. He was fond of hearty dishes like pig's feet with sauerkraut and purée of peas, and would get a childish pleasure out of devouring two full portions of pig's feet while his friends were having trouble finishing one. Only one man could beat him at this: Robert Bialek, who could eat three portions. Colleagues who knew about the tension between them used to say facetiously that Honecker could never get over the fact that Robert's stomach was bigger than his.

Erich Honecker was always a very moderate drinker. He would take a couple of glasses of beer now and again, but he was not very fond of hard liquor such as schnapps or vodka. The countless toasts that had to be drunk in vodka at all the receptions he attended caused him some difficulty, and as there was no way out, he was usually ill after these affairs.[79]

7. The "New-Type" FDJ

Withdrawal of the Bourgeois Representatives

THE YEARS 1948–50 took Honecker higher up the ladder leading to the control center of the Social Unity Party. He became one of Ulbricht's principal allies and, as president of the Free German Youth, head of the SED's most important auxiliary. Nonetheless, after the stormy events of 1946 and 1947, 1948 inevitably brought him some reverses, too. At the meeting of the secretariat of the FDJ Central Council on January 28, 1948, the long-awaited break with the bourgeois representatives finally occurred. Two representatives of the Christian Democratic Union (CDU) and the Liberal Democratic Party (LDP), together with their colleagues from the Central Council staff, announced their resignation from the FDJ.

The withdrawal of four bourgeois representatives from the Central Council secretariat had repercussions lower down. In most *Land* secretariats and many district directorates it was followed by the resignation or expulsion of all those bourgeois representatives who were no longer willing to go along with the FDJ's more and more obvious espousal of the SED party line. The members of the LDP and CDU who remained—whether out of opportunism or because they thought they could reconcile the new direction the FDJ was taking with their own *Weltanschauung*—were the ones who felt themselves to be FDJ functionaries first and members of their party only secondarily.

While the FDJ's nonpartisan character had once again been

97

formally preserved, Honecker had some trouble with the SED leadership. Ulbricht and Pieck took the attitude that this clearing of the air in the FDJ was useful because it had to come sooner or later. Ulbricht assured Honecker that the exposure of this "split in youth" could only strengthen the FDJ's fighting potential.[80] Other members of the party secretariat, however, especially former Social Democrats, criticised Honecker for having been in too much of a hurry and thus letting slip a chance of unification with the youth organizations in the Western zones.[81]

But much weightier problems faced him inside the FDJ. As we have mentioned, the *Land* branches had developed quite autonomously during the first few years of their existence, because the Central Council regarded the retention of the bourgeois representatives as its primary responsibility and therefore could not offer very effective central leadership. This had to be changed. But the *Land* directorates were accustomed to independence and often treated instructions from Berlin with contempt or even ignored them completely. The Berlin headquarters had a hard time asserting its authority over the lower levels of the organization. At this time it had no central program that the *Land* branches were bound to support, and there was also a shortage of functionaries who could influence half a million young people ideologically or organize them into an effective force. Further, there were great fluctuations within the functionary apparatus, chiefly because, simultaneously with its own expansion, the FDJ had to supply the party and governmental machine with more and more officials. In 1948 alone three thousand FDJ officials were transferred to high-level bureaus in the economy, the mass organizations, and the parties—the majority of course going to the SED. A large number of FDJ members also joined the People's Police.[82]

So at the end of 1948 the FDJ found itself in a real growth crisis. At the sixteenth session of the Central Council (November 18–19, 1948) Erich Honecker felt compelled to voice some sharp criticisms, which were reflected in the Council's resolutions.[83] While he deplored the fluctuations in the cadre structure, which made sustained work impossible, he did not dare to mention the real reason for them, which was that every FDJ official whose performance brought him to the attention of the party directorate in that field was immediately transferred from the FDJ to a position in the party or the governmental machine. Here Honecker displayed a weakness which was often noticeable at this stage of his character development. While he recognized the youth organization's mistakes, weaknesses, and difficulties and criticized their effects, he never openly identified their causes, because he knew very well that to do so could easily lead to conflict with the party.

This was the case in the matter of working-class participation in the FDJ. At the sixteenth Central Council meeting, Honecker complained that despite the founding of 850 new factory groups, there had been only a slight rise in the working-class percentage of the total membership. Although he did remark that working-class youth was not adequately represented in the FDJ, he avoided any admission that the reason for the disproportion lay in the already overt conflict between the trade unions and the FDJ—a conflict which was to become considerably more acute in the next few years. Honecker could not find the courage to say openly that the FDJ was handicapped in its work in the factories by the Free German Trade Union Federation (FDGB) and that the bad working conditions and unpleasant atmosphere in the factories and the negative attitude of many older employees toward the FDJ, which they regarded as a troublemaker and agitator, were the reasons for its unsatisfactory showing in the factories.

The foundations of the People's Democracy were then being laid. The introduction of a centrally planned economy, with the Half-Year Plan of 1948 and the Two-Year Plan of 1949–50, the promotion of the Activist movement, the expansion of the People's Police by the addition of the KVP and the frontier and criminal police forces, the establishment of people's control commissions, the expansion of "worker and peasant faculties," the training of new teachers and judges, the organization of sports committees under the auspices of the FDJ and the FDGB—all this, and more, was accomplished between 1948 and 1950 with the help, direct or indirect, of the FDJ. In addition, it had to build up its own organization and take part in innumerable mass activities such as the soliciting of signatures in connection with the "people's congress movement," for which the FDJ arranged 21,000 meetings, demonstrations, leaflet campaigns, etc., and collected two million young people's signatures.[84]

The size and strength of this three-year-old youth organization is shown by a list of achievements which is impressive in itself, quite apart from their value and usefulness: first state youth conference in Schönebeck on the Elbe (November, 1947); first young workers' congress in Zeitz (April, 1948); establishment of 1,348 activist youth groups in 1948; assistance in meeting the quotas of the Two-Year Plan amounting to 35 million hours of voluntary work; and above all the building of 13,821 new farmhouses and the completion of holiday camp facilities for 110,000 boys and girls in the summer of 1948.

It is not the purpose of this book to present a complete history of the Free German Youth or a chronicle of the Soviet Zone. These scanty and incomplete facts are simply intended to indicate the role and importance of the FDJ during those years. This in turn will give some idea of the ever increasing influence the president of such an organization exerted upon the social development of the Soviet sphere of power in Germany.

No Competition Tolerated

The process of turning the FDJ into a reservoir for the SED was completed by the foundation of the Young Pioneers at the seventeenth Central Council meeting of December 11–12, 1948,[85] the incorporation of the sports movement through the establishment of the German Sports Committee, whose chairman was appointed by the FDJ (October 1, 1948),[86] a tremendous demonstration campaign to commemorate the thirtieth anniversary congress of the Komsomol in which "more than 600,000 young people participated,"[87] a big "educational campaign on the significance of the Soviet Union in the struggle for a lasting peace and human progress in the world,"[88] the admission of the FDJ to the World Federation of Democratic Youth,[89] and its extensive reorganization on the Komsomol model—to name only the most important events. At the third congress in Leipzig at Pentecost, 1949, Honecker could announce with pride:

Since Meissen our organization has undergone a development which has enabled it to become a great formative force in the life of our people. It has also consistently strengthened its role as the instrument and reserve of the progressive forces in our nation [i.e., the SED]. . . . This is most clearly shown . . . by the fact that in the period covered by this report, and more particularly since the middle of 1948, more and more young forces from the ranks of our militant alliance have moved up into responsible positions in the democratic organizations, parties and administrations, or have left their jobs to go back to school so that they may later render great service to our nation as scientific workers.

. . . We have a right to be proud of this record. One hundred and four of the friends who have left us have assumed responsible positions in the state and central administrations. Four of them: namely, Edith Baumann, Hermann Axen, Paul Verner, and Ernst Hoffmann, have been working in responsible positions on the executive of the Social Unity Party of Germany.[90]

This was the beginning of the phase in Erich Honecker's career that saw him become a candidate for the power-control center: the Politburo of the SED. As a member of the secretariat of the FDJ Central Council from 1951 to 1953 and as second secretary and deputy to Honecker, I was very close to him throughout this period. In late July, 1948, the SED had used the Russian attacks on Yugoslavia as an excuse for a purge of "hostile elements" within the party, in which many Social Democrats, trade unionists, opposition Communists, and other "opponents of the party" were expelled. It stands to Honecker's credit that he prevented the purge from being extended in any significant degree to the FDJ. He resisted strongly when, in 1949, the Central Party Control Commission and the cadre division of the SED ordered him to expel all former Hitler Youth leaders from the Central Council apparatus and to dismiss youth officials who had emigrated to the West from responsible positions in the central apparatus. He refused not because he was in any way opposed to the purge but because the personnel situation of the FDJ was extremely serious, and he took the view that the youth organization ought to be judged by special standards. All the same, this stand certainly revealed his growing self-assurance—no doubt a result of his closeness to Ulbricht. He simply declined to negotiate with the cadre division, for instance, and submitted the cases in question directly to Ulbricht—which often aroused ill-feeling among his opposite numbers on the Central Committee. As a popular variation on Goering's saying put it: "I'm the one who decides who's an enemy of the party."

For Honecker too the First SED Congress (January 25–28, 1949) was the signal to step up the transformation of the FDJ into a disciplined mass organization whose primary task was to put the party's resolutions into practice among young people and to create a cadre reserve for the party and the governmental apparatus. This required a competent central apparatus and a corresponding leadership center, which would have to be set up before the third FDJ congress at Pentecost, 1949. So in the first half of 1949, one of Honecker's chief responsibilities was to draw on the *Land* branches for manpower for Berlin. He also had to supply the German Sports Committee and the Young Pioneers with competent officials. The Free German Youth in West Germany was also to be centralized, having previously been affiliated only on a zone basis. This necessitated a central FDJ office for West Germany.

Honecker solved this problem in a way that typified his method of making political appointments. Two functionaries were available: Robert Bialek, whose career as an inspector in the People's Police had been cut short by conflict with Erich Mielke and Walter Ulbricht and who was awaiting a new appointment, and Kurt Goldstein of Thuringia, a native Rhinelander who was undoubtedly of top-functionary caliber. Bialek was the candidate Paul Verner favored to head the FDJ in West Germany. Verner thought that the dynamic, undisciplined, impulsive Bialek might just as well let off steam in the Western zones; he was the right type for the position. Honecker raised an unexpected objection to Verner's proposal, saying that they might just as well turn Bialek over to the West German police, because it was common knowledge there that they would arrest him on sight.[91] This led to a dispute between Verner and Honecker. Honecker also rejected Goldstein on many different grounds. One was that he had not forgotten Goldstein's undisciplined behavior in the premature founding of the FDJ in Thuringia in 1945. But his main argument was this:

As head of the FDJ in West Germany we need a personality who can arouse enthusiastic loyalty in all strata of youth. Kurt Goldstein is a Jew. His name sounds Jewish, and I'm sorry to say that he also looks very Jewish. This would certainly give rise to resentment in some quarters and might force the FDJ into isolation.

He said this without any noticeable personal animus, and his remark did not seem to me to stem from any basic anti-Semitism.

But it does offer a clue to his concept of a top FDJ official: big, blond, and blue-eyed. The man he chose to succeed himself when he left the FDJ in 1955 looked like that. Karl Namokel was a big, blond, blue-eyed functionary—and those were his only qualifications for succeeding Honecker.

A year passed before Honecker decided who was to head the FDJ in West Germany: Jupp Angenforth. Although Angenforth wasn't tall, he was blond and blue-eyed. He was appointed to this responsible position regardless of the fact that he had only just returned from Russian captivity, where he had taken courses and later taught seminars at *Antifa* School No. 2041. He had no practical experience in youth or party work. When I pointed out the disparity in experience between Goldstein and Angenforth to Honecker, he said Goldstein could be second or third secretary of the West German FDJ, but for first secretary he preferred an ex-army man who would be more familiar with the problems of his generation and better able to evaluate them.

Honecker's orders from the party were gradually to adapt the FDJ to the Komsomol model, without at this point changing the nonpartisan façade it was still maintaining. The new line was quite obvious in his speech at the third congress. Sharp attacks on "United States imperialism" reached a climax in this sentence: "For German youth united in the national front there is only one enemy: the policy of the dismemberment of Germany now being pursued by the Anglo-American imperialists and their stooges!" He then dealt exhaustively with relations with the Soviet Union. Without mentioning Titoism—for the FDJ had not yet taken an official stand against Yugoslavia—he branded every form of anti-Sovietism as enmity toward Germany.

In the ranks of the Free German Youth there is no room today for anti-Soviet elements. . . . May this new spirit shape the consciousness of all German youth! May German youth as a whole recognize that to tolerate anti-Soviet agitation is to sin against the national interests of the German people! All the German people's interests demand friendly cooperation with the Soviet Union and its allied people's democracies in Eastern and South-Eastern Europe. The German economy cannot exist without sound commercial relations with Eastern and South-Eastern Europe. The foreign policy interests of our nation coincide with the Soviet Union's desire to strengthen peace. Anyone who refuses to recognize this is either unconsciously ignoring the nation's interests or is an out and out enemy of our nation.[92]

This policy faithfully reflected Honecker's world view. He was proud of being a German and a Saarlander, but at the same time had deep sympathy and respect for the Soviet Union. Even in the most intimate gatherings he would not tolerate criticism of conditions in Russia. If such criticism was ever cautiously expressed—for instance, when participants in courses mentioned backward conditions in Russian party and youth schools—he would usually intervene with a didactic explanation that these were merely transitional weaknesses and legacies of the war.

Striving for Monopoly

At the third congress in Leipzig at Pentecost, 1949, Honecker spoke openly about the FDJ's difficulties in relation to the German Trade Union Federation. He had tried to get Walter Ulbricht to make the FDGB give up all youth work, but Ulbricht had simply told him to come to some agreement with it. He therefore passed the word along inside the FDJ that the FDGB was to be infiltrated with activist FDJ members. The new slogan was: "FDJ members, become the most militant unionists!" The FDGB Youth Commission was a thorn in his flesh, so to tie it more closely to the FDJ he agreed with the FDGB executive that "the Youth Commission and the factory-groups committee of the Free German Youth should in future hold joint instead of separate meetings, in order, through this concentration of forces, to be better able to accomplish the great tasks in industry."[93] And he did not hesitate to say outright that this was the only effective means of "further strengthening the unity of working-class youth."

During this phase Honecker jealously guarded the FDJ's monopoly of youth recruitment. This obvious striving for power can hardly be attributed to motives of practical politics. All independent bourgeois forces had been forced out of youth work, and the FDGB, like the FDJ, was a Communist-directed organization.

Honecker's one and only concern was to have no competition in youth work. This became particularly obvious in the battle over student groups. He was furious when he found that the FDGB had organized trade union groups at some technical colleges and universities, and that some of them were working more successfully than the weak FDJ student groups. He immediately declared that these trade union student groups might become revisionist centers, threatening the unity of student youth and offering opposition to the FDJ. In the Central Council secretariat he openly expressed his suspicion that these FDGB units were camouflaged Social Democratic groups, because the whole trade union organization was still infested with Social Democrats. He tried—again through Ulbricht—to have the FDGB prohibited from engaging in any activity at all on the college level.

Obviously Ulbricht still did not feel strong enough to take a purely administrative decision of this kind on his own. He was well aware that there were elements in the party leadership who were keeping a critical eye on the FDJ's monopolistic position and who were glad to see the Federation engaging in youth work too, in some areas at least. He therefore told Honecker to work out a solution with the FDGB. This was done in May, 1949, at a meeting in Hiddensee, where it was decided that while the Federation's college groups need not be dissolved, they were to confine themselves to the students' social needs, leaving political and cultural activities in the universities exclusively to the FDJ. Honecker was not very happy with this solution, but he had to accept it.

His desire for monopoly showed itself in other areas too. He succeeded in having the youth paper *Start* suspended, because he regarded it as a competitor of the FDJ's *Junge Welt*. Editorially *Start* was a much better paper than *Junge Welt* and was widely read in colleges and schools. It sold well and after 1955 was the only youth paper to survive on a very small subsidy. Honecker was suspicious of the cluster of bright young intellectuals on the staff of *Start*. He read every issue, criticizing everything that in his opinion diverged from the FDJ line. He used to collect this material to show to Walter Ulbricht, taking advantage of the golden opportunity offered by the Cominform resolution against Yugoslavia. The chief editor of *Start* was Arne Rehan, a capable young journalist who had acquired his experience in anti-Nazi radio work in England. Honecker's charge was: *Start* is an independent youth journal which does not always follow the FDJ line. Its chief editor was once a refugee in England. This was sufficient to induce Ulbricht to suspend the paper. Honecker transferred Arne's assistant, Joachim Herrmann (now chief editor of *Neues Deutschland*), to a position on the FDJ paper *Junge Welt*.

Having more or less forced the trade unions out of youth work and eliminated the competition of *Start* in the field of journalism, Honecker faced only one more adversary in youth work: the SED youth secretariat. In 1948 he was already beginning to collect his material, although he did not yet dare to make the decisive move. As he liked to say, he could wait, and in 1952 he finally succeeded in having this agency of the party dissolved. In 1949, however, he was still using the youth secretariat in his struggle with the party leadership over the recognition and consolidation of the FDJ's position within the SED. Here again he successfully used the technique of collecting his material and then waiting for the right moment. He had compiled the material in 1948 and 1949; after the third congress in Leipzig, the right moment seemed to have come. He presented to Pieck and Ulbricht and the whole central secretariat a report listing serious deficiencies on the part of low-level party units in regard to the FDJ. The result could be scored as a success for Honecker. Wilhelm Pieck and Otto Grotewohl addressed an open letter to all SED members sharply criticizing the organization's youth work:

Some of our functionaries and members fail to understand the role of the FDJ as the most progressive youth organization and an ally in our party's struggle. . . . Others, disregarding the FDJ's politically indispensable autonomy, think they can step in and issue orders. . . . It is essential that we win over and boldly integrate young people into the activist, responsible work of our party organizations.[94]

"The Saar Is German"

The year 1949 also brought Honecker and the FDJ an international success. For the first time since World War II, a strong German delegation was able to participate in an international meeting. Seven hundred and fifty boys and girls, all members of the FDJ, attended the second world youth festival in Budapest from August 14–28, presenting their own cultural program and taking part in the athletic contests. The group had previously taken a training course of several weeks to ensure a unified stance.

The West German delegation included a group from the Saar, and alongside the FDJ flag they carried a French tricolor. The leader of the delegation, Heinz Merkel, took the view that the

Saar would never return to Germany and that its youth movement was closer to the French Republican Youth (a mass organization similar to the Free German Youth) than to the West German FDJ. When Honecker learned of this, he became very angry. I have rarely seen him lose his temper so violently. He called in the whole group, and there was a heated argument, in which he talked about the struggle of the KPD and the Communist League of German Youth during the occupation of the Saar in the 1920s. As a climax he declared that the Saar was and would always remain German and that he forbade the display of the tricolor.

The astonished Merkel tried to point out that it was not really of much significance, since they were all internationalists anyhow, and in any case the much stronger Communist movement in France could be of more help to them than the West German KPD and FDJ, which would probably be prohibited sooner or later. Honecker cut him short, refused to discuss it, and categorically declared that the group could be included in the delegation only if it gave up the French flag. In the 1920s and 1930s too, he said, the socialist movement had been strong in France, and the KJVD and KPD had collaborated with the French comrades, but their goal had always been to keep the Saar for Germany. They should not lose sight of this today. I have rarely seen Honecker so personally involved as he was in this affair. The Saarlanders were not so easily convinced. They relinquished the flag, but they wanted to march with the French delegations in Budapest and were only prevented from doing so after considerable trouble.

At the third congress in Leipzig, a similar dispute had arisen between Honecker and Ulbricht, on the one hand, and Jacques Denis, representative of the World Federation of Democratic Youth (and now a member of the Central Committee of the French Communist Party), on the other. I witnessed an argument in which the French Communists took the position that the Saar must remain French, while the two German Communists protested that it was and always would be German. This discussion, which started in the lounge of the hotel, began harmlessly enough, but Ulbricht, backed up by Honecker, soon became extremely aggressive. Denis argued that even though France and West Germany were capitalist countries, the socialist movement was much stronger in France than in the Western zones of Germany. The French comrades could give their comrades in the

Saar far more help. Besides, the formation of a popular front government in France was just a matter of time, while it was quite uncertain whether the German Communists would ever reach that point. If the Saar were awarded to West Germany, that country's already strong industrial potential would become even stronger, and this could not be advantageous to the Soviet Zone. Ulbricht described this view as chauvinistic and arrogant, and Honecker added that it was still by no means certain who would be the first to succeed in changing the distribution of power.

8. The FDJ and the Founding of the DDR

The Pledge of German Youth

AFTER THE FOUNDING of the German Democratic Republic, the FDJ was hastily reorganized on the model of the Komsomol and developed into a "new-type" youth organization.

The "Max Reimann Announcement" promulgated at the third congress—Max Reimann was chairman of the KPD in the Western zones—which culminated in a "peace meeting," was not significantly different from an activist demonstration of the Communist League of German Youth in the old days. Indeed, in his address Honecker drew parallels with the situation before the Nazis' seizure of power, stressing that the Germany of today was not the Germany of 1932.[95] The proclamation of the German Democratic Republic revealed the full significance of his words.

Honecker, president of the FDJ, was designated by Walter Ulbricht to call upon the secretariat of the German People's Council in the name of the Central Council of the FDJ "to take immediate steps to form an all-German government."[96] During the evening of October 7, after the proclamation of the DDR, tens of thousands of FDJ members who had been hastily transported to Berlin by the truckload, filed past Grotewohl's newly formed government and President Wilhelm Pieck in a torchlight parade and made the pledge of German youth to Honecker: "We, German youth, pledge allegiance to the German Democratic Republic because it wants to bring youth peace and a better life—and will do so."[97]

A month later Honecker wrote in a leading article in the functionaries' journal *Junge Generation:*

It is therefore desirable that our Free German Youth, which has so often proved itself in the past as the advance guard of German youth at the side of the progressive and leading forces of our nation, should now proceed, on the basis of the document of the National Front of Democratic Germany accepted by the German People's Council, to enlist German youth as a whole for the completion of its historic tasks.[98]

So far as the FDJ was concerned, these "historic tasks" consisted chiefly in strengthening the organization ideologically by intensifying its training programs and creating a competent leadership which would adapt itself to the Bolshevist working style. After the Third SED Congress, which voted for the final Stalinization of the organization and declared war on "the relics of social democracy" and the "Tito bandits," the FDJ openly initiated the study of Marxism and Leninism.

Working Style and Struggles for Power

After June, 1949, Erich Honecker worked with a secretariat without bourgeois representatives in which Hermann Axen was the only survivor of his old guard. Most of the new secretaries came from top positions in state FDJ branches. Gerhard Heidenreich, previously first secretary of the strongest *Land* organization, Saxony, was now responsible for organization. Heinz Kessler, head of the Berlin organization, took over working-class youth. The new secretary for student affairs, Peter Heilmann, was the former first chairman of the student council of the University of Halle. Ernst Horn, Irmgard Spillner, Klaus Herde, and I came from the Thuringian branch, and Karl Morgenstern had previously been in the Saxon *Land* organization. All these *Land* secretaries had been used to working independently. They now had to adapt themselves to a collective body whose functions were radically different from anything they had been engaged in before.

For over three years Honecker had been dealing in the secretariat with officials with little experience in organization. This new situation led to all kinds of complications and clashes, whose cause Honecker obviously could not or would not recog-

nize. At all events, he did nothing to smooth out incipient conflicts and continued to run things in his usual style. This soon led
to discontent and poor morale. Honecker did not keep the members of the secretariat sufficiently well informed about overall
concepts, especially in connection with the party leadership's
plans in youth politics. He preferred to discuss all important decisions in party matters with Edith Baumann and Paul Verner—
or at most with Hermann Axen and Heinz Kessler too. As time
passed, even this collaboration no longer worked, because Honecker received his directives straight from Ulbricht and never
gave either the SED youth secretariat or the FDJ Central Council
secretariat the full story. There was also personal friction. Honecker did not understand this situation and even aggravated it
by a certain arrogance, which probably stemmed from his own
insecurity at having to deal with a new staff. This was also noticeable in his attitude to the SED bloc in the Central Council.

Honecker fully acknowledged the SED's authority, and his
party loyalty leaves nothing to be desired; nonetheless it was
quite obvious that he made a clear distinction between the party
laws that applied to the rank-and-file membership and the rules
governing its leaders. This was evident when, in July, 1949, the
SED executive decided that in the mass organization apparatuses,
both on the central level and on the *Land* and district boards, the
members were to be organized in party groups. The function of
these party units was to implement SED authority in those organizations that were still officially nonpartisan.

An SED group was even established within the Central Council
apparatus. It is true that it was far from effective, because Honecker rarely informed it of Central Council policy, but it certainly led not only to duplication but also to friction, especially
in the matter of political appointments. Honecker considered
himself responsible only to the party leadership. In his own
sphere of influence he did not accept the principle of democratic
centralism and control from below, which the formation of party
groups within the central directorates of the mass organizations
was intended to demonstrate—at least formally. As he saw it:

The comrades of the party group should concern themselves with
social questions, problems of internal organization, and the implementation of the resolutions passed by the secretariat of the Central
Council acting on behalf of the party leadership. It does not behoove

the comrades of the party group to criticize these resolutions, since they lack the necessary perspective.

At that time there were still no political conflicts within the Central Council secretariat, but because of their practical experience, individual members approached many questions of tactics and methods differently from Honecker. Honecker tolerated no criticism. He would not be contradicted, and when he failed to convince other members in argument, he would simply say that the matter had been discussed with the party and must be dealt with accordingly. Again and again he made it plain that he would engage in political argument only so long as he saw a chance of winning it. As soon as he realized that he couldn't win, he would break off the discussion and fall back on his position of power.

The secretaries put up with this treatment for a few months, but discontent grew. Cliques formed within the secretariat, generally composed of functionaries who had worked together in the *Land* branches. The irritation was not confined to the Central Council secretariat. The members of the youth secretariat of the SED executive, headed by Paul Verner (to which Edith Baumann and the Saxon FDJ functionary Erich Hönisch had in the meantime been appointed) were dissatisfied because they, too, were kept uninformed about youth policy. Honecker always conferred directly with Ulbricht or Pieck without passing on the upshot of their conversations to the youth secretariat. He himself did not seem disturbed and acted as if nothing were wrong.

Things changed abruptly when the preponderantly Saxon group decided to take action. They agreed to appeal to the party over Honecker's head, report the untenable situation in the secretariat, and demand Honecker's dismissal. Kessler, Morgenstern, Brasch, and Hönisch held conspiratorial discussions on "Peacock Island" in the Treptow section of Berlin. Heidenreich was to be co-opted later. Heidenreich, however, did not trust Kessler and Brasch and criticized his friends Morgenstern and Hönisch for becoming involved in such an affair. He was proved right in the end. Honecker got wind of the plan to demand his dismissal.

(Heidenreich later said that Horst Brasch "got scared at his own courage" and informed Honecker.) His reaction was characteristic. He remained impassive but changed his working style with the secretariat, keeping its members better informed and even engaging in a little self-criticism. He also had many individual talks with the very men who had conspired against him, courting their favor until the front collapsed and their planned initiative came to nothing. Then, however, he transferred them one by one to different fields of work—which was not difficult, since the party and governmental apparatus urgently needed officials.

He dealt first with Morgenstern and Hönisch, his two weakest opponents, transferring one of them to the KVP, the paramilitary police, and the other to the *Land* directorate of the Berlin SED. He did not dare to demote Heidenreich directly, but arranged to have him transferred to the cadre division of the Central Committee. (He later took charge of personnel appointments in the DDR's foreign espionage service, the *Institut für Wirtschaftswissenschaftliche Forschung,* which was then being established.) In the case of Kessler, Honecker accepted with alacrity the Russian request that he be made available to the KVP to build up the DDR's air force.

It took Honecker just over a year to eliminate the "conspirators" from the FDJ leadership, one after another. Brasch fared the worst. He was "exiled to the provinces," to become minister of education in Brandenburg. Later the youth secretariat was dissolved. Honecker's personal relationship with Kessler and Heidenreich remained unchanged. He spent many hours hunting or playing *skat* with Kessler at the Central Council secretariat's recreation lodge on the Döllmsee. Heidenreich, too, was often a guest in his home. The painful affair was never mentioned, but Honecker does seem to have learned one lesson from it. As long as he remained president of the FDJ, he never again appointed to the secretariat an official who could match his party experience or was ideologically stronger than himself.

Honecker's approach to personnel appointments during this phase was generally ambivalent. On the one hand, it was strongly emotional, so that he was capable of ignoring SED cadre directives if they conflicted with his own wishes. On the other hand, he had a deep dislike of intellectuals, even those with excellent political training and an unblemished past in the party. What his own selection process usually came up with was mediocrity—and he was constantly complaining about this. He once told me with considerable self-pity that he was the party's elementary school-teacher who did nothing but teach every new generation the three R's of leadership.

This build-up period between 1949 and 1951 provided innumerable examples of Honecker's pronounced mistrust of intellectuals. He got a kind of malicious satisfaction out of Wolfgang Leonhard's defection to Yugoslavia in 1949 and told Gerhard Heidenreich and me that he had always known there was something fishy about Leonhard and that was why he had put up so much resistance when the party tried to force the man on him. Anton Ackermann, he said, had tried to sell Leonhard to him "like hot cakes" for secretary for culture and education, but he had refused, because Leonhard, though he may have known something about theory, knew nothing about practice.

A short time later his secretary, Reinhard Biehl, went off to West Berlin and invited several members of the Central Council to clandestine meetings at the Zoo subway station. Honecker was terribly upset and refused to believe that Biehl had gone over to the West of his own free will. He kept repeating that he must have been kidnapped or was acting under some kind of pressure. This was partly because he had thought highly of Biehl but chiefly because he did not want to admit to an error of judgment in a staff appointment. From then on he was even more suspicious of intellectual functionaries.

His behavior in the case of Heinz Stern, son of the "Old Communist" Viktor Stern, was equally characteristic. Heinz Stern had grown up in the Soviet Union and attended a Russian university. The party and the Russians wanted to make him chief editor of *Junge Welt*. Honecker was immediately put off by Stern's outward appearance; he looked like an absent-minded professor, and Honecker used to refer to him by that nickname. Although Stern had good qualifications for the job, Honecker took a skeptical attitude from the start. It wasn't long before he told me in private that he "couldn't stand the fellow." As long as Stern was chief editor of *Junge Welt*, Honecker continually found fault with the paper. When he thought the list of Stern's misdemeanors was long enough to justify getting rid of even a Soviet-trained functionary, he did so and replaced him with big, blond, blue-eyed Joachim Herrmann, whose promotion to chief editor of *Neues Deutschland* he approved in 1971.

But Honecker's willfulness in political appointments did not go to the extent of risking personal difficulties. Several such cases arose in 1949 and 1950 in connection with the Cominform resolution against Yugoslavia. A talented young caricaturist of upper-class Jewish background came to Berlin from Holland to help build up the FDJ. He was as naïve as he was committed and had worked on the laying of the Yugoslavian youth railway from Samac to Sarajevo and had come back full of enthusiasm. This communal achievement by young people from many different countries was the most exciting experience he had ever had. For this reason he treasured the decoration awarded to him by Tito for having participated in the project. He hung it above his desk and never stopped talking about his experiences. Then came the break with Tito, which he simply could not understand. Because of the medal, which he still insisted on displaying, he was arrested and disappeared without a trace. Honecker did nothing. Even when the boy's brother came from Holland to ask Honecker for help, he refused.

In May, 1950, it became known that Kurt Müller, deputy chairman of the KPD, had been arrested by the DDR security agency. Honecker had known Müller from the pre-1933 days, when Müller was president of the KJVD and Honecker was a member of the Central Committee. He had often talked to me about him and would say: "If you can't get anywhere with Max Reimann [of whom he had a low opinion], go to Kurt. He's sympathetic toward youth." When we learned of the arrest, I asked Honecker for an explanation. He did not answer. He seemed embarrassed, but quickly pulled himself together and said noncommittally: "If the party takes a step like that, it must know what it's doing." He declined to intervene or even look into the matter. I saw him behave in a similar way in the case of Fritz Sperling, another of his very close friends.

In March, 1951, Peter Heilmann was arrested, after having served for two years as head of the department of student affairs in the secretariat of the Central Council. The only thing that seemed to disturb Honecker was that a colleague from his secretariat should be an "enemy of the party." At first he acted as if he knew nothing about it and was just as surprised as anybody else. Then he suggested that this might be just one more mistake, and finally he came out with an explanation he must have known to be false. For him the case was now closed. Heilmann's name was never mentioned again.

In the matter of the Cominform resolution against Yugoslavia, he followed the party line unswervingly. As recently as the second congress in Meissen he had given the Yugoslavian delegation an especially warm welcome, yet he never uttered a word to question the justification for the attacks.

So the early 1950s saw the development of an authoritarian tendency in Erich Honecker, which increased when he was nominated as a candidate for the Politburo at the Third SED Congress. He tolerated no contradiction in the secretariat, dropped all attempts to introduce collective leadership, which he had played up for a time after the clash with the "conspirators," and resumed his old style of government-by-decree. On Tuesdays, when he returned to the secretariat from the Politburo meeting, he would merely summarize his notes. The only thing the secretariat could discuss with him was how to translate some party measure or thesis into language youth would understand or into appropriate practical terms. Discussions of basic principles and criticism were a thing of the past.

The "All-Germany" Meeting of the FDJ

As far as Honecker was concerned, the greatest event of 1950 was undoubtedly the All-Germany Meeting. At Pentecost a million young people from all parts of Germany were to proclaim their support of the DDR and the National Front of Democratic Germany in a fashion that could not be ignored. Honecker insisted on going to West Germany to present the FDJ's invitation to West German youth personally at the delegates' conference of the North-Rhine-Westphalian branch of the FDJ and at a demonstration in Duisburg. As secretary for West German affairs I accompanied him.

As soon as we reached the Ruhr, I noticed a conspicuous change in Honecker. We were staying with Ewald Kaiser, then a member of the KPD *Land* directorate, whom Honecker had known during his underground days in the Ruhr in the 1930s. Kaiser had been county secretary of the Ruhr branch of the KJVD in Essen even before 1933. In this capacity he had managed to maintain relatively good contacts with groups of young Catholic workers in the

Ruhr which had formed principally around Chaplain Rossaint (now vice-president of the West German Committee for Victims of Nazism) in Oberhausen and later in Düsseldorf.[99] When the National Socialists came to power in 1933, collaboration between Rossaint's Young Catholic Workers and Ewald became even closer. Honecker now got to know Dr. Rossaint, who had been a great source of help and protection to endangered young Communists. From conversations between Honecker and Kaiser in late 1949 I gathered that Honecker owed a great deal to Dr. Rossaint during his underground days and had never forgotten it. When he spoke of him, it was clear that he saw Rossaint as a personification of the kind of united front he really seemed to believe in. He kept emphasizing Rossaint's courageous, unselfish behavior during the Nazi period: "If all Christian forces were inspired by the same spirit as Dr. Rossaint, the establishment of the National Front wouldn't be so difficult."

For Honecker that trip was an excursion into the past. I have rarely seen him so emotionally moved. He had cast off the dignity and burdens of the first secretary of the FDJ, who in the DDR was one of the political decision-makers. In his evening and late night talks with Ewald Kaiser, Josef Ledwohn and others, when the past would come to life again, as well as in his appearances at the conference and demonstration, he seemed much more relaxed than at home, spoke with more enthusiasm and let himself be carried away in the general excitement. On our return journey he told me that he would really like to nominate himself for president of the West German FDJ, because there were simply no other candidates at that time. On that trip I got to know a different Erich Honecker, who reacted spontaneously, whose temperament ran away with him and who seemed to enjoy direct confrontations.

Spontaneity and Putschist Tendencies

This spontaneity increased as the All-Germany Meeting approached. The nearer it came, the more dramatic became Honecker's style. At a meeting on February 6, 1950, he declared that at Pentecost the boys and girls would give the warmongers an answer "the like of which Germany has never yet seen." A few weeks later, at the functionaries' conference in Berlin on March 1, he boasted that if necessary the FDJ would "set up democratic conditions in West Berlin."[100]

These and similar remarks by other top officials, together with a leaflet put out by the Berlin FDJ saying that "Berlin must be ours," created the impression in the West that the FDJ was planning to turn this meeting into an assault on West Berlin. A song with words by the national prizewinner Kurt Barthel (Kuba) and music by the national prizewinner André Asriel and a chorus that went: "The FDJ Storms Berlin" was thought to offer additional evidence of *putschist* intentions.

It is difficult to determine today whether this fear really existed in the Federal Republic and West Berlin or whether it was deliberately whipped up as counterpropaganda. Certainly neither the Russians nor the SED—least of all the FDJ—had any concrete plans of this nature at the time. All the announcements to this effect, most of them claiming that the FDJ intended to stream into the Western zones by the thousands and to provoke incidents that would justify the intervention of the People's Police, were based on speculation. That they could arise at all and be exploited was the doing of Erich Honecker. He had worked himself up into the state of excitement he thought was needed to get the FDJ moving (because preparations for the All-Germany Meeting were lagging behind in the DDR *Land* and county organizations). So with the knowledge and approval of the SED, but without calculating the consequences, he was deliberately heightening the excitement. Only when the reaction in the West could no longer be dismissed was the publicity stopped, and by that time there was considerable uneasiness within the FDJ and among the general population in the DDR, too. Rumors were circulating about the imminent outbreak of war, the intervention of the Western powers, and clashes between Russian troops and the Western allies.

Honecker was dismayed; he had never expected this. He was criticized by both the Soviet Control Commission and the SED leadership for his impetuous behavior and had to take hasty measures to calm public opinion. The song "The FDJ Storms Berlin" was rechristened "The FDJ Greets Berlin."[101] Top FDJ and SED officials hurriedly explained that the meeting would be conducted with order and discipline. Prime Minister Grotewohl said reassuringly on May 24: "No one is thinking of misusing young people of our nation . . . for a surprise attack on the people of West Berlin."[102]

When the West German participants were leaving (all wearing the blue shirts and waving the blue flags that had been issued to them), an incident that Honecker was to exploit occurred at the Herrenburg-Lübeck crossing point. The West German police had been concentrated at the frontier and were demanding that all young people coming from Berlin register and undergo medical examinations. This led to protests and some preliminary clashes. Refusing to comply with the police orders, the young people left their special trains and besieged the checkpoints. Apparently this was exactly what Honecker was waiting for. He kept in constant touch with the situation through the national railways telephone service. When reports of the confrontation with the West German police reached him, he gave orders that the young people were not to comply with police demands, called a hasty staff meeting, and dispatched tents, straw mattresses, and field kitchens to the frontier so that emergency camps could be quickly set up. He called on the press and radio to go to the border and tell the world about this "resistance to the police forces of the West German puppet government." Honecker was delighted by this move by the West German police. The All-Germany Meeting got some publicity from a sensational development after all. He thought that if the young people had simply been checked through, the whole affair would not have caused a ripple.

Two factors in this incident are noteworthy. First, Honecker took a very prompt decision to exploit the propaganda value of an obvious blunder by the West German security agency, and second, he had trouble in getting the party to accept his plan. It was still perturbed by the assertions of West German public opinion that the SED and the FDJ intended to take Berlin by storm, and at first took a dubious view of Honecker's demand that they should not give in at Herrenburg but keep the camp set up until the West German police capitulated. Some party secretaries argued that provocations or attempts to cross the frontier by force (which was in effect what Honecker was proposing) might lead to bloodshed, which would again be used to discredit the All-Germany Meeting and the FDJ.

The hesitations of the party leadership made Honecker very angry. "We, the FDJ, must galvanize the old comrades and confront them with a *fait accompli*," he said disparagingly. And that is exactly what he did. With the help of the People's Police, camps were set up at top speed, and groups of agitators and a press corps were dispatched to interview the returning delegates. Honecker then reported this to the party, which could do nothing but give its belated sanction to the operation. Events developed as might have been expected. The aggressive mood of the young people was heightened, and they held out for two days, when the police finally gave in.

The propaganda value of the "victory of Herrenburg" was exploited to the full. The Central Council report, written by Honecker himself, stated:

> Today at 2 A.M. the West German authorities capitulated to the legitimate demands and the resolute will of the FDJ, to the powerful solidarity of all German militant pacifists, and to the seventy million supporters of the World Federation of Democratic Youth. The police were forced aside, and the ten thousand enthusiastic young militant pacifists were permitted to march across into their West German homeland.[103]

Stalin's Telegram

Particular importance was attached to Stalin's answer to the greeting sent to him from the All-Germany Meeting. It read:

> I thank the young German militant pacifists participating in the All-Germany Youth Meeting for their greetings. I wish German youth, the active builders of the unified, democratic, peace-loving Germany, new successes in this great work. J. Stalin.[104]

In an open letter to the members and officials of the FDJ concerning the "mobilization of German youth for peace," which had been decided upon at the All-Germany Meeting, Erich Honecker said:

> The significant telegram of Generalissimo Stalin, leader of the worldwide peace camp, is an acknowledgment that as a result of your actions at a decisive moment in the struggle to preserve peace, German youth has won a great victory over the pernicious, doomed forces of war. The words of the great Stalin calling German youth the active builder of the new democratic, peace-loving Germany also mean that German youth is competent—and obliged—to achieve other, still greater successes in the struggle for a unified, peace-loving, and democratic Germany.[105]

This was said to be the first telegram Stalin had ever sent to a foreign organization. All youth newspapers and magazines in the DDR published it as the leading item on their front page, together with a big picture of the secretary general of the FDJ. *Neues Deutschland*, the official organ of the West German FDJ, printed the telegram as a minor news item. This made Honecker furious. He took it not merely as a slight to Stalin but also as the expression of a hostile attitude to party policy.

At the Third SED Congress in July, 1950, Honecker was nominated as a candidate-member of the Politburo—a conspicuous indication of the special position enjoyed by the FDJ.[106] Not the numerically far stronger Free German Trade Union Federation but the FDJ, as the direct cadre reserve for the SED and the whole governmental apparatus, was now to be represented, by its own president, on the top decision-making body. Honecker proudly announced this to the secretariat of the Central Council. Through this action, he said, Ulbricht and the party leadership had singled out the FDJ. It would now show what it could do.

9. At the Power Center

Ulbricht's Aide

HONECKER'S NOMINATION as a candidate-member of the Politburo changed his style of life and work, and this in turn affected his manner and personality. It began with outward details. As a candidate of the Politburo, he was given a new car of Russian manufacture and a "shadow." The shadow was a young member of the Ministry of State Security's watchguard responsible for the personal safety of top SED and government functionaries. A party resolution inspired by a Russian recommendation required every member and candidate-member of the Politburo to have such a bodyguard. Honecker's shadow bothered him. It was not that he felt that he was keeping a check on him, and certainly not that his way of life would not bear scrutiny. He was simply not yet accustomed to his new position of power. He first tried to get rid of his young escort by putting him on indefinite leave of absence, but this had to be reported and led to a reprimand from Otto Schön, secretary of the Central Committee secretariat. Then he tried to put him to work for the FDJ. This too came to light, and he received another friendly reminder to observe the party's resolutions. When he realized that he was never going to be able to shake off his shadow, he decided that he would just have to put up with him. But he was always perfectly friendly. On trips he ate with him in restaurants, and at receptions he would make sure that his shadow got something to eat, too. He never kept him waiting outside in the rain, and rarely asked him to do the kind of personal errands other members of the Politburo had long taken for granted.

There was another change, too. Honecker could no longer devote himself exclusively to the FDJ. Several times a week a Politburo courier would arrive with a locked leather briefcase, for which Honecker would sign a receipt. It contained innumerable files on matters to be discussed at the regular Tuesday-morning meeting of the Politburo: the members and candidate-members had to familiarize themselves with all this material in advance. Dealing with these voluminous files and attending the weekly meeting made Honecker unavailable for FDJ business several days a week, and in addition he often had to do extra work of one kind or another for the Politburo. This forced him to change his working style, to give the individual secretaries more scope for initiative, and to expand his personal staff. During this phase Honecker learned to delegate work to others and to entrust the writing of his speeches to his personal secretary, Hans Schönecker, a former Hitler Youth leader. Until then he had always written his own speeches, and at first it was hard for him to let anyone else do it. He obviously didn't like this, and was constantly apologizing for it. He would sit down with Schönecker and sketch out his ideas, which Schönecker would develop. Then Honecker would add stylistic touches of his own and a few new thoughts.

When Honecker began work in the Politburo, the question of who was to replace him in the FDJ became acute. As a rule the second secretary in charge of the organization and cadre division served as deputy president. In July, 1950, this was Helmut Hartwig, formerly *Land* chairman for Saxony, who was not on the best of terms with Honecker and in any case was not qualified to replace him. Honecker unhesitatingly overrode the rules of order and made Heinz Kessler his deputy. When Kessler was transferred to the People's Army, he was replaced by Margot Feist (Honecker's future wife), director of the Young Pioneers, who had been promoted to the Central Committee secretariat in 1950.

But the biggest change was in the working style of the secretariat. The FDJ secretariat usually met the day after the Politburo. The session would begin with a political briefing by Honecker on the outcome of the last Politburo meeting so that the Central Council secretariat was kept up to date on the party line. Then Honecker would give the individual secretaries their assignments, which consisted in reformulating the questions that fell within their particular field as proposals that could be submitted at the next session. The next meeting would again begin with a report by Honecker on the Politburo session of the day before, and then the proposals arising out of the last meeting would be discussed. Obviously this procedure did nothing to challenge the initiative of individual secretaries or promote a feeling of collective leadership. The Central Council secretariat became a sort of branch office of the SED. Original ideas became fewer and farther between. The secretariat's only function was to translate Ulbricht's ideas, as relayed by Honecker, into the language of youth—or what it imagined to be the language of youth. There was rarely an occasion to criticize or add to what Honecker had said, because he merely passed along the thoughts of the secretary general of the party—and nobody was going to question those.

The new working style had its effect on Honecker personally. He relied increasingly on the Politburo's directives and concentrated on implementing them within the FDJ. The FDJ's highest-level committee was being turned into a body of young party functionaries. After Honecker became a Politburo candidate, his attitude to the FDJ and the collective leadership began to change conspicuously. Although he always acted as though he couldn't understand why he had been so honored and why Ulbricht made so much of him, he was more concerned than ever to live up to expectations by faithfully carrying out party policy within the FDJ. This led inevitably to a growing estrangement from his immediate colleagues, who felt that their role was being reduced to taking orders. As some members of the Central Council secretariat said in a private conversation: "Erich is really only half with us. He seems to regard the youth organization as just a springboard for getting ahead in the party."

This became increasingly evident right up to the first FDJ functionaries' conference on November 26, 1950. At the sixth Central Council session, on July 13, 1950, a fundamental resolution was adopted providing for the improvement of the FDJ's work in political education and calling upon the organization to utilize "the experience of the Soviet Union and of the vanguard of world democratic youth: the Komsomol" and to cement its close friendship with the Soviet Union and the other people's democracies.[107] Honecker was sharply critical of inadequate political training in the FDJ, which he said was the cause of errors of political judgment. He thought the danger of another war was generally underestimated, and that the FDJ was not showing enough initiative in "unmasking the German taskmasters of the American and Anglo-French imperialists in their policy of colonization and war in West Germany."

The resolution concerning the FDJ's first-year training was passed at this same Central Council conference. From that day on, the pressure that party headquarters in Berlin brought to bear on the lower levels became heavier and the FDJ's assent to the leading role of the SED more obvious. Finally, at the eighth session of the Central Council on October 27, 1950, Honecker issued a directive calling for an "unequivocal declaration of support of bolshevist principles."[108]

During this period Honecker devoted much attention to the development, selection, and assignment of cadres. He vigorously opposed the "raiding" of FDJ departments by low-level party agencies. The high turnover on local committees, in particular, needed to be checked. It was therefore decided, with Ulbricht's approval, that every transfer of a secretary on the local level or of a secretary or section head in a *Land* committee must be approved by the secretariat of the FDJ Central Council. Erich Honecker was extremely proud of this rule; he had great difficulty in getting it passed and succeeded only because of his position as a Politburo candidate. He said afterward in the secretariat of the Central Council: "I had to bring it home to the comrades very forcefully that you don't kill the cow you want to milk." Only because he was already sure of Ulbricht's unfailing support could he permit himself remarks like that.

At the first FDJ functionaries' conference in November, 1950, the Stalin cult began to assume unprecedented proportions. Honecker never ended a speech without expressing the love and respect of German youth for "the beloved leader of the workers of all the world" and "the great teacher of the German people." FDJ training programs included topics such as "Stalin, the Builder of Socialist Society," "Stalin in the Period of the War for the Fatherland," and "Stalin, the Best Friend of the German People."[109] All FDJ officials also had to take required courses in the history of the Soviet Union (the standard Short Course on the History of the Communist Party of the Soviet Union) and the Komsomol, and on Stalin's speeches on the twenty-fourth, twenty-fifth, twenty-sixth, and twenty-seventh anniversaries of the October Revolution.

The FDJ's relation to the SED was also finally clarified when Ulbricht declared: "The FDJ can fulfill its function only if it recognizes the leading role of the SED, the only party guided by the scientific theory of Marx, Engels, Lenin, and Stalin, the party which . . . has proved itself to be the highest organization among all organizations."[110]

Nationalist Euphoria

For the FDJ and therefore for Honecker too the year 1951 was one of great nationalist activity. Up until the world youth festival Honecker added fuel to the nationalist campaign in the Federal Republic with constant references to the repeated occupation of the island of Helgoland, which the British Royal Air Force was using for target practice. The public-opinion poll "against remilitarization and for a peace treaty" was intended to mobilize large segments of youth in the West against rearmament, which was then a very controversial subject.

At the same time the West German FDJ began preparations for going underground, since most of the *Land* governments in the Federal Republic had declared it unconstitutional. Here Honecker was in his element. Remembering his underground work during the Third Reich, he developed all kinds of ideas for illegal agitation that would be effective yet not too risky for the individuals involved. He spent a lot of time on these problems, although they were not really his responsibility. He obviously enjoyed these strategic games; his temperament and character were better suited to active duty than to the bureaucratic routine in the DDR.

How strongly he was still influenced by KJVD thinking from the old days can be seen from his attitude to the West German trade unions. Although he was always calling upon the West German FDJ to become active in the unions and work with their youth organizations, early in 1951 he personally directed the FDJ to establish committees of young miners and metalworkers in the Federal Republic. He was not to be convinced that such political activity within the unions would naturally arouse opposition. How seriously he took this question is shown by the fact that he broke his usual rule of not submitting questions concerning the West German FDJ to the whole secretariat, and sought an official resolution on it. He even arranged for Paul Verner to go to the Federal Republic to attend an illegal conference of young metalworkers in the Taunus mountains. Honecker's plan came to nothing. Neither the young miners' separatist movement nor the young metalworkers ever achieved anything. This committee failed to give him a toehold in the unions. By 1952 the groups had ceased to exist.

At the end of January, 1951, Honecker tried, within the framework of the national campaign against the remilitarization of Germany, to get in touch with a group of former Hitler Youth leaders. On January 29 and 30, in a parish in the French sector of Berlin, Erich Honecker and Margot Feist met with some former Hitler Youth leaders and members of other National Socialist organizations. The results were meager, but they did include a communiqué demanding the rejection of remilitarization and exploration of the possibilities for "fruitful joint work toward the reunification of Germany." The meeting had no lasting effects, but, lacking anything better, Honecker cited it in his speech to the Berlin branch of the FDJ at the Friedrichstadt Palace commemorating the FDJ's fifth anniversary:

We note with pleasure that ever broader segments of our people are being drawn into the movement against the remilitarization of West Germany, and that people who were once members and leaders of the Hitler Youth now realize that the road of Truman, Adenauer, and Schumacher is leading Germany to ruin and are therefore enlisting in the common front against remilitarization and for a peace treaty in 1951.[111]

The World Festival of Youth in Berlin

The high point of the FDJ's work in 1951 was the World Festival of Youth in East Berlin. The program included all kinds of sports and cultural events and debates, and it was generally agreed, especially among the foreign participants, that it was a powerful and imposing mass demonstration. But those in a position to know soon realized that the FDJ was not up to the tremendous organizational demands. There were shortages of food and housing. Grotesque blunders were made; for instance, Premier Grotewohl was refused admittance to a reviewing stand because he had no ticket. The chaos was so great that the party had to intervene and assign functionaries from the Central Committee, including Gerhard Heidenreich, to help out the FDJ organizing committee.

The party, particularly Franz Dahlem, criticized the carelessness and inadequate supervision of the FDJ leadership. The lack of organization was so obvious that in this case even Ulbricht could not protect Honecker; in fact, he himself criticized the work of the secretariat and the organizing committee. Politically the most damaging factor was that some FDJ members took this opportunity of going over to the Western sectors to eat and sleep, and participated in events there. This was a hard blow to Honecker. The criticism of the SED leaders concentrated on this point, and Honecker was told that he should have foreseen it. Suddenly it was suggested that the morale of the FDJ was not all it had been claimed to be. Honecker, it was said, was responsible for this. He ought to have known how "his FDJ" would react. According to Oelssner, Dahlem, Jendretsky, and others, all the crossing over into West Berlin showed that Honecker had disregarded this danger when he developed the festival on such a grandiose scale for the sake of personal publicity.

Honecker decided that the best defense against this criticism would be attack. Whatever happened, he wanted to prevent the FDJ members from crossing over into West Berlin, and he hoped that a dramatic action might divert criticism from himself. His idea was simple enough: "Mayor Reuter's City Council has invited us. We shall come. But not as they expect, singly or in groups. We shall march into the Western sectors in closed formations, with our blue shirts and our flags. Then we'll see what they'll do."

Honecker was obviously counting on clashes whose propaganda value he could exploit. Then the West would put a stop to the FDJ's excursions into West Berlin. When he was pressed, he tended to make hasty decisions without thinking through all the possible consequences. He brushed off all warnings that such an action might end in bloodshed. As a counterargument he recalled his experiences in the great strike of 1923: "At that time we children protected the comrades from the police. Why shouldn't our girls do the same in this case? The police would think twice before beating up girls and boys singing youth movement songs in a peaceful demonstration."

On August 15 several columns, each of five to ten thousand young people, marched across the sector border and were terribly beaten up. Robert Bialek, who was attending the festival as leader of a delegation of ten thousand young Saxons, wrote an eyewitness account of the action:

We were told that after crossing the sector border we should break up our close marching order and link arms in groups of three boys to two girls, making sure that the girls were in the middle. Bialek asked whether they ought to take the girls along at all, because there was no doubt that the West Berlin police were not going to stand quietly by and watch.

Honecker replied: "We won't provoke any clashes. We're coming in response to Herr Reuter's invitation. But if the West Berlin police want to disgrace themselves by beating up defenseless boys and girls, the whole world will condemn these 'friends of freedom.' In my opinion there's no reason to march in without the girls, because that would look as if we wanted to provoke violence. We have no such intentions."

Later, Honecker came up to me and said angrily: "Why ever did you raise that stupid point? Even if you're a hundred percent sure that there'll be clashes, you don't need to drive everyone else crazy."

After several hours' march, we assembled in the Treptow Park. Erich Honecker came rushing up, called for me and said: "Robert, you take immediate command of the ten thousand marchers and walk on the left at the head of the procession. Things are getting serious, and there will probably be serious clashes. Several columns have already marched in, and you're to follow immediately. Keep the girls well in the center and protect them. I rely on you to bring everyone back safely."

Before I could reply, Honecker was gone. I decided to lead the demonstrators forward very slowly in the hope that the whole thing would peter out. Suddenly, when we were about five minutes away from the sector border, boys and girls in torn FDJ shirts came running toward us. A boy I knew shouted: "Robert, don't go in there. They'll beat you to death. We went across and they beat us back. It's no good. You won't get anywhere. They'll use rubber truncheons, pistols and water cannons on you."

We slowly approached the crossing point. To my relief I saw some People's Police officers coming toward me. A captain shouted: "Comrades, you can't possibly march into the Western sector. All the crossing points have been cordoned off by the police. We can't help you, because we can't leave our sector. We'd just have to stand and watch them beat you up. So stay here whatever happens."

By now we were thirty yards from the border. I stopped the marchers and walked up to the crossing point. Here there was a double rank of West German police, chin straps buckled, night sticks in hand, holsters unbuttoned. The People's Police officer next to me said: "You

see what it's like. But that's not all. The twenty policemen you see
here are just a blind. The side streets are full of loaded troop-carriers
and water guns."

While they were still talking, Honecker drove up. Bialek's account continues:

He came up to me and said: "It's a good thing you haven't gone
across. We can't keep it up. We've got hundreds of wounded already. I'll make a speech here, and then you must go back to the
camp."
When I objected that this might have been expected, he replied:
"Don't forget the propaganda value of this action in the eyes of young
people who've come to Berlin from all over the world. Besides, Robert, we've just proved that with hundreds of thousands of determined
FDJ members we could occupy West Berlin in two hours if we organize
it properly and if we really want to. That's worth something."[112]

So much for Robert Bialek's account. It is true that the number
of serious injuries was excessively high.
At the concluding ceremonies on August 19 Honecker said:

The whole German people looks up with love and admiration to
those German boys and girls—more than a hundred thousand of
them—whose courageous demonstration for peace on August 15 in
West Berlin, then still under the scepter of the Reuter clique, proved
that no sector boundaries or prohibited areas can prevent German
youth from defending peace to the last.
But the love of the German people and its youth for these brave
young fighters for peace is inseparably linked with a burning hatred
for those inhuman hordes that ran amok with their clubs, pistol whip-
pings, nightsticks, and squad cars and fell upon our peace-loving
boys and girls, who had come to West Berlin with joyous songs and
cries of friendship on their lips to talk to the peace-loving people
there about the preservation of peace.[113]

In this way Honecker tried to turn an out-and-out failure into a
victory, but his position in the party had suffered. Until the festival most Politburo members had believed that he was invulnerable, both because of the FDJ's impressive achievements and
because he enjoyed Ulbricht's special protection. What happened
at the festival seemed to change their minds. Certainly Honecker
was exposed to criticism in the Politburo much more often after
the World Youth Festival than before. After this debacle, his op-

ponents in the Politburo again began to ask whether it would not be useful to revive the youth secretariat of the Central Committee. This was particularly embarrassing to Honecker, because he had just succeeded in having it abolished, so that the FDJ reported directly to Ulbricht.

One notable thing about the third World Youth Festival in East Berlin was that the Stalin cult reached almost unsurpassable heights, especially as practiced by Erich Honecker.[114] In his speech marking the conclusion of the "mobilization for Stalin" he exclaimed: "Long live the standard-bearer of peace and progress in the world, the best friend of the German people: Josef Vissarionovich Stalin!"[115]

It is worth remarking that these tributes to Stalin have been deleted from the archives of the history of the FDJ, which were not published until the 1960s.[116]

10. Honecker and the Building of Socialism

Signs of Crisis

AT THE TENTH SESSION of the Central Council conference on September 1, 1951, the results of the festival were assessed, and Honecker soberly admitted that the work of educating "the broad masses of youth and the population in general on the peace-threatening character of American imperialism's intervention policy in West Germany and on the restoration of German imperialism and militarism" had been completely inadequate. This had been demonstrated by the large numbers of FDJ members who had been misled into crossing over into the Western zones. Furthermore, the world festival had shown that the organization's leadership training was still underdeveloped, as could be seen in the disregard for discipline and the neglect of principles of criticism and self-criticism.

Although the party passed no formal resolution on the failure of the FDJ leadership, harsh words are said to have been spoken in the Politburo. When Honecker returned from the first Politburo meeting after the festival, he was bad-tempered and depressed. He reported excitedly that some of the comrades had made unfair attacks on him, and mentioned the names of Fred Oelssner, Wilhelm Zaisser, and Hans Jendretzky. Jendretzky especially had charged him with irresponsibility and declared that the arrogance of the FDJ leadership and its unwillingness to cooperate with the Berlin party organization had reached an almost unsurpassable level. But according to Honecker, Jendretzky

Im Namen

des Deutschen Volkes

In der Strafsache gegen

1.) den Elektromonteur Bruno B a u m aus Berlin, Usedomer Straße 19, geboren am 13.Februar 1910 in Berlin, ledig, bestraft,

2.) den Dachdecker Erich H o n e c k e r aus Berlin, Brüsseler Straße 26, geboren am 25.August 1912 in Neunkirchen (Saar), ledig, unbestraft,

3.) die Medizinstudentin Sarah F o d o r o v á geborene Libun aus Prag-Podoli, Doudova 23, geboren am 21.Juni 1912 in Spola (Ukraine), verheiratet, tschechoslowakische Staatsangehörige, unbestraft,

4.) den Feinmechaniker Edwin L a u t e n b a c h aus Berlin-Charlottenburg, Herschelstraße 12, geboren am 18. April 1909 in Berlin-Neukölln, ledig, unbestraft,

        sämtlich zur Zeit in Untersuchungshaft,

wegen Vorbereitung zum Hochverrat unter erschwerenden Umständen und schwerer Urkundenfälschung,

hat der Volksgerichtshof, 2. Senat, in der öffentlichen Sitzung vom 8. Juni 1937 auf Grund der mündlichen Verhandlungen vom 7. und 8. Juni 1937, an welchen teilgenommen haben.

ABOVE:

Photographs of Erich Honecker after his arrest in December, 1935

BELOW:

Verdict of the People's Court, 2nd Division, against Bruno Baum, Erich Honecker, and others, June 8, 1937 (extract)

Gründungsbeschluß
======================

Die am 26. Februar 1946 im Sitzungssaal des Magistrats
der Stadt Berlin, Parochialstraße, anwesenden Mitglieder
des Zentralen Jugendausschusses für die sowjetische Besatzungszone Deutschlands bekunden hiermit einmütig
ihren Willen, sich zwecks Gründung einer überparteilichen,
einigen, demokratischen Jugendorganisation

"Freie Deutsche Jugend"

an die sowjetische Militärverwaltung in Deutschland zu
wenden.
Die Grundlagen hierzu bilden die von allen Unterzeichne-
ten angenommenen und der Urkunde beigefügten Ziele und
Satzungen der Freien Deutschen Jugend.

Berlin, den 26. 2. 1946

Resolution to establish the FDJ (showing all thirteen signatures)

Gründungsbeschluß

Die am 26. Februar 1946 im Sitzungssaal des Magistrats
der Stadt Berlin, Parochialstraße, anwesenden Mitglieder
des Zentralen Jugendausschusses für die sowjetische Besatzungszone Deutschlands bekunden hiermit einmütig
ihren Willen, sich zwecks Gründung einer überparteilichen,
einigen, demokratischen Jugendorganisation

"Freie Deutsche Jugend"

an die sowjetische Militärverwaltung in Deutschland zu
wenden.
Die Grundlagen hierzu bilden die von allen Unterzeichne-
ten angenommenen und der Urkunde beigefügten Ziele und
Satzungen der Freien Deutschen Jugend.

Berlin, den 26. 2. 1946

*Doctored facsimile of the resolution to establish the
FDJ as published in* Zur Geschichte der Arbeiterjugendbewegung in Deutschland

Signing the FDJ charter, March 7, 1946
Left to right: Theo Wiechert, Erich Honecker, Paul
Verner

Erich Honecker at the first FDJ congress, 1946

ABOVE:

The first leader's conference of the FEJ, November, 1950. From left to right: the author (Heinz Lippmann), Walter Ulbricht, and Erich Honecker.

BELOW:

Heinz Lippmann congratulating Erich Honecker on his election as chairman of the FDJ Central Council at the fourth congress, Leipzig, 1952

*Walter Ulbricht, Erich Honecker, and Friedrich Ebert,
1968*

Erich Honecker

had made a mistake when he attributed this arrogance to the fact that the party was no longer kept informed of the FDJ's activities. Jendretzky had complained that not even the Politburo knew exactly what was going on, because Honecker discussed everything with Ulbricht personally. "And that's what saved us," said Honecker. "That got me off the spot. Walter took this as a personal attack and really put Jendretzky down."

Honecker tried to put the blame for the FDJ's failure on the raiding of its staff by the party and governmental apparatus, and he did in fact succeed in having several officials who had already taken over party functions returned to the FDJ.

At this time Honecker was trying to launch a campaign against the European Defense Community (EVD), the so-called West German general defense treaty. Pastor Herbert Mochalski, a Darmstadt student chaplain who worked closely with the FDJ, had called a meeting, attended by some 1,200 members of various youth groups and some youth organizations, in Darmstadt in early March, 1952. As a result a "Presidium for a Meeting of the Young Generation" was formed, and committees to oppose recruiting were established in all states of the Federal Republic. They called a great peace march on Essen for May 11, 1952. Of course the FDJ had already mobilized all its forces for this mass demonstration. On the occasion of the march, the bourgeois members of the Presidium met in Essen with Erich Honecker, Gerald Götting, Manfred Gerlach, and Margot Feist.

Negotiations did not go smoothly. The West German group was not prepared to go along with all the FDJ's demands. They reached agreement on the need for four-power talks, German reunification, the establishment of a German national assembly through free elections, inter-German talks on the parliamentary and nonparliamentary level, and the rejection of the general treaty. No agreement was reached on German neutrality. The West German delegation demanded that the Western powers as well as the Soviet Union must be assured that the German armaments potential would not pass into the hands of any hostile group of powers.

Here Honecker again showed his ability to stick to the party line while remaining flexible. Although he was not willing to sign any document that deviated in the slightest from the official Russian and SED line, he was anxious to achieve some concrete result. He therefore had the controversial points (including a section on the rejection of rearmament for Germany as a whole) separately listed in the communiqué and added a supplement saying that the DDR delegation believed that a peace treaty of the kind the Soviet Union had in mind would prevent a revival of German militarism. On the question of rearmament in part of Germany or in Germany as a whole, the DDR delegation declared, again in a separate statement: "In case the general treaty is not averted and the danger of war is thus increased, the DDR sees itself compelled, in the interest of maintaining peace, to organize its own armed defense."[117]

In connection with the Essen peace march, Honecker gave a classic demonstration of "innocent prevarication." The march had been scheduled under the auspices of the Presidium, but had later been canceled by order of the Essen chief of police. The bourgeois members of the Presidium thought that in these circumstances it should not take place and asked Honecker to persuade the West German FDJ not to hold an illegal militant demonstration. After some discussion Honecker promised the West German delegation that he would do so, although he knew very well that at this point the demonstration could not be stopped. His promise sounded so sincere that other members of the Central Council secretariat took it seriously and called him to account. He replied with a grin: "You can pass the order on, but after all it's not your fault if it doesn't arrive in time."

The demonstration was held in spite of the prohibition and resulted in the most serious clashes so far encountered. For the first time the police used guns, and a Bavarian FDJ official, Philipp Müller, was killed. At the fourth congress Honecker made a martyr of Müller and misused his name to whip up militancy in the FDJ in connection with volunteers for the KVP. To quote from a letter headed "To German Youth," which Honecker directed the Central Council secretariat to send out: "We greet the young fighters of Essen! We call upon the youth of all Germany to follow the courageous example of their determined fight! . . . Forward, German youth, under the banner of national resistance that the courageous youth of West Germany unfurled in Essen."[118]

The first half of 1952 confronted the FDJ with conflicting tasks. On the one hand, like the SED, it had to support the Soviet Union's diplomatic offensive over Germany, aimed at preventing the creation of the European Defense Community. In its famous note to the Western powers of March 10, 1952, the Soviet Union had demanded a peace treaty providing for a neutral, united Germany possessing limited national military forces, and had suggested the possibility of negotiations over free elections. On the other hand, under the slogan of "Stop the general defense treaty," the FDJ had to make moral and political propaganda among young people for the rearmament of the DDR, train them in "vigilance and defensive preparedness," and engage in recruiting for the armed services currently being built up by the DDR.

In the resolution of the eighth session of the SED Central Committee on February 23, 1952, the FDJ's task was formulated as follows:

To safeguard our democratic order, the organizations of the Free German Youth must constantly reinforce the vigilance of members of the FDJ and other young people. They must help to unmask enemies of the people, saboteurs, spies, wreckers, revisionists, and other agents of Anglo-American imperialism, thus everywhere and at all times supporting the responsible work of the People's Police and the agencies of the Ministry of State Security in defense of democratic order.

In particular the organizations of the Free German Youth should develop a broad educational program among youth, presenting the People's Police as upholders of the people's interests. They should inculcate in youth a spirit of friendship and respect for the People's Police and give extensive help to the *Land* directorates and local committees of the FDJ and to the FDJ groups within the People's Police in improving ideological work and solidifying the organization.[119]

This referred not to the local police forces but to the KVP, the cadre reserve of the future People's Army. On January 2, 1952, these police units, now called divisions, were armed with Russian weapons.[120]

An important instrument in preparing youth for its coming militarization was the FDJ's fourth congress, held in Leipzig from May 27–30, 1952. Once again the FDJ had to act as an advance guard and publicly bring up questions that the SED did not discuss openly until its second party congress in July, 1952. This produced a curious situation in that the FDJ delegates returned home with ideas and resolutions for which the lower-level SED units were quite unprepared.

It is worth quoting fairly extensively from Honecker's report to the fourth congress, because here certain aspects of the character and philosophy of the forty-year-old leader emerge more clearly. He began with a declaration of loyalty to the SED, thus finally dropping the FDJ's mask of nonpartisanship, which had been so essential when it was founded:

In this situation the Free German Youth is entrusted with the proud responsibility of proving itself to be the loyal helper and reliable fighting reserve of the party of the working class, and of wholeheartedly supporting the government of the German Democratic Republic in the execution of all measures designed to reinforce and strengthen our German Democratic Republic and also the successful prosecution of the campaign to defeat the general defense treaty and promote the signing of a peace treaty with Germany.[121]

Then came the obligatory tribute to Stalin—another demonstration of the FDJ's now openly admitted subordination to the SED and the Soviet occupation authorities:

In the great Stalin, millions of young German patriots today revere the leader and teacher of all progressive mankind, the genius who created the tremendous edifice of Communism, the organizer and inspirer of all the victories of the world peace camp. Wherever in the world the word "peace" is spoken, Stalin is present. To him belong our thanks, the thanks of millions of young Germans, for everything that has made our life more beautiful and more meaningful since the destruction of Hitlerism. To him we owe our commitment, in the present phase of the struggle to preserve peace under the leadership of the Socialist Unity Party of Germany, to help to remove every obstacle to the unification of our fatherland. . . . Long live the indestructible bulwark of peace, the great socialist Soviet Union, and the inspirer of all our victories, the great and wise Comrade Stalin! Hurrah! Hurrah! Hurrah![122]

After violent attacks on the West German government and the European Defense Community as it was then being planned, Honecker indulged in some open propaganda for military service and premilitary training:

We have never made a secret of the fact that if West Germany should be turned into a base for aggression against peace-loving nations, we are prepared to organize the armed defense of our homeland. As long ago as 1950 the FDJ Central Council stated, in view of growing provocation from the imperialist camp, that peace-loving German youth must regard it as a high honor and obligation to defend peace at the side of the Soviet Union in case of aggression.

So it represents only a continuation of our resolute championship of peace when, in the present situation and in the interest of safeguarding peace, the security of our homeland and our achievements, our Free German Youth assures the President of our German Democratic Republic, Wilhelm Pieck, and Premier Otto Grotewohl that in organizing the armed defense of our homeland they can rely implicitly and to the utmost on the youth of the German Democratic Republic.

First and foremost, therefore, we must strengthen, through youth, our German People's Police, who, weapons in hand, stand guard over the peace. For every member of the FDJ, service in the German People's Police is a proud service to the German people.

In seeking to promote readiness to fight for peace, there is no reason why we should not encourage those forms of sport that, besides training the eye, give youth an opportunity to prepare itself to defend its homeland. We therefore propose to the congress that all motions concerning the introduction of the sports of target shooting, gliding, and parachuting be combined in one resolution. We further propose in connection with the discussion of the report on the implementation of the law to promote the welfare of youth, that the deputy of Premier Walter Ulbricht be asked to support youth by instituting measures that will permit it to achieve a high standard of performance in the above-mentioned sports.[123]

Even children of six to fourteen were to be trained in the spirit of patriotism within the framework of the Young Pioneers: "The twelve-year-old Young Pioneer Hannelore Wottke of Berlin-Lichtenberg took part in the great peace demonstrations of German youth on August 15, 1951, in West Berlin. . . . Our Young Pioneers are prepared, if called upon, to defend their homeland and save human lives."[124]

Honecker then openly called upon the FDJ to support the state security organization:

Youth is confident that the agencies of the state security service will continue their successful prosecution of gangs like the "Bloodhounds" and will conscientiously fulfill their mandate from our government, and hence from the people, by preventing the infiltration of agents into our Republic. The young people assembled here today express their thanks to the Council of Ministers of the DDR for the measures it has taken [the closing of zone frontiers, the resettlement of people living within the five-kilometer prohibited area, etc.] and assure the Premier that they for their part will do everything in their power to give these measures vigorous support.

In all factories and machine rental centers, in the city and the countryside, but especially in areas along the line of demarcation, there now falls to youth the honorable task of increasing vigilance to a significant degree and thus making a decisive contribution to the annihilation of American agents and Adenauer's saboteurs. We at this congress renew our appeal to German youth to track down the agents of American imperialism and liquidate the wreckers.[125]

At the fourth congress Honecker also made the clearest statement so far of his concept of socialist morality. (He summed it up even more explicitly fourteen years later, when he was head of the security and cadre division of the SED.)

The youth of West Germany is being ideologically prepared for the American war by the pornographic trash and filth being published in millions of copies. Over 420 firms in West Germany have been ordered by the American occupation authorities and the Kaiser government to demoralize German youth by publishing this trashy, filthy literature in the hope of degrading youth to the spiritual level of the U.S. mercenaries and the criminal methods of warfare practiced by Plague-General Ridgway in Korea.

In the name of the young generation we protest vigorously and angrily against the criminal attempts of the American monopolists to distort the moral countenance of German youth through trash and pornography, brothels and crime films. We vigorously oppose the Kaiser government's recent attempts to impair the moral fiber of youth in the DDR by smuggling in trash and pornography.

The ideals of German youth are not those of the warped old men in the Kaiser government in Bonn. German youth is engaged in making the German nation's great cultural heritage its own and drawing from it the strength for its daily work, its daily struggle.[126]

Honecker's address, every detail of which he had discussed with Ulbricht, and Ulbricht's own speech, which dealt with the same questions, formed the basis of the FDJ's work until the "New Course" of June, 1953. These speeches also anticipated the resolutions of the second SED party congress of July 9–12, 1952. Honecker and Ulbricht spoke the same language of unrealistic *putschism*. Both concentrated on the same points: defensive preparedness and vigilance. Ulbricht became even more explicit. He accused an organization named Young Congregation with various acts of sabotage, and after citing many examples of alleged secret-agent activity, declared:

I just want to mention a few facts as a warning against any kind of carelessness. In some places even ministers of religion have tried to support the enemy forces. . . . Representatives of a so-called Young Congregation have appeared in a number of places. Investigations have shown that they were connected with the so-called youth of Berlin-Lichterfelde, the organizing center for hostile agitation in the schools of the German Democratic Republic. The Free German Youth must pay a little more attention to these happenings in the schools and not continue to tolerate enemy activity of this kind. If such vigilance is exercised, it will not be difficult to liquidate the agents' contacts inside our schools and colleges and in the factories. That will prevent such elements from doing any damage to our economy through sabotage.[127]

Shortly afterward the FDJ began a campaign against the Young Congregation, which was to have serious consequences, and a purge of allegedly unreliable elements in the high schools and universities.

On another important subject Honecker's and Ulbricht's remarks coincided almost exactly: in their strategic and tactical plans for Germany and their objectives in regard to the Federal Republic. They used almost the same words: "The Adenauer government must be swept away if the German people wants to live in peace."

Honecker openly called for the overthrow of the West German government:

From the platform of this congress we call upon German youth to unite in the spirit of the young patriots of Essen and under the banner of national resistance, with the object of turning the general defense treaty into a scrap of paper by overthrowing the Adenauer regime. The general defense treaty must go so that Germany may live.[128]

The call goes out to the youth of West Germany at this grave hour to organize mass demonstrations and strikes in West Germany under the leadership of the working class and on such a tremendous scale that Adenauer, along with his American backers, may be swept away before it is too late for the German people.[129]

On Ulbricht's instructions, the KPD had to include the demand for the overthrow of the Adenauer regime in its program of national resistance, without consulting its own executive committees or those of the SED. So it can be legitimately said that responsibility for the banning of the Communist Party in West Germany rests chiefly on Walter Ulbricht and Erich Honecker, who presented the evidence to the courts of the Federal Republic on a silver platter.

The fourth congress was a classic example of how well Ulbricht and Honecker could collaborate even then, when it came to by-passing the party leadership, the Central Committee, and the Politburo. This technique became habitual during the second half of 1952 and in 1953.

The Militarization of the FDJ

Immediately after the fourth congress, the militarization of the FDJ began. The big campaign for "volunteers"—whose service was often anything but voluntary—for the paramilitary police units was initiated in line with the FDJ's agreement, reached at the fourth congress, to sponsor KVD units. It was plainly stated that it was the duty of every unit of the Free German Youth to delegate its best members to the People's Police divisions. Every member had a patriotic obligation "to acquire technical knowledge in the field of shooting, gliding, communications, parachuting, terrain, and topography, in order to be better able to defend the peace."[130]

The Second Congress of the SED legalized what Ulbricht had referred to at the fourth FDJ congress as "new tasks" arising out of "the changed situation," and renamed them "the building of socialism in the DDR."

After these two congresses, when "the building of socialism in the DDR" was well under way, Honecker's sense of reality appeared increasingly disturbed. Organizationally the FDJ was in a state of crisis. The permanent competition from mobilizations for Stalin or mobilizations for peace and from participation in the endless SED campaigns for collectivism, activism, etc. made regular work impossible. The constant personnel changes were no help either. Many FDJ leaders resigned or tried to get transferred to one of the plentiful openings in the governmental apparatus, the party, or the mass organizations. Others succumbed to corruption and began to falsify their reports and meet their work quotas without moving from their desks.

Honecker was so fascinated by "the building of socialism in the DDR" that he never noticed the signs of crisis at the lower levels. He would not recognize that the understaffed functionary apparatus was overloaded with directives from the central organization. Centralized planning allowed no latitude. If the secretariat of a local FDJ headquarters wanted to read, discuss, and answer all the directives, queries, requests for reports, etc. it received every month from higher bureaucratic departments such as the Central Council apparatus or the county directorate, and if the individual functionaries wanted to fulfill their numerous obligations to various county institutions (commission meetings, reports to the party, district assembly, People's Police, Society for Sports and Technology, sports clubs, etc.) they needed to spend eight to ten hours a day at their desks and barely had time to attend the compulsory weekly meeting of the secretariat. If this—and the reason for it was pointed out to Honecker, he would get angry and talk about the extracurricular working parties organized by the best group functionaries. But setting up these extracurricular groups required a lot of work, and the country functionaries lacked the time to direct them properly. So Honecker came up with another universal remedy: no official was to devote more than 50 percent of his time to desk work. But at the same secretariat meeting at which he proposed this magic solution, many motions were passed that would tie the secretaries down to their desks even more effectively.

At that time Honecker seemed to have no sense of reality. This was evident in other areas, too. He regularly made decisions over the heads of fellow members of the secretariat. And when groups came to him with requests for material help in the way of tents or building materials for youth hostels, he would make big promises—probably out of a desire for popularity—without first checking whether sufficient funds were available.

Distrust in the Politburo

Honecker's successes with spectacular affairs like the All-Germany Meeting, the World Festival of Youth, and the fourth congress, and especially his increasing closeness to Ulbricht, had obviously gone to his head. In the Politburo, too, he threw caution and reserve aside. Only belatedly did he realize that his special position vis-à-vis Ulbricht aroused mistrust and resentment in other members of the Politburo. They suspected that Ulbricht might be building him up as an aide with the idea of bypassing the Politburo on important power issues, especially security and cadres.

Moreover, these Politburo members had their own sources of information and knew that the FDJ's work was not going too well. Recruiting for the People's Police had not been as successful as had been hoped. At the second session of the Central Council in Halle, Honecker had to admit that while increasing youth's preparedness for defense and "swelling the ranks of our armed forces, the basis of our future People's Army," was a glorious task for the youth organization, it was also a difficult one.[131] The cadre situation was catastrophic. At that same session Honecker announced that "many functionaries from the basic units, instructors from the local branches, donned the proud uniform of the People's Police. They were replaced by new, younger cadres, and above all by our girl members."[132] Obviously a development of that kind is not beneficial to an organization of a million members.

Certain members of the Politburo took advantage of these acute difficulties. Morale there was in any case not very high. Opposition to Ulbricht was crystallizing—though still beneath the surface. Paul Merker had been ousted, and Franz Dahlem, generally regarded as Ulbricht's strongest opponent, was eliminated in 1952. Some members thought Honecker had a hand in this. The opposition began to concentrate its fire on Honecker as the safest and most effective way of getting at Ulbricht. Although its front changed constantly, the opposition was usually made up of those individuals who specialized in criticism of Honecker; among them were Wilhelm Zaisser, Rudolf Herrnstadt and Hans Jendretzky, and also, though with certain limitations, Fred Oelssner and Elli Schmidt. Ebert, Grotewohl, Matern, Rau, Mükkenberger, and Wilhelm Pieck never voiced any such criticism.

The case of the Wilhelm Pieck Training College will serve as one of the many examples. The college was housed in a former castle of Josef Goebbels, but since its enrollment was to be increased 300 percent, the castle had become too small. The architects Kurt Liebknecht and Herrmann Henselmann had been commissioned by the Central Council to design a new building, and Honecker approved their plans. The two architects, Honecker, and I then submitted the plans to the Politburo, because the project, particularly its funding, had to be approved by the SED leadership. Professor Liebknecht made a report. Honecker offered explanatory comments on both the building and the financial plans and recommended the sketches without reservation. The new buildings were intended to blend with the landscape and with the style of the existing one and to create a feeling of a spacious school in a woodland setting. A lot of wood would be used, in addition to concrete and stone.

Even while Liebknecht and Honecker were still speaking, it became obvious from Ulbricht's remarks that he disliked the plan. This made Honecker so unsure of himself that he began to question the project he had just been recommending. When the professors finished what they had to say, Ulbricht stood up. They were not planning a convalescent home, he said, but a training school for youth, an institution of socialist education, a monument of socialism. This must be evident in its architectural style. Disregarding the architect's drawings, he sketched Greek temples with Ionic columns in red pencil on graph paper. Developing his basic concept of socialist architecture, he drew new socialist cities, yet to be built, repeatedly referred to the Stalin Allee in East Berlin, emphasized the gigantic model of the Soviet Union, and concluded by saying: "This, Comrades, is how you must build. Only in this way can a socialist style of architecture be developed." The architects were told to submit new plans in four weeks. Honecker did not dare to raise any objection. On the contrary, he hastily assured Ulbricht that he would see to the preparation of new plans and avoided all mention of funds.

Four weeks later the new plans in the requested monumental style were submitted and, apart from some minor changes that Ulbricht made for the sake of his own prestige, were approved in principle. No other member of the Politburo took part in the discussion at these sessions. Zaisser read the newspaper; Rau went through the papers in a folder; all the rest gave their attention to other things.

Late in 1952 we were called before the Politburo again and confronted by a completely changed situation. As was to be expected, the building, only 60 percent complete, had already cost three times the original total appropriation of six million marks. In the meantime, however, the party had begun its economy drive: "Economize on every gram, every *pfennig*, every minute." Ulbricht's and Honecker's opponents in the Politburo seemed to have been counting on this. Choosing a moment when Ulbricht was away on a trip to the Soviet Union, they put on the agenda the item "Youth Training College; Financial Estimates." Matters of this kind were regularly dealt with by Otto Schön, secretary of the Politburo and the secretariat, who, in conjunction with Honecker's first wife, Edith Baumann, seemed to be the coordinator of the anti-Ulbricht forces. A motion had been proposed in the Politburo to investigate the construction of the Bogensee Youth Training College in which the FDJ had been accused of wasting funds, misplanning, etc. Ulbricht, just back from the Soviet Union, had no chance to prevent this item from being raised. Honecker and I were called again before the Politburo, this time without the architects and accompanied only by the Central Council's financial expert, Heinz Wenzel.

Both Ulbricht and his opponents behaved in an absolutely typical manner. Realizing that he was in a weak position, the secretary general tried to get out of it in his own way. Although the whole Politburo knew that he had been responsible for the rise in construction costs, no one dared to mention it. All the accusations and harsh criticism were directed against "the leading comrade of the youth organization," who was charged with extravagance and with wasting the workers' hard-earned money. Ulbricht acted as if he were in no way concerned, listened to the charges, and immediately took the lead in criticism. He censured the Central Council secretariat as irresponsible and wasteful, accused it of disregarding and misconstruing party orders and of neglect and inadequate expertise in supervising the project. Everyone in the Politburo knew that this was a complete distortion of the facts, but most members seemed glad that Ulbricht had been forced to wriggle out of a predicament.

Honecker was in the most awkward position of all. He listened grimly to the criticism but could not summon up the courage to contradict Ulbricht and remind him that he himself had been responsible for the expensive revision of the plans. He could not dismiss his fellow members' charges, because they were justified by the facts. When we left the Politburo, he could no longer contain himself and began to curse and swear. His anger, however, was not directed at Ulbricht, but at Jendretzky, Herrnstadt, and Oelssner, who had been among the sharpest critics. When I asked why Ulbricht had played this double game, he told me I wouldn't understand. This was part of an underground fight, and Walter

Ulbricht, not the school building project, was the target. But the day would come when he would strike back.

The opportunity arose when Oelssner, speaking to some party and FDJ officials about the role of the FDJ in the rural areas and especially in the agricultural collectives, suggested that there should be only one FDJ group, which would have to take in both the young people and the agrarian collectives. Only in this way could the unity of youth be ensured. Honecker took a different view. He believed that the FDJ should establish the basic units, especially within the agrarian collectives, as well as maintaining its own local groups in the villages.

Honecker himself was not present at the conference where Oelssner expressed his views. When he heard about it, he went straight to Ulbricht. He had learned that Oelssner's speech was to appear in the next issue of *Neues Deutschland*. I was present at this meeting between Ulbricht and Honecker and could observe how close their relationship was. Ulbricht listened to Honecker's criticism of Oelssner and took immediate action. He called for the proofs of Oelssner's speech, read the passages in question, crossed them out in red pencil, and gave orders that the speech was not to appear at all in its present form. Then he telephoned Otto Schön and angrily asked why the speech had not been cleared with him. Any statement of principles, especially any statement of ideological principles, had to be approved by him in advance. Schön must have objected that Politburo members were excepted from this rule. Ulbricht angrily retorted that it applied to all Politburo members, including Comrade Oelssner.

Honecker obviously enjoyed the whole scene immensely, and I understood the reason for his changed demeanor in the Central Council secretariat. His constant awareness of Ulbricht's absolute power, in which he himself could bask, inevitably impaired his realistic assessment of the forces operating in his own area of work and also diminished his loyalty to his colleagues. I realized then why Ulbricht's and Honecker's opponents had waited for an occasion when Ulbricht would be absent to launch an attack on Honecker. In Ulbricht's presence they seemed either to be afraid or to recognize that their plans were doomed from the start. Honecker once said: "They're lying in wait for a chance to get me, but they'll find out that I have more staying power than they do."

"Service for Germany"

Before long Honecker learned that he would do better to take his opponents seriously. This was brought home to him by the trouble over the Service for Germany, a labor corps set up in a very hasty, dilettantish fashion. The Service was officially founded on July 23, 1952, by order of the Council of Ministers, but in fact it already existed in skeleton form. Its director and top officials had been appointed, and uniforms, membership cards, and equipment had been procured, so that its first two brigades, each composed of ten thousand boys and girls, could begin work. Erich Honecker proudly announced at the second session of the Central Council in Halle on August 14, 1952: "As we all know, the first Service for Germany brigades have already started work."[133]

It had begun very mysteriously. No one in the Central Council secretariat knew when Ulbricht and Honecker had discussed the establishment of such an organization or when Honecker had quietly begun to organize it. Most of the Politburo members had been kept in the dark, too, and were all the more astonished when they learned about it. All the bureaucratic work had to be done virtually in a month. Within that time the ten thousand members had to be selected, uniformed, equipped, and instructed in their duties. Camps had to be set up, at least on a temporary basis. The officials could not be properly trained in so short a time. The result was disastrous. The boys' and girls' camps were set up in impassable terrain in the neighborhood of Pasewalk, close to several barracks and camps of the KVP, which was to build roads and do the landscaping for the labor corps units. Honecker was on vacation and had left no explicit instructions. In his absence, ominous reports poured in. Sanitation facilities in the camps were inadequate; there were many cases of illness; food and clothing were in short supply; moral standards were catastrophic. The troops located near the girls' camps made the most of this welcome opportunity for intimate relations. The result was numerous cases of venereal disease and the collapse of the already weak discipline.

Since Ulbricht was on vacation, too, leaving Otto Schön in charge of the secretariat and Wilhelm Pieck of the Politburo, I sent a report on the situation and asked for help from the SED leadership. It was decided to send a Politburo delegation to inspect the camps. The conditions it found were absolutely appalling. Wilhelm Pieck, leader of a group that included Hermann Matern,

Pieck's secretary, Walter Bartel, Hans Jendretzky, and Elli Schmidt, tried to allay the delegation's obvious anger, because he knew that it would be directed primarily against Ulbricht and Honecker. While the group was inspecting a camp of the para-military police they discovered that they already had Russian T-34 tanks. Matern exclaimed resentfully: "Let's hope that if war breaks out tomorrow they'll let us know!" In fact none of the Polit-buro members knew that the KVP was already equipped with heavy weapons. Even Pieck himself could not calm their resent-ment.

Immediately after the delegation returned, a special session of the Politburo was called. Secretaries of the FDJ Central Council and Generals Heinz Hoffmann and Rudolf Dölling of the KVD attended this meeting, where the findings of the site visit to the Service for Germany camps were discussed. It emerged that Ul-bricht had not informed the Politburo of the original resolutions and that it did not even know of the existence of the girls' camp. The comprehensive report on the conditions the delegation had found was devastating: moral degeneracy, venereal disease, ap-palling sanitary conditions, lack of discipline, and inadequate food supplies. The Politburo criticized these conditions with the utmost severity. Hans Jendretzky proposed that proceedings be instituted against the responsible parties in the Central Party Control Commission. The evidence was so overwhelming that even Ulbricht's supporters voted for the motion, with the excep-tion of Wilhelm Pieck, who tried to calm down the excitement and postpone action until Ulbricht's return. Everyone knew that Ulbricht and Honecker were responsible. Exceedingly critical re-marks were made by Wilhelm Zaisser, Elli Schmidt, and Hans Jendretzky, and by Heinrich Rau who normally held aloof from all factional disputes. Now, however, it was Rau who declared:

If we punish workers in our factories as saboteurs for failing to ful-fill their quotas, then we should do the same with those who at the same time are doing the same thing on a much wider scale, involving more than ten thousand boys and girls. I therefore support the mo-tion to institute an investigation of those responsible for these abuses.

Everyone knew whom he was attacking, but no one dared to mention the names of Ulbricht and Honecker.

Zaisser took this opportunity to extend the attack to the direc-

tors of the Society for Sports and Technology and the Government
Committee for Sports and Physical Culture. His exposé was so
convincing that the Politburo voted to remove these two organizations from Honecker's jurisdiction (previously shared with Ulbricht). No names were named in this resolution either. The
Politburo simply ruled that in future only the entire party leadership, that is, the Politburo as a whole, could make fundamental
decisions concerning these organizations. Nevertheless, it was
clear to everyone that this meant a limitation of the power of Ulbricht and Honecker.

Honecker returned to Berlin shortly before Ulbricht, and Matern immediately brought him up to date on the investigation.
Honecker put the blame on the army, which was responsible to
the Council of Ministers for food and housing. He told me that
there was no reason to worry: "When Walter gets here, everything will be cleared up." He was quite right. Ulbricht returned
from vacation, read the report, and threw it in the wastebasket.
Neither the Central Party Control Commission nor the other members of the Politburo dared to protest. Ulbricht justified his conduct to the Politburo on the grounds that "that's the way the Russian comrades wanted it." The Service for Germany was abolished
in 1953. This episode is clear proof that no one could make a move
against Honecker so long as Ulbricht remained at the head of
the party.

Honecker himself realized this and began to ignore rules ap-
plying to high-ranking comrades. In 1952 every top functionary
was required to participate in some way in the SED educational
program. The high-ranking comrades were assigned to "directed
studies," meaning that they were given a reading list which they
had to complete within a certain time. A scholar or scientist was
supposed to hold regular individual sessions with them to satisfy
himself on their progress. Honecker, like everyone else, had a university lecturer assigned to him, but he saw little of him and never
completed the required reading. For one thing, he had no time,
because of his dual responsibilities in the Politburo and the FDJ;
for another he had little enthusiasm for studying and even less
for academic supervision. So when the party leadership set the
dates for these informal examinations, he and I would write excuses for one another. As Honecker saw it, he had made a thorough study of the Short Course in the History of the Communist

Party of the Soviet Union, and, together with his practical experience, that would suffice for the time being. He would leave studying to others. This attitude was no secret in the party. One of his opponents, Otto Schön, was always inquiring how his studies were progressing. Then through intermediaries he would inform Ulbricht—who would do nothing.

So at the beginning of 1953, despite serious symptoms of crisis in the FDJ and despite his enemies in the party leadership and the Central Committee apparatus, Honecker's position was stronger than ever—thanks to his alliance with Walter Ulbricht.

Honecker and the Seventeenth of June, 1953

Early in 1953 Honecker quietly married for the second time. Edith Baumann had long resisted a divorce and had yielded only in response to pressure from Ulbricht and Pieck. Honecker's second wife was Margot Feist, then director of the Thälmann Young Pioneers, now the DDR's minister of education. She was born on April 17, 1927, in Halle on Saale, where her father, a cobbler, was a pre-1933 member of the KPD and the Red Trade Union Organization. Margot's brother Manfred, three years her junior, was made a candidate of the SED Central Committee at the party's Eighth Congress and is now director of the foreign information division in the Central Committee apparatus.

Margot Feist-Honecker often talks about how, as a school child, she would carry messages for her father, then a member of an underground Communist group in Halle, and keep watch when the comrades held meetings in their apartment. "It was less suspicious if a child—and a girl at that—went rushing about Halle with those hot messages," she said with a smile. After finishing grammar school, she was employed in business. Immediately after the collapse of the Third Reich she became a co-founder of the Halle Anti-Fascist Youth Committee. She joined the KPD in 1945 and the SED later.

As for her political career, after the establishment of the FDJ, she became a member of its Halle district board; in 1947 she was made director of the cultural and educational division of the state secretariat, and by 1948 she was FDJ secretary for culture and education. During 1948 she attended a special course at the party training school in Liebenwalde. After the third congress in 1949, she was transferred to Berlin, where she became director, and shortly afterward secretary, of the Young Pioneer division. From 1949 to 1954 she was a member of the *Volkskammer*, the East German parliament. Since 1950 she has been first a candidate then a member of the Central Committee, to which she was re-elected at the Eighth Congress in 1971. In 1953 she was sent to Moscow for a year at the Komsomol training college. On her return, she left the FDJ to become director of the central division of teacher training in the Ministry of Education; in 1958 she was made deputy minister. In November, 1963, she succeeded Professor Alfred Lemnitz (under whom she had taken courses at the party training college in Liebenswalde) as minister of education. In May, 1963, she was made deputy chairman of the DDR's UNESCO Commission.[134]

Margot Feist-Honecker is extremely enterprising—not to say ambitious, but this in no way decreases her feminine charm or her capacity for warm human decisions. At the time when she worked closely with Erich Honecker in the Central Council secretariat, she influenced him considerably even in personal decisions, and he valued her judgment. Her combination of intelligence and warm cordiality is appealing. Functionaries who hesitated to turn directly to Honecker would come to her with their problems in the hope that she would put in a word for them. Margot Feist-Honecker is a hard worker, knows what she wants, and has no trouble making her way in a society largely dominated by men. How much of a moderating influence she still exerts over the sometimes irascible Honecker is uncertain. In well-informed circles of East Berlin and the DDR, the rumor persists that they have been separated for a long time.

Although Honecker's marriage introduced order into his private life, which had been a constant subject for attack, it did not save him from other conflicts. The scandal over the Service for Germany was by no means forgotten when, in January, 1953, his opponents made another attempt to get at Ulbricht through him. This time the attack originated with the Free German Trade Union Federation. In defiance of the 1949 agreement, the FDGB executive announced, without informing Honecker and Ulbricht, that in future the Federation would maintain its own youth groups in the factories, independent of the FDJ groups. The reason given was that FDJ activity in the factories had been a failure and the

FDGB could not stand by and see large segments of youth remain indifferent to socialism merely because the FDJ did not know how to appeal to them. This was an overt attack on Honecker, which struck at Ulbricht too. It was designed to break the FDJ's monopoly. There would now be a competing youth organization in the factories, and it would probably soon become stronger and more influential than the FDJ. The FDGB youth would give a hundred thousand young workers an opportunity to organize politically without the strict Stalinist control exercised by the FDJ and a chance to stand up for their social rights.

Honecker informed Ulbricht, who promised to leave no stone unturned to have the resolution rescinded. And in fact the FDGB was forced to call another executive meeting at which the leading trade unionists had to disclaim a resolution they themselves had passed. They passed a new one to the opposite effect, stating that the Federation's principal task was to support the FDJ groups, renouncing all independent youth work of its own.

Honecker's alliance with Ulbricht proved its worth again, but an uncomfortable feeling remained. It seemed to me that Honecker's self-confidence was slightly diminished. At the beginning of 1953 the situation in the FDJ was anything but satisfactory. The same was true of the situation among the general population. On January 1 the SED declared 1953 the Karl Marx Year. Little did it realize that developments in the DDR would follow the laws of Marx and it would turn drastically against the Stalinist interpretation of his theory. The omens were not auspicious. Coercive measures to ensure the fulfillment of centrally imposed plans, an increase in basic food prices, ruthless measures to raise production, and the strengthening of the surveillance apparatus were arousing increasing insecurity and passive resistance among the people. Instead of seeking the reason for this in its own policy, the Ulbricht leadership regarded the restiveness as the work of foreign agents. Ulbricht saw agents, saboteurs, and enemies of the party everywhere. In 1953, realizing that the elimination of the alleged deviationists Leo Bauer, Willi Kreikemeyer, Lex Ende, Paul Merker, and others in 1950 and 1951 had not put a stop to opposition in the Politburo, he decided to strike back. In late 1952 the information office directed by Gerhard Eisler had been abolished because many of its staff (appointed by Ulbricht's own cadre division) had spent the Hitler years in emigration in the

West, and Ulbricht regarded them as a conspiratorial concentration of hostile elements. On February 21, 1953, the Association of Victims of the Nazi Regime was dissolved because it had allegedly become a focus of oppositional Communists. Ulbricht was most disturbed by the large numbers of Spanish civil war veterans who had made this association their formal organization.

On March 5 Stalin died. His death increased the insecurity of the leading functionaries. Honecker was profoundly shaken. When the doctors' bulletins first announced the gravity of Stalin's illness, I was able to observe his reaction. He seemed unable to grasp the news. Obviously it had never occurred to him that Stalin —who after all was seventy-three—must die too some day. When he called the secretariat together, his voice faltered, and tears ran down his cheeks. All the other secretaries were equally unable to hide their deep emotion.

When I told Honecker how Minister of Culture Johannes R. Becher had reacted to the news of Stalin's illness, his indignation was undoubtedly genuine. I had gone to Becher's apartment to ask him to be chairman of the national committee for the next world youth festival. He said he hadn't much time, because he had to work on a poem as an obituary tribute to Stalin. When I remarked with some surprise that Stalin hadn't died yet, Becher replied without any emotion, in fact almost serenely: "He will. And after all I've got to be the first." When I told Honecker about this he was stunned, and then his dislike of intellectuals and artists exploded. They were callous and ungrateful, he said, and had no loyalty to the party. They knew nothing about readiness for sacrifice or service. What came first with them was egoism, dishonesty, and personal ambition.

When the news of Stalin's death broke, Honecker became very serious and said that very difficult times lay ahead, which we could survive only if we held closely together. Now everyone must give his utmost, and so on. I felt that he was afraid that everything that had been achieved since 1954 was about to collapse. Naturally we were all deeply upset over Stalin's death, but it had not occurred to us that it might change everything. Our confidence in the Soviet Union was so strong that we took it for granted that even Stalin's death could not interrupt the sustained upward course of the USSR. Honecker must have seen things differently. When he returned from his first talk with Ulbricht, he seemed thoughtful and still gloomy. He spoke of the possibility of another war and of the opportunity the American imperialists would exploit to fall upon "the world peace camp, now left without a leader." For this reason it was imperative to increase vigilance against our enemies, inside and out. The FDJ press was instructed to play up the intensification of the class war and alertness in recognizing enemies of the working class, and to publish reports about the exposure of agents. Attacks on the Young Congregation were intensified, and, after a brief interruption, the witch-hunting of internal enemies of the SED and FDJ was resumed even more vigorously.

On May 14, 1953, Franz Dahlem was expelled from the Central Committee and relieved of all his functions because of "political blindness toward the activity of imperialist agents and an attitude toward his errors unacceptable by party standards." The SED leadership and Honecker along with it were so much caught up in the constantly accelerating struggles for power that they failed to recognize how serious the situation of the DDR had become.

On May 14 a 10 percent rise in work norms was ordered.[135] This drastically reduced the standard of living, particularly of the workers, and inflamed the political climate. Although the Soviet Control Commission was about to be disbanded (May 27, 1953) and replaced by a high commission headed by Ambassador Extraordinary and Plenipotentiary Vladimir Semyonov, it was very well informed about the growing discontent among the population. It proposed to the SED and to the FDJ Central Council that their methods of ascertaining the mood of the population and the effectiveness of their own work be revised on the Russian model. Over several months, teams of interviewers operating in specific areas of the DDR were to make carefully planned surveys of the mood of the population and the reasons for it, and so far as possible take remedial measures on the spot. Their reports would provide the Politburo and the Central Council secretariat with an analytical basis for improving their work.

The reports unanimously showed a general indifference to the work of the SED, open hostility among the workers toward the measures taken by the party, the government, and the mass organizations, and hopelessness and apathy among the functionaries of the factory and district branches. Honecker's reaction to these disastrous findings shows how much he relied on Ulbricht's protection. He denounced the lengthy reports, in which every point was fully documented, as defeatist humbug, as a sign of surrender in the face of hostility, as unjustified pessimism, and as an antiparty expedient.

The Russian functionaries in Karlshorst, on the contrary, took the results of the survey very seriously. They interpreted them to mean that the mood of the people was steadily deteriorating and that a change of policy must be prepared. They obviously did not agree with Honecker's attitude, because before going to Moscow Semyonov invited me instead of Honecker for a talk. When I asked in surprise why the Russians did not invoke their right to issue directives and force the SED and the FDJ to treat the reports seriously, Party Secretary Orlow replied: "We want to see if the German comrades can manage to handle their own problems. If they can't, we can always help them out. Besides, we've been instructed, in line with our changed status, not to intervene any more in the DDR's internal affairs."

Honecker was very upset that he had not been invited to Karlshorst for this talk. He said didactically that while the Soviet Union's leading role was beyond dispute or attack, the SED was a sovereign party and the chain of command could run only from the Presidium of the Communist Party of the Soviet Union to the Politburo of the SED. "Where does it leave us if every comrade deals directly with the Soviet comrades?" he asked. In April, 1953, Semyonov returned to Moscow, taking with him all the reports—at least all those prepared by the FDJ.

The New Course, announced on June 9, came as a surprise. Although it was supposed to ease and improve conditions, it actually did the reverse. The discontented population regarded the concessions as inadequate and took them as a sign of weakness and indecision in the leadership. Low-level functionaries felt themselves betrayed by the executive boards. Suddenly all the unpopular measures they had been supposed to enforce under pressure from above had been declared a mistake. They felt they had been unfairly treated, used as scapegoats and made ridiculous in the eyes of the people. Moreover they received no directives on the new line of argument. So they withdrew and so far as possible avoided discussion.

On the morning of June 16 construction workers marched on the ministerial building to call Ulbricht and Grotewohl to account.

Honecker was at the regular Tuesday meeting of the Politburo. According to him, this is what happened. The meeting began in routine fashion. Among other items on the agenda was the problem of work norms and morale among the construction workers on the Stalin Allee, who had recently been indulging in open criticism of the SED and its trade union policy. While the agenda was being dealt with in the normal way, the first reports began to come in of a big demonstration of construction workers marching from the FDGB building toward the ministerial building on the Leipzigerstrasse. The Politburo meeting was broken off. An emergency information and messenger service and a direct telephone line to the ministerial building were set up. In this way the Politburo learned that the demonstrators were calling for Ulbricht and Grotewohl. Fritz Selbmann, who happened to be in the ministerial building at the time, urged Ulbricht to speak to them and quiet them down. He described the critical situation and his own unsuccessful attempts to restore order. The only way of pacifying the workers, he said, was for Ulbricht to appear.

According to Honecker, Ulbricht refused on the grounds that the Politburo meeting was more important. He was sure the demonstrators would disperse and go home if no one paid any attention to them. His position was strengthened when it began to rain. The Politburo thought that all provocation should be avoided, and that if nothing was done to excite the men they would disperse of their own accord. Accordingly, the police were ordered to avoid clashes as far as possible, to give the demonstrators their head, and on no account to use weapons.

About noon Honecker made a brief appearance in the Central Council secretariat, which was also continuing its meeting, although it was keeping a radio tuned to the American station RIAS, the only station that was broadcasting news. Honecker issued instructions for securing the building and sent out all available functionaries to mix with the demonstrators in small action-groups. He refused to inform the county directorates. And he said —and as the Politburo agreed—it would be better to confine the affair to Berlin and not "start a stampede in the DDR."

Ulbricht's hope that the trouble would end with the demonstration outside the ministerial building was not fulfilled. More and more segments of the population joined the workers, who were now demonstrating all over the eastern sector of Berlin.

The antiregime slogans were growing sharper in tone. Shouting and chanting of "The Goatee [Ulbricht] must go! We want free elections!" was becoming more widespread. In the meantime Honecker had returned to the Politburo and arranged a messenger service between the Central Committee and the Central Council. In view of developments, the party leadership decided to rescind the increase in work norms, effective immediately. Ulbricht thought this would put an end to the whole affair, because the workers had now achieved what they wanted. But this was his second fatal error of judgment. The norms were no longer the crucial issue. The workers were already making political demands: the overthrow of the regime and free elections.

Ulbricht made his third mistake on the evening of June 16, when he called a conference of the Berlin SED functionaries at the Friedrichsstadt Palace to establish their position on the day's events. This meant calling the functionaries away from the factories, where, as representatives of SED policy, they could have stirred up opinion against the preparations for a general strike. Through this action Ulbricht left the rebellious factory workers to their own devices and allowed them to prepare for the demonstrations of June 17 undisturbed. The political bodies were left without leaders. No instructions were issued to their organizations and affiliated associations. When the demonstrations ended at about 10 P.M., there was no one left in the factories who could have acknowledged such instructions.

Ulbricht's report also showed a complete misjudgment of the situation. All he did was go into an explanation of the New Course, already proclaimed on June 9 and familiar to everyone present. He did not devote a single word to the day's events. The construction workers' demonstrations were ignored as though they had never happened, giving the functionaries the impression that nothing of significance had taken place. Inquiries from the county functionaries, who had learned of the day's events over RIAS, evoked similar answers: the demonstrations were over; the RIAS reports were exaggerated; they shouldn't allow themselves to be provoked but simply keep quiet; the SED leadership hoped to be able to localize the disturbances in Berlin the next day.

Although the Central Council had heard quite a different story from the DDR—reports of isolated strikes, increased unrest in the factories, etc.—and although he himself was not so sure that all would be quiet the next day, Honecker rejected every proposal to take precautionary measures on the county level. The reason he gave was that that was what Comrade Ulbricht had decided.

During the night Honecker himself visited the Berlin headquarters, which was on alert. His account of what he found there was anything but flattering. With a certain malicious pleasure he discovered that in the Service for Germany camps, which Comrade Jendretzky had made so much fuss about and which were located at a distance of several hundred kilometers from the Central Council, the disorder was not as great as in Comrade Jendretzky's own offices. The secretariat was completely isolated. All attempts to keep in touch with the big industrial plants had failed. The SED leaders in Berlin were totally cut off not only from the workers but from their own subordinates as well. Some of these could not be contacted, others had left word that they were out, others made excuses to avoid accepting any responsibilities. The secretariat was not even properly informed of the situation in the various sections of Berlin, because its messenger service could not furnish regular reports.

The Politburo met all through the night. Although outwardly it maintained an optimistic front, negotiations had been begun with Russian representatives to evacuate members' wives and families to the Soviet Union. On Ulbricht's instructions Lotte Kuhn asked Margot Feist the next day if she wished to be included. She indignantly refused. Late that night I witnessed the first quarrel between Margot Feist and Erich Honecker, when he tried to justify this resolution as necessary.

June 17 also confronted Erich Honecker with a personal decision that was to influence his whole future life. The events of June 16 and 17 brought the anti-Ulbricht feeling, long smoldering beneath the surface, into the open. Herrnstadt and Zaisser appointed themselves its spokesmen. They were supported—more or less reluctantly—by Jendretzky, Elli Schmidt, and Oelssner. Other members and candidates of the Politburo took a wait-and-see attitude. I spoke briefly to Honecker at noon in the Central Committee, having had considerable trouble making my way there to bring him the report he was expecting. He thought there were others who sympathized with the Zaisser-Herrnstadt group but were waiting to see what would happen, because they were "cowards." He was undoubtedly referring to Grotewohl, Ackermann, Ebert, and Rau.

The opposition attributed the events of June 17 to Ulbricht's

high-handed policy. His working style, they said, had led to bureaucratization and inflexibility in the party. The party cadres
were intimidated and lacked the courage to turn in honest reports. The party bore down heavily on the masses and was totally
isolated from them. There were no real ideological discussions
within the party leadership and mass organizations. From the
Politburo down to the basic units, the principle of one-man leadership prevailed. This erroneous style of working was also responsible for the Service for Germany scandal. For this reason a "re-
newal of the party" was imperative.

The Central Committee building was surrounded by tanks. I
had Honecker called out of the Politburo meeting for a moment.
He seemed nervous and was apparently not listening to what I
said. When I asked if he were ill, he shook his head and said re-
signedly: "They're all attacking Walter. He'll probably be defeated. But the worst thing is that I don't know what I should do
myself." He sounded weary and depressed; I had never heard him
talk like that before. He was in no hurry to go back into the meeting—almost as if he hoped to avoid having to make a decision.

Everyone knows how it ended. Ulbricht won, because he was a
more skillful tactician and because the rebels indirectly helped
him out. When he realized that he no longer had a decisive majority, he postponed a decision by demanding that the opposition
put its views in writing and discuss them with a commission.
Meanwhile he was negotiating with Semyonov, who deliberately
strengthened his position because he did not want to change leaders at this juncture. When Honecker returned to the Central
Council secretariat late that night, he seemed relieved and also a
little ashamed that he had entertained the idea of leaving his pa-
tron in the lurch and going over to the opposition.

The fate of the opposition and the end of all the hopes vested in
the revolt are common knowledge. But how did Erich Honecker
behave after June 17? Did he really believe that this workers'
rebellion was the work of a handful of agents and paid *provoca-
teurs*? At the sixth session of the Central Council on August 21,
1953, he stuck to the official version:

The events of June 17 show that a number of members of our organization did not immediately recognize the nature of the fascist
provocation and were therefore not in a position to counter enemy
propaganda with effective arguments. This is to be attributed to lack

of political knowledge and to the lack of well-organized, youth-oriented political training within the organization. Obviously in our educational program we have not succeeded in making the acquisition of political knowledge an integral part of the life and duties of youth.[136]

In the private conversations with all county secretaries that he held in July and August, Honecker was more explicit. Here he admitted that many FDJ boards had failed radically. Many officials had not even defended their own offices but had disappeared when the excited crowds approached. Thousands of FDJ members had actually taken part in the demonstrations. A considerable percentage of FDJ units collapsed completely during the rebellion, merged with the crowds of strikers and made common cause with them. In the private conversations Honecker denounced all these things, and every official had to express criticism and self-criticism.

Here Honecker was the reliable functionary, holding to the party line and conscientiously executing party resolutions. But what did he really think? He had always proudly emphasized his proletarian origins. What were his feelings when he confronted the fact that it was primarily the working class that had revolted against the "workers' and peasants' state"? There is no way of knowing. After June 17 he became unapproachable—something that had never happened before. Once only, when he was telling me about Ulbricht's closing words at the fifteenth plenary session of the Central Committee (July 24–26, 1953) did he disclose what he really thought. At the end of his speech Ulbricht had discussed the Zaisser-Herrnstadt faction. He reproached Herrnstadt with having used "the intelligence techniques of so-called active reconnaissance within the party leadership" and with "playing one comrade off against another." Zaisser, he said, believed he could "put pressure on the members of the Politburo." Instead of turning antiparty documents over to the Politburo, he had participated in the conspiracies. Ulbricht's closing words were: "They began with Ulbricht. Then came Matern, then Grotewohl, Honecker and the rest. Then Comrade Herrnstadt let fly against the party apparatus he hates so much."

Honecker commented: "When you see how despicably those fellows behaved and how they twisted and turned, you understand why many workers have no confidence in our party. They think they're typical of the party." He was obviously aware that the workers' rebellion could not have been the work of infiltrated agents and saboteurs, but he was so firmly convinced that Ulbricht's policy was right that he could do nothing but blame the "deviationists."

Nevertheless the events of June 17 radically changed his manner in the Central Council secretariat. He seemed more suspicious and smelled treason everywhere. He was more reserved and completely dropped his old, slightly boastful communicativeness. He had definitely decided to move upward at Ulbricht's side.

The All-German Election Scare

On August 15, 1953, two months after the workers' revolt of June 17, the Soviet Union sent the three Western powers a note on the German question. Like the note of March 10, 1952, this one provided for the calling of a peace conference, the formation of a provisional all-German government, the holding of free elections, and some relief of financial and economic obligations connected with war damage.[137]

The announcement hit Berlin like a bombshell. The self-confident façade vanished. No one could understand why the Soviet Union should deliver such a note so soon after the revolt of June 17. Honecker was as perplexed as everyone else. The Politburo met more frequently than usual, and there was hectic activity everywhere. When the news was announced, the top representatives of all mass organizations were summoned to the SED Central Committee and ordered by Hermann Axen to work out, within a few days, an election plan for their own organization using all the means at their disposal. Even functionaries who had never deviated from the party line or doubted the infallibility of the Soviet Union or the party now began to ask uneasily what would happen if the Western powers accepted the Russian proposal. Honecker too was asked these and similar questions, and I still remember his embarrassed answer: "Then we'll just have to fight and, if it comes to the worst, die like heroes."

I had learned from the leaders of the underground unit that maintained liaison with the West German Communist Party, Hans Rosenberg and Richard Stahlmann, that an emergency staff within the Central Committee was already working on plans for the SED to go underground without losing its effectiveness. When I mentioned this to Honecker, I could see that although he obviously knew about it already, my remark had embarrassed him. Everything indicated that the party leadership took this note and the whole question of the elections extremely seriously. Erich Glückauf, head of the division of all-German affairs, openly expressed what we were all thinking. "They'd be complete fools not to accept that kind of offer at this time. They know what we're up against now, since June 17. If they don't jump at the opportunity, they're really beyond hope." Only a minority took the view that the Soviet Union "knew what it was about," as a slogan in the current election campaign in West Germany put it.

Shortly after the publication of the Russian note, Schelepin arrived in East Berlin, having been ordered by the Central Committee of the Soviet Communist Party to transmit a resolution to send twenty to thirty thousand young people over into the Federal Republic to distribute more than a million leaflets with the text of the Russian note of August 15. Cultural and theater groups and glee clubs were to help them. Most of the Central Council secretaries pointed out that such a drive would cost a tremendous amount of money and probably bring very meager results, because it would be impossible to select and brief so many young people and get the campaign under way without the West German security agencies finding out. Honecker, however, insisted that the Soviet comrades' suggestion must be carried out. Only to a handful of friends did he admit that they could hardly hope for any success.

When Honecker came to the office in a bad temper, it always meant that he had dreamed that Adenauer had resigned. The consensus was that Adenauer was the only halfway reliable guarantee that this Russian offer would be declined. But the SED did not have to drain this cup of bitterness after all.

Decline and Preparation for New Tasks

For Honecker 1954 brought a hard struggle to ensure the FDJ's survival, to restore the prestige it had enjoyed until 1952 in the party and in political opinion, and to fight off unending personal attacks and criticisms of his performance. The Service for Germany had been abolished on March 1, three months before the

Seventeenth of June, but even in late 1953 its dissolution, along with the behavior of many FDJ units during the June crisis, was still taken as proof that the FDJ was by no means living up to its strong, dynamic image.

For Honecker 1954 was to be devoted to whipping up young people's hatred for the "Adenauer regime," improving the FDJ's political work with the masses, eliminating the bureaucratic type of work, increasing the effectiveness of the ideological training of functionaries and members, and stabilizing the cadre situation.

At the seventh session of the Central Council in January, 1954, Honecker referred to Adenauer as "the Hitler of today," who intended to "drive the German people into the catastrophe of a new war." He also attacked the big West German youth organizations whose cooperation he had hitherto sought so assiduously:

> Youth should not trust the treacherous leaders of West German youth organizations like the League of German Catholic Youth—leaders who, at the last meeting of the Federal Youth Association, permitted Dr. Schröder, Bonn's Minister of the Interior, to expound the Adenauer clique's program of aggression and who, following the directives of Bonn's Minister of War Blank, try to lure youth into the American army of mercenaries with phrases like "European Defense Community" and "democratic military service."[138]

Honecker felt called upon to immunize East German youth against the system in the Federal Republic and to shield it from Western influences. The West German government, he said, was a cabinet of capitalist magnates and landowners and the Bundestag in Bonn its "docile instrument." Only 3 percent of the members of the Bonn parliament came from the working class, and most of those were "right-wing Social Democratic Party and trade union leaders, who make every effort to tie the working class and the unions, as well as the members of the SPD, to the war policy of the West German militarists."[139] But this hate campaign, initiated at the seventh session of the FDJ Central Council, failed to activate the organization.

To help the FDJ fulfill its functions, the Russians sent a big Komsomol delegation to the DDR—thus calling renewed attention to Honecker's failure. The delegation found that much of the FDJ's educational program existed only on paper, and even Honecker had to admit that the 1954 program had been prepared far too late.[140]

To improve the SED's relations with the FDJ and to remind the party of its obligations to the youth organization, Honecker even cited the Russian example. In a basic article in the SED's mouthpiece *Neues Deutschland* entitled "Duties and Responsibilities of the Party toward Youth," with the subtitle "How the Communist Party of the Soviet Union Offers the Komsomol Constant Help and Leadership," he said that the Russian Communist Party continually confronted the question of educating and training youth and was permanently involved in the Komsomol's activities. The party secretary's door was always open to the director of the Komsomol. "The Communist Party functionaries study Lenin's and Stalin's directives concerning youth, as well as the Central Committee's resolutions on questions of Komsomol work. As a result the party's leadership of the Komsomol is concrete and purposeful, which is obviously not the case with the SED."

He stressed that instead of constantly taking officials away from the youth organization the Russian Communist Party strengthened it with "experienced cadres."

In Georgia, for example, ninety-seven Communists were recently assigned to Komsomol work. The Communist Party of the Soviet Union is exemplary in its support of the Komsomol and its work with the masses of youth. The SED, by contrast, neglects its obligations to youth. It should help more with the patriotic education of all young people. Not yet are all party organizations aware of youth's mood and interests, or its attitude to vital problems of our nation.

He admitted that mistaken and hostile ideas, which many party functionaries and organizations were unaware of, were still to be found among young people. It was not enough to support FDJ meetings in word and deed. The party must become the constant helper of youth.[141]

To counteract the general indifference of the SED and other organizations toward the FDJ, and also to prepare gradually for Honecker's transfer from FDJ to party work, Ulbricht brought him increasingly to the fore as a Politburo candidate. On the thirtieth anniversary of Lenin's death it was Honecker who made the commemorative address in the name of the party. This was the first time he had appeared on such an occasion. He used the opportunity for vigorous attacks on "the rightist Social Democratic leaders—the Ollenhauers, the Neumanns and their associates—

who, as faithful lackeys of their imperialist masters, give full support to the international forces of reaction."[142]

The first signs of cautious de-Stalinization were now becoming visible in the Soviet Union and in most European countries, and Stalin's successors in the Kremlin were beginning to shake off his heritage. For Honecker, however, he was still "the great Stalin, the great continuer of Lenin's work."

Taking as its point of departure the great Stalin's brilliant work *Economic Problems of Socialism in the USSR*, the Communist Party of the Soviet Union is organizing the gradual transition from socialism to communism through the continuing upswing in the Soviet economy.

He concluded this speech with the words: "Forward, Comrades, in the spirit of the invincible theory of Marx, Engels, Lenin, and Stalin!"[143]

In 1954 Honecker also published occasional basic articles in the SED's official paper *Neues Deutschland*. "Master-Builders of a New Life" (May, 1954) and "Fifty Years of Struggle for the Happiness of the Young Generation" (October) are typical examples.

Yet all these efforts, which Ulbricht supported, could not hide the fact that Honecker's position in the SED had been weakened and that the FDJ's role in the party was controversial. The following extract from an article in *Neues Deutschland* gives an idea of the criticism concentrated upon Honecker and the FDJ at this time by influential elements within the SED leadership:

It is urgently necessary that the sectarianism still evident in the FDJ be quickly overcome. This applies particularly to the secretariat of the Central Council. . . . As of August 29, 1954, one single secretary of the FDJ Central Council had addressed a gathering of young people. Central Council Secretaries Werner Felfe and Hannes Keusch had never spoken at a business meeting or attended a young-voters' forum. This indicates grave deficiencies within the secretariat of the Central Council. . . .

The executive committees of the FDJ, from the Central Council secretariat down, lack a stable orientation to this goal. They are dilatory about exploiting youth's creative ideas. . . . It is therefore desirable to make it a regular principle of the party's work that the party executives and organizations are to assist the youth organization. . . . The whole FDJ, right down to the comrades in the basic units, must feel the helping hand extended to it by the party's executive bodies.[144]

This criticism contains a strong hint of the necessity for closer supervision of the FDJ by the party. One year after Zaisser's and Herrnstadt's attack on Ulbricht's work style, high-handedness on the part of Honecker and Ulbricht was again under fire.

Another of Honecker's hopes to restore the FDJ's prestige through its all-German activity was dashed when an attempt to hold conversations with the Federal Youth Association failed in the spring of 1955. A meeting did take place on March 17 in Bad Godesberg. The agenda proposed by Honecker in a letter of March 7 to Heinrich Köppler, chairman of the Association, included the rejection of the Paris Agreements, exchange of opinions on German reunification and measures to combat German militarism, and arrangements for a referendum. But this agenda was never adopted, although Honecker declared that:

> We see new possibilities of mutual understanding in the proposals for a national referendum submitted to the *Volkskammer* of the German Democratic Republic. Such understanding will be fostered by (among other things) the proposed general guarantee of the right to free expression of opinion and will, freedom of activity for all parties and organizations, freedom to distribute printed matter, and complete freedom of movement and personal inviolability in Germany as a whole.[145]

The Federal Youth Association, however, declined to combine the four agenda items it had suggested with a referendum and a rejection of the Paris Agreements, and made the following demands: (1) freedom of activity for all democratic youth organizations in the Soviet zone; (2) renunciation by the FDJ of its privileged position as the state youth group; (3) release of all young people imprisoned on political charges; (4) free circulation of all youth newspapers and magazines.[146] Honecker himself did not go to Bad Godesberg but sent Hannes Keusch, head of the division of youth affairs in the Premier's office (now East German ambassador to Bulgaria), and Hans Wolfram Mascher, then a member of the central committee of the *Volkskammer* and also a member of the executive board of the Eastern branch of the Christian Democratic Union, who was sentenced to several years penal servitude in the early 1960s.

The fifth FDJ congress (May 25–28, 1955) was supposed to round out Honecker's decade of service to the youth policy of the KPD/SED and conclude a decisive phase in his career. First he made an urgent appeal to youth to arouse and strengthen a spirit of defensive preparedness. The theme of vigilance formed a kind of transition to his later function in the SED Politburo, where he was responsible for internal and foreign security. At this congress he said:

Everyone who carries a gun of the armed forces of the German Democratic Republic actively serves the defense of peace, the protection of our republic's achievements and the struggle for the united, democratic, peace-loving Germany. That is why we are doing all we can to strengthen the armed forces of our republic and give our youth military training that will equip it to defend its homeland. We call upon youth to perform its two years of service in the KVP with discipline and honor, just as a young man must be a master of his trade in his daily work. We call upon youth to close its front against those who allow themselves to be used as advocates of the weakening of our workers' and peasants' state.[147]

To conclude his work in the FDJ, Honecker set the official seal on its transformation into a youth unit of the SED. The new statute of the FDJ stated: "The Free German Youth regards the Komsomol as the vanguard of democratic world youth. It emulates its example . . . and recognizes the leading role of the working class and its party, the Socialist Unity Party of Germany."[148]

So ended another phase in Honecker's life. As a functionary he had proved himself loyal to the party and unconditionally prepared to recognize the leading role of the USSR. But he had not succeeded in building up the FDJ into a strong all-German organization or making it representative of all young people in the DDR. On the contrary, since the FDJ had been forced to assume to an ever greater degree the functions of a party youth organization and supply cadres for the party and governmental apparatus instead of actively working with young people, a paralyzing bureaucracy had set in.

Nevertheless, Honecker was retired with honor. The Politburo voted to award him the National Gold Medal for Merit, thus scotching the rumors that he had failed as president of the FDJ. He was then sent for a year to the party training college in Moscow, where for the first time in his life he had to grapple seriously with Marxist-Leninist theory, strategy, and tactics and was forced to learn Russian.

No sooner had he arrived in Moscow than Albert Norden (now a member of the Politburo under Honecker's direction) devastatingly criticized the work of the FDJ before the twenty-fifth session of the Central Committee. He began by saying that the increase in emigration of young people to the West was to a great extent the fault of the FDJ leadership. His criticism was directed against the way the FDJ was run under Honecker—but at the same time against Walter Ulbricht. All Norden's suggestions for improving youth work were in fact an indictment of the FDJ's one-sidedness under Ulbricht and Honecker, of the bureaucratization of its apparatus, and of its lack of independence arising out of its subordination to the party:

The FDJ secretary shouldn't confront young people as a politician. He should be their friend and fool around with them a bit. His speeches shouldn't consist entirely of great political theorems. There's no harm in beginning with a joke and throwing in a few witticisms. At dances, instead of acting as if he were making a big sacrifice by being there at all, he should join in the fun. . . . I think the comrades in the Central Council apparatus need to change their attitude and ask themselves whether in this respect the structure of the youth organization is not perhaps too closely adapted to the structure of the party.[149]

III. A Functionary in the Apparatus

11. Preparation and Practice

Training in Moscow

FROM MID-1955 to 1956 Erich Honecker took a full year of courses at the Soviet Communist Party training college in Moscow.[1] For the first time in his life he had to make a thorough study of Marx-ist-Leninist theory as interpreted by the Soviet Union. The cur-riculum included the following subjects: history of Russia and of the Russian Communist Party; dialectical and historical materi-alism; political economy and practical economic problems; inter-national communism and the history of the international labor movement; political and economic geography; international re-lations at the government level; and literature and art. A thorough study of the Russian language was also required. Honecker is said to have audited courses at other Russian academic institutions too, chiefly on problems of military policy and security. There is no record of how well he did, but hard-working and ambitious as he is, he no doubt met the party's standards.

In Moscow he was given an opportunity to reinforce his ten years of practical experience in the field of party youth policy with a theoretical background and to equip himself for the work he would do in the future. As a candidate of the Politburo of the So-cialist Unity Party and the former head of the Free German Youth, he enjoyed a privileged position at the training school and was in effect the leader of the German student group. However, other East Germans who were studying in Moscow at that time and saw him occasionally say that he seemed very isolated. It was obvi-ously not easy for him to adjust to his new student role.

This year at the college was a crucial one for Honecker because he witnessed for himself the process of de-Stalinization
both before and after the Twentieth Congress of the Communist
Party of the Soviet Union, which took place while he was in Moscow. Even before Honecker left for Moscow in 1955, the SED had
had to come to terms with the new Russian policy toward Yugoslavia indicated by Khrushchev's and Bulganin's visit to Belgrade
in May, 1955. At the party training school he had a close-up view
of a radical change in Soviet society, which included economic
decentralization, the dissolution of Russian business corporations
in the people's democracies and the DDR, the dismissal and even
execution of leading officials of the Commission for Internal Affairs (NKVD), the proclamation of an amnesty for Soviet citizens
who had collaborated with the German occupation forces during
the German-Soviet war, and the condemnation of the grandiose
Stalinist style of architecture.

Party training schools function as political seismographs. Government and party decision-makers who teach there keep the students oriented to significant new political developments and their
ideological interpretation. Honecker learned at first hand of the
new trends in ideology and the interpretation of history that in
the autumn of 1955 were already being discussed in basic articles
in theoretical journals.[2]

The SED delegation to the Twentieth Congress, which included
Ulbricht and Politburo members Grotewohl, Schirdewan, and
Neumann, told Honecker what went on there, so he learned of
the revelations about Stalin while he was still in Moscow. This
must have meant the collapse of his world, because all his political thinking bore Stalin's indelible stamp. When Honecker joined
the party, Stalin had already overcome most of his opponents in
the Russian Communist Party. In the early 1950s, when Honecker was promoted to the control center of the SED, the Russian
dictator was at the height of his power. Honecker felt genuine
grief at the passing of this "wise leader and standard-bearer of
peace and progress all over the world," as he liked to apostrophize
him in speeches and articles.[3] Up until the Twentieth Congress
he had seen one straight line leading from Lenin to Stalin, whom
he regarded as the executor of Leninism. Suddenly he was told
that it wasn't like this at all. Stalin, they said, had ignored the
Leninist principles of collective leadership, willfully misused his

power, violated socialist legality, and committed serious errors in his direction of the government and military affairs.

It was certainly a good thing for Honecker's future development that he suffered this shock while he was still in the Soviet Union. The leaders in the DDR had to face the new situation abruptly, but Honecker was able to adapt himself gradually to the new era of Soviet reality. He had a chance to convince himself more deeply and thoroughly that this de-Stalinization phase was a vital necessity for a modern Soviet Union capable of coping with twentieth-century conditions, and he learned more about its background and effects than many of the other SED leaders. This explains why his fundamental belief in the leading role of the Soviet Union was not shaken but only modified by Stalin's fall. He must have realized that although the future of the DDR was inseparably linked to that of the USSR, it required a different approach.

Return to Berlin

Honecker's return to Berlin and his integration into the apparatus of the SED Central Committee were hardly noticed by the general public. In the DDR, too, the political landscape had changed. The condemnation of Stalin had plunged the SED into general confusion. The SED leadership was totally committed to Stalin; even in its congratulatory message to the Twentieth Congress it had paid tribute to "the invincible theory of Marx, Engels, Lenin, and Stalin."[4] It therefore wanted to conclude the discussion of Stalin's crimes as quickly as possible in order not to jeopardize its own authority.

In this situation the sphere of responsibility assigned to Honecker in the Central Committee apparatus was of particular importance: he was put in charge of the nation's security. This included responsibility for the armed services (the National People's Army) and the police, including the frontier and secret police (the State Security Service). Since the expulsion of Wilhelm Zaisser from the party leadership, these services had been under the personal control of Ulbricht. By entrusting this important field of responsibility to Honecker, Ulbricht demonstrated his confidence in him and at the same time strengthened his own position through an unconditionally loyal subordinate. Many people who had believed that Honecker's career was over when he left the FDJ were forced to change their minds. After a year's interruption, the old Ulbricht-Honecker alliance had been renewed at a higher level. Ulbricht had realized that in this difficult de-Stalinization period he needed allies who were deeply devoted to him yet did not threaten his own power. Honecker knew that without Walter Ulbricht he had no chance; on the other hand, Ulbricht had nothing to fear from him. During the next few years this alliance based on mutual need proved advantageous to both of them.

Honecker's initiation test came in October, 1956, with the revolts in Hungary and Poland. Those two events shocked the whole Eastern bloc. The SED, still shaken by the workers' rebellion of 1953, was particularly worried. In October, 1956, Honecker reappeared in public, making speeches in factories as part of the SED campaign to combat the effects of the Hungarian rising. At the Nationalized Electricity and Coal Combine in Berlin he organized the writing of a letter to the workers of the Inota-Gyartelep Combine, a Hungarian light-metal company with which the Berlin firm did business. In his speech to the workers he indirectly admitted that the unrest had spread to the workers of the DDR. "Certain people in West Berlin and West Germany," he said, "are nervous because things are quieter in the DDR. Now they are trying vigorously to transplant their nervousness to the DDR through RIAS and the Western press." He protested against alleged attempts by the Western press "to transform the counter-revolutionaries into heroes through the sensational slanting of news reports" and reduced the Hungarian revolt to simple terms: "What those gentlemen really want is to restore the old relationship of exploitation."[5]

But the main thrust of Honecker's work during this period was not visible to the public eye. In October, 1956, as the functionary in charge of state security, he was occupied with campaigns against dissident intellectuals who, after the Twentieth Congress, had begun to revolt against the dogmatic leadership methods of the party apparatus. The dissent was concentrated in a few universities, particularly Humboldt University in East Berlin. To what extent Honecker was responsible for the use of armed detachments against a student meeting there has not been determined.[6]

In October, 1956, the State Security Service began a wave of arrests which, according to *Neues Deutschland* of November 1, 1956, resulted in the arrest of seventy-three "agents."[7] The arrest of the "subversive group" led by Wolfgang Harich must also be credited to Erich Honecker. In February, 1957, Honecker was publicly identified with this purge. Reporting for the Politburo to the thirtieth conference of the Central Committee, he dealt in detail with "the counterrevolutionary coup in Hungary." Asserting that the Hungarian Communist Party had been guilty of political and economic errors, he said that it was the SED's task "to step up ideological and organizational work . . . and bring it much closer to the masses, as well as to increase vigilance against the reactionary forces of imperialism."[8] The serious view the party took of the situation in the DDR can be seen from these words: "These [West German] circles cherish the false hope that events like those in Hungary might occur in the DDR."[9]

Honecker's responsibility for the arrest of dissident party members is again revealed in the passage of his report where he appeals for "the maintenance of party unity." Many party organizations, he said, had not been resolute enough in the struggle for party unity. The principal task of the Party Control Commissions was "to wage war on subversive activity within the party."[10] On the other hand, he admitted that the Party Control Commissions themselves had in recent years issued false or exaggerated reports, which must now be corrected.

At the thirtieth session of the Central Committee, Honecker also made his first official appearance as the party functionary responsible for the National People's Army. He informed the Central Committee that the Politburo had given great attention to improving the political and military training of the combat groups and their weapons and equipment, and said that in the first half of 1957 it would be essential to give the armed forces of the National People's Army "all possible support in the fulfillment of their duties." In 1957 National Army Day would be celebrated for the first time. "In instituting all these measures, the Politburo was acting on the assumption that an increase in the preparedness of our armed forces and of the agencies of the Ministry of State Security is vital to the maintenance of peace at home and abroad."[11]

One remark that Honecker made underlined his own importance in the party hierarchy:

The German working class would never forgive us if at this juncture we were to forget even for an instant the strengthening of our republic's defensive forces. We bear a heavy responsibility for ensuring that the armed forces of our workers' and peasants' state, the National People's Army, the German People's Police, and the militant groups of the working class are at all times in a position to uphold law and order with the means at their disposal and to nip in the bud, suppress and wipe out any counterrevolutionary provocation that might occur.[12]

From this time on Honecker made more and more public appearances advocating defensive militant preparedness. A month after his report to the thirtieth plenary session of the Central Committee, *Neues Deutschland* published seven columns of extracts from his speech at a party meeting in the Railway Repair Depot in Halle, in which he compared the party task forces with the militant companies of workers of 1923 and appealed to youth "to enter the ranks of the National People's Army and fill the places of those soldiers who will be honorably discharged this year upon completion of their service to their fatherland."[13]

One year after his return from Moscow, Honecker was already playing an important role in the party leadership, which he continued to strengthen and develop during 1957 and 1958.

Conflict with the Schirdewan Group

In 1957 Honecker's relation to Ulbricht and his policy was put to the test. De-Stalinization had produced conflict within the party leadership, too. The leader of the opposition group was Karl Schirdewan, who at the time was still Ulbricht's second in command, in charge of the party organizations and cadre division of the SED Central Committee. Schirdewan was committed to "a return to Leninist party norms"[14] and believed the replacement of Ulbricht to be a necessary consequence of the doctrine laid down at the Twentieth Congress. He tried to obtain the support of Khrushchev, who was said to have approved fully of his plan at the time and even to have "tried to further it," because he regarded Schirdewan as the German Gomulka.[15]

When Honecker returned from Moscow, the conflict between Ulbricht and Schirdewan was already in full swing, though still beneath the surface. Schirdewan and a few associates, including

Ernst Wollweber, Minister for State Security, and Gerhard Ziller, secretary for economic affairs in the Central Committee,[16] wanted to continue the de-Stalinization process, while Ulbricht was trying quietly to end it. The Schirdewan group advocated "a slower tempo in socialist development" and was prepared to make certain concessions to promote a détente between the two Germanys. In this it was supported to some extent by Fred Oelssner, member of the Politburo and the SED's chief ideologist, and by the economic expert Deputy Premier Fritz Selbmann, both of whom regarded Ulbricht's economic policy as fatal for the DDR's development.[17]

Ulbricht firmly rejected this readiness to compromise, which he denounced as a "third way" policy.[18] Nevertheless, for the time being he gave the opposition its head, because it had some backing from Khrushchev and his staff. Whether he was also waiting for Honecker's return before dealing with the opposition is uncertain. But there is no doubt that Ulbricht's position in the Politburo was then anything but strong and that he urgently needed all the personal support he could get. Certainly without Honecker he would have found it difficult to replace Schirdewan in the secretariat and Politburo. Honecker was exactly the person Ulbricht needed: loyal but not nearly strong enough to pose a threat to the party chairman himself. There was little likelihood that Honecker, reserved to the point of secretiveness and as isolated personally as his master, would become a serious rival to Ulbricht in the foreseeable future.

Soon after his return, Honecker was drawn into the turmoil. To be given such an important assignment so soon must have strengthened his self-confidence enormously. At the same time he must have recognized the risk he was taking when he decided to stand by Ulbricht in attacking his opponents. In 1956 it could not be predicted with any certainty that Ulbricht would emerge victorious, as he had in 1953. If he had not been backed by Moscow, he would certainly have been defeated, which would have been the end of Honecker's career. But Honecker had no alternative. There was no place for him in the opposition, because Schirdewan had already rejected him when he was still president of the FDJ and Schirdewan himself was in charge of party organizations and Western affairs (between 1953 and 1954). Even in those days Honecker had often made disparaging comments, sometimes in my presence, about the "debating society" in Schirdewan's division. Schirdewan had also been responsible (in 1953) for reestablishing the Central Committee's youth secretariat under Horst Schumann for the purpose of keeping a closer check on the FDJ and on Honecker himself. A few years previously Honecker had managed—with considerable difficulty—to have this secretariat abolished. The ostensible reason for Schirdewan's action was that the party must exert a stronger influence on the FDJ and youth policy must again become the responsibility of the party as a whole.

The risk to Honecker was diminished when Khrushchev's opponents in the Soviet Union, apparently strengthened by Molotov's promotion to Minister of State Control in November, 1956,[19] began to blame Khrushchev's de-Stalinization policy for the outbreak of the Hungarian revolt. Ulbricht was able to isolate his opponents, and here Honecker gave him active assistance.

The thirtieth session of the Central Committee (at which, as we have already noted, Honecker called for "the maintenance of party unity") was where it began. For the new security chief, the period between February, 1957, and the thirty-fifth session of the Central Committee in February,1958, when Honecker was able to announce the victory of the Ulbricht forces over the Schirdewan group, was one of bitter conflict and fluctuating warfare. After his time at the party training college, this was an important year in Honecker's career. If it had not been for his tactical skill and the firmness of his principles as Ulbricht's ally, he would certainly not be secretary-general of the SED Central Committee today.

At the thirtieth session, Ulbricht—and Honecker along with him—had won his victory over the Schirdewan faction but by no means put it out of action. The Ulbricht-Honecker group did, it is true, get Alfred Neumann appointed to the Central Committee secretariat, thus making him a member of the central party apparatus. But while Neumann was a loyal, uncritical supporter of Ulbricht, he was still very much under the influence of Schirdewan. Moreover, the opposition was much stronger than it had been in June, 1953. Besides Schirdewan, Wollweber, Ziller, Oelssner, and Selbmann, it included many decision-makers in almost every branch of the governmental apparatus, who more or less consistently demanded some modernization or liberalization of the system, at least in certain departments. The only ones who need to be mentioned here are the Central Committee secretaries Paul Wandel and Kurt Hager; the economists Friedrich Behrens and Arne Benary; Kurt Vieweg, director of the Institute of Agrarian Economics in the Academy of Agricultural Sciences; and (with some reservations) the Minister of Culture, Johannes R. Becher.[20]

The opposition was not confined to the Central Committee apparatus but had penetrated the county and district leaderships, including those of Dresden, Halle, Gera, Suhl, Schwerin, Potsdam, and East Berlin.[21] The executive levels of the mass organizations were not free from anti-Ulbricht influences either.[22] At the thirty-fifth plenary session of the Central Committee, Honecker gave an indication of the extent of the opposition's activity when he said that Karl Schirdewan "tried to deny the existence of subversive groups, although their plans were already being put forward, both openly and camouflaged, in many newspapers and magazines such as *Sonntag* and *Wochenpost*."[23]

Honecker's qualifications as a functionary in the apparatus came to light during this phase in his career. Having been taken away from his FDJ work and sent back to school, having been retired with what amounted to a negative appraisal of his achievements, he could count on little sympathy in the SED secretariat and the Politburo, except from Ulbricht, Neumann, and Pieck. His return to the party leadership in a completely new capacity left him no time to look for allies and build up his own empire, as he had done in the FDJ. The only support he could rely on was Ulbricht's. As the functionary in charge of security, he had to work closely with a minister—Wollweber—who was to be counted among his opponents. At the thirty-fifth session Honecker said:

His [Wollweber's] false appraisal of the situation and his erroneous ideas prevented the state security agencies from performing their duties as they should have been performed. The struggle against subversive elements was criminally neglected by Comrade Wollweber. Investigations showed that he had failed in his duties. Instead he tried to recruit other comrades for the divisive work of the Schirdewan group. This divisive activity was conducted with a lot of talk. Oppositional agencies were able to acquire information about internal party matters and use it against the party.

Regardless of the justification for these charges, Honecker's words suggest the difficulties he faced in the first phase of his new assignment. Because of the structure of the apparatus, responsible functionaries in the Politburo and Central Committee secretariat must rely heavily on the performance of ministers who, although technically their subordinates, control the apparatus and can therefore decide whether a party functionary is to succeed or fail. Because of the structure of the SED, the functionary in charge of security depends, for better or worse, on the proper functioning of the minister of state security, the minister of defense, and the official responsible for party organizations and cadre affairs. When Honecker took over security, two of these vital positions were occupied by opponents who wanted to get rid of Walter Ulbricht and his young cohort.

Isolated as they were, Ulbricht and Honecker ensured the neutrality of the working class by a series of social measures, of which only the forty-five hour week and the establishment of worker committees need be mentioned here. Between 1957 and 1958 the SED leadership did in fact succeed in neutralizing much of the population. In 1958 the number of refugees leaving the DDR was lower than it had been since 1950. The country had achieved a certain measure of stability.[24]

Ulbricht had realized that he could overcome the opposition only if all remained quiet in the DDR and if labor did not become involved in the conflict. In June, 1953, he had been saved by the workers' revolt. This time he won out because the unrest in Poland and Hungary had not spread to the DDR, and the Russians, as well as certain party leaders, were afraid that to replace the head of the SED might precipitate such an escalation. Khrushchev is said to have told Schirdewan that there must be no new disturbances in the DDR. "The change of leadership must go smoothly. You must give me your word on that."[25]

The Schirdewan group was defeated because it misjudged this balance of power and paid too little attention to the party hierarchy's fear of the much stronger West and to its uncertainty concerning its own population. At the thirty-fifth plenary session of the Central Committee, Honecker made the following charges against Schirdewan:

1. An incorrect evaluation of the situation; an underestimation of the NATO policy and of the German militarists' extensive attempts to undermine the German Democratic Republic.

2. There was talk of democratization but not of the necessity for taking security measures against the opposition's subversive activities.[26]

Honecker had already conceived the idea that the division of Germany must be a prerequisite for any policy of détente. Now that he is First Secretary of the SED Central Committee, this idea is a fundamental principle of his policy. Schirdewan, he said, "did not realize that a lessening of the tension in Germany can never be achieved unless the German Democratic Republic is secured and strengthened on all sides."[27]

On the same occasion Honecker clearly enunciated the remedy he is still recommending against the threat of Social Democratism:

We have not allowed counterrevolution to organize beneath the cloak of the fight against dogmatism. Without neglecting the fight against dogmatism, we opened a major attack on the foremost danger: revisionism. We did not allow ourselves to be forced into any discussion of mistakes. Comrade Schirdewan's erroneous evaluation of the situation would have led the party and the working class into the greatest difficulties. . . . Actually the only important question—then and now—is whether we look at and solve problems from the class standpoint or just act as if we knew all the answers.[28]

At the thirty-fifth session Honecker won a great victory. His loyal service to Ulbricht was rewarded. In addition to security, he was given charge of the division Schirdewan had headed: the division of leading party organizations and SED cadre policy. This made him the most powerful man in the SED leadership after Ulbricht. Never before had Ulbricht demonstrated his confidence in another functionary by delegating so much authority to him. From the first he had been careful not to allow any Politburo member but himself to control the party organizations, the cadres, and the armed services simultaneously. From the thirty-fifth session on, it was certain that Honecker would some day become Ulbricht's successor, at least in the party.

12. From the Fifth Party Congress
to the Building of the Wall

Member of the Politburo

THE FIFTH SED Congress of July, 1958, confirmed Ulbricht's now unchallenged position. The Schirdewan group was eliminated, and the SED leadership set its sights on "the completion of socialist reconstruction."[29] Ulbricht proclaimed the utopian goal of "reaching and surpassing the West German per capita consumption of food and the most important industrial consumer goods by 1961."[30]

Honecker's position, too, was strengthened at the Fifth Congress. He became a full member of the Politburo and shortly afterward secretary of the National Defense Council. In his new capacity he was one of those chiefly responsible for purging the party of supporters of the Schirdewan-Wollweber group. As a full member of the Politburo and Central Committee secretary for party organizations, cadres, and security matters, he made more public appearances, wrote position papers, headed delegations to other countries of the Eastern bloc and to the West, including one to Copenhagen in April, 1959, and appeared in public at Walter Ulbricht's side with calculated regularity. He spoke at many meetings during the campaign for the *Volkskammer* elections of November 16, 1959, including meetings of the employees of the potash works in Bad Salzungen and the Simson works in Suhl and another at the Illmenau Electro-technical College.[31]

The constant theme of all these speeches was that the party organization must pay more attention to the workers' criticisms and utilize workers' and engineers' experience more fully. Honecker's profile as functionary in charge of the leading party organizations and his ideas concerning a different life-style began to emerge more clearly from his position papers on the leadership functions of the party and the governmental apparatus. Here he always stressed the deepening of propaganda work and the improvement of agitational and press activity. At the seventh meeting of the SED county leadership in Gera in June, 1959, he said in this connection:

It also seems to me desirable to shift the emphasis of our press' agitational and propaganda efforts more than ever before toward providing answers to the concrete questions that life poses. Since space is so limited in the local papers, it seems to me essential that they should concentrate on problems of economic and cultural reconstruction. Our press should also give more coverage to workers—on the job, during coffee breaks and talks, and so on. We have still not succeeded in making this shift. Sometimes you do find two to three pages on world politics, but for that, after all, we have *Neues Deutschland* and we have the radio. It is of the greatest importance that we learn to combine these wider problems with the successful performance of our local tasks. We must link all our agitation and propaganda much more closely to life.[32]

In later years Honecker went more deeply into this subject and still continues to do so.

Honecker and the People's Army

On January 18, 1956, a few months before Honecker left for the party training college in Moscow, the paramilitary police force (KVP) was renamed the National People's Army (NVA). When Honecker returned and was made head of security in the SED Politburo, he automatically assumed control of the armed forces, that is, of the army, air force, navy, and frontier troops.

He was quickly at home in his new field of work because he had had very close contacts with the KVP during his FDJ days, when he had served on the various committees responsible for recruiting, armaments, and political direction of the armed forces. The central problem—relations between the army and the party—

had long been familiar to him. While he was president of the FDJ, he had observed from various minor events that the KVP was developing an independent life of its own. At that time he had often criticized the arrogance many officers displayed toward the civilian political authorities in the party and the FDJ. The fight over the Service for Germany had offered him an excellent opportunity to study the KVP bureaucratic apparatus. He had given many warnings that the army—for even then it was referred to by this name in private—would tend to become a state within a state if the party and the youth organization did not exercise their authority. For this reason he strongly insisted on establishing FDJ groups in every KVP unit and encouraged the youth officers of the central political administration to stimulate these groups to criticize the way their army units were run.

Honecker was able to utilize this experience in his new position. Despite his close involvement in the conflict with the Schirdewan group, he very soon began to look into the role of the party within the NVA. He discovered that the army was left very much to itself and that the party did not exercise sufficient control or leadership. One reason for this was that the armed forces were directly under Walter Ulbricht and the security division of the Central Committee had no authority over the leadership of the NVA. When Honecker became head of security, the director of the Central Committee's security division was the "Old Communist" Gustav Röbelen, who had served in the Spanish civil war as an officer in the International Brigade. Because of his anti-bureaucratic attitude, Röbelen could not work very effectively with Ulbricht or with the expanding apparatus of the armed forces. Honecker therefore replaced him with Walter Borning.

Honecker had little liking for the deputy minister of national defense, Lieutenant-General Heinz Hoffmann. His reservations dated back to FDJ days. Honecker assumed that Hoffmann had denounced him to the Politburo in the Service for Germany affair in order to foist off his own responsibility for this scandal on to the FDJ. During this controversy Honecker had accused Hoffmann of a tendency to place himself above the party. The central problem that confronted Honecker in the NVA was in fact to reconcile the necessity of upholding military discipline by giving the officer corps unrestricted authority with the party's demand that its leading role extend to the armed forces. Honecker's stocktaking also showed that relations between officers, noncommissioned officers, and enlisted men fell far short of the party's expectations. At the SED delegates' conferences that Honecker called in all NVA units in preparation for the Fifth Congress, he said:

There are still officer-comrades who fail to see their enlisted men as class comrades and co-fighters for the cause of socialism and peace on an equal footing with themselves, who pay no attention to their personal needs and troubles and treat them condescendingly even off duty. With the help of our party organizations, we must all quickly rectify this unhealthy state of affairs, which is incompatible with the character of our armed services.

At the delegates' conferences a number of comrades made the valid criticism that top officers . . . do not always respond to suggestions from the youth groups for improving military training and political work and suppress unfavorable comments on the way they perform their duties. Some officer-comrades were criticized for assuming that while the men can learn from them, they cannot learn anything from the men. During the discussions several comrades openly posed the question of these officer-comrades' relation to the party.[33]

These conditions in the army, especially its negative attitude toward the party's leading role, led Honecker to determine in late 1957 "to strengthen the role of the party organizations within the armed forces through a general improvement of party work."[34] He therefore submitted an extremely critical analysis to the Politburo, as a result of which the party leadership passed a resolution on January 14, 1958, "on the party's role in the National People's Army." Among other things it required officers regularly to include the secretaries of the party organizations affiliated with battalions, regiments, and independent units in their staff talks and to consult them before taking important decisions. "Every officer must recognize that he is first and foremost a political functionary in the service of the party of the working class."[35]

This resolution gave the party organizations the right "critically to evaluate, at party meetings, the results of education and training, the level of morale, and the performance of all officers, and to make suggestions for improving their work."[36] While these drastic measures were not intended to affect the unquestioning execution of orders, "the results of orders should be critically assessed once they have been executed." Theoretically at least,

Honecker had found a compromise which safeguarded the role of the party within the armed forces without jeopardizing the system of command or military discipline.

In his speech introducing the discussion at the SED's Fifth Congress, Honecker gave a very open and critical account of what he had found in the National People's Army: "In the past some officer-comrades in the armed forces had a tendency to underestimate the opinion of the party as a whole. Some officer-comrades believed that to strengthen the party's leading role would weaken individual performance and discipline in the armed forces."[37] This criticism was obviously directed partly against the army leaders, including the commander in chief of the army, Lieutenant-General Hoffmann. But Honecker came to terms with him too, and Hoffmann finally realized that Honecker's position was unshakable. During the next few years Honecker continued to expand the security division, taking care never to let the principle of the party's dominant role be questioned.

Master-Builder of the "Anti-Fascist Protective Wall"

Erich Honecker's role in the building of the Berlin Wall cannot be ascertained from primary sources. A study of all the available documents, materials, and research suggests that Walter Ulbricht conceived the idea and obtained Khrushchev's agreement to it. The decision was a joint one.[38]

But it was Erich Honecker who actually built the Wall. It was he who took charge of all the organizational and military preliminaries, supervised security while it was being built, and planned and directed the political and propaganda campaigns connected with it. The coordination of the vast military, organizational, and political plans that culminated in the utterly unexpected erection of the first barricades was entirely in his hands. During the preliminary period he had at his disposal a staff of selected functionaries from diverse fields, including, as we now know, several Russian advisers.

The plans were not developed hurriedly just prior to August 13, as SED propaganda now claims, but had been completed several months previously. In reply to a question by the correspondent of the *Frankfurter Rundschau* at a press conference on June 15, 1961, Ulbricht said: "I take your question to mean that there are people in West Germany who want us to mobilize the builders in the capital of the DDR to erect a wall. . . . I am not aware of any such intention."[39] This was an unintentional admission that the idea of erecting a barrier in the form of a wall had long been maturing within the SED leadership. Plans to build it must certainly have been completed by this time, because the correspondent's question had been whether Ulbricht had decided to make the Brandenburg Gate the city limit and "to accept the full consequences of this."[40]

In 1952 and 1953, when the number of refugees jumped sharply in comparison with previous years, certain groups within the leadership were already discussing how this stream of emigrants might be stopped. The experience gained during the World Youth Festival of 1951, when young people crossed over to West Berlin, was evaluated. It was found that all checks of subway and metropolitan trains by police and FDJ auxiliaries at sector crossing points were ineffective. Later, plans were discussed to issue special permits and keep a closer watch on the main traffic routes from the DDR to Berlin. Some of these measures were even tried out but none of them was effective. Erich Honecker was convinced even then that the only thing that would work was to seal off the frontier completely. He compared the situation in Berlin with that of the Paris Commune in 1871 and took the view that the defeat of the Commune was partly due to the failure of the Communards to barricade themselves from their enemies in a material sense, too.

To have planned an operation of this magnitude successfully down to the last detail and to have carried it out under the watchful eyes of the general public in the West and of all the news services in West Berlin was a triumph of organization, even though experienced Russian functionaries did contribute to it. Ten years after the building of the Wall, General Hoffmann could say with justifiable pride: "Even the uninitiated will have some conception of the amount of preliminary work, coordination, political maturity, and military expertise required to carry out this security measure swiftly and decisively, taking the enemy completely by surprise."[41]

In spite of his Russian backing, the surprise move of August 13 involved considerable uncalculated risk for Honecker. Moving the frontier troops and workers' task forces up to the sector frontier was hazardous enough in itself. They had of course taken part in maneuvers and exercises, but they had never been put to the test in an operation of this kind. There was no knowing how they would conduct themselves if it came to a clash with Allied troops or the West Berlin police. Honecker was well aware of the physical and psychological strain the troops would be under; this is why he attached so much importance to political and ideological work and to the efficient servicing of the operation. The dispatch of numerous *Agitprop* units, the provision of cultural entertainment, even arrangements for the presentation of bouquets and gifts by Pioneers and FDJ girls, were all part of a great plan to maintain the troops' morale, and this plan was probably originated by Erich Honecker. Five months before August 13 he had said in an address to the "fighters and officers" of the "Youth" task force at the national BKW plant:

The 1961 school year confronts us with new, higher tasks. First of all we must achieve a new quality of political education in military training, decisively improve the quality of the training every fighter receives, and increase the military effectiveness of all units still further by means of rigid discipline.

Knowing full well that it would not be long before these task forces would be put to the test, he added: "To fight and win requires a high standard of individual training in our fighters, and precise, combat-type action by our platoons and companies in all circumstances, day and night."[42]

After the successful conclusion of this operation, Honecker made a tour of frontier towns as part of the preparations for the municipal elections of September 17, 1961. He took part in election rallies, visited units of the frontier police, shook hands, chatted with men and women workers, and inquired about morale among the border troops. "Your duties are hard," said Comrade Honecker to an assembled company, "but they are very important. When we were carrying out our measures to safeguard peace in Berlin, the party and government placed great trust in you. You have proved yourselves worthy of that trust."[43]

To the workers of the Kaltwalz plant in Bad Salzungen he said: "Things have been a lot better since August 13, when we taught the militarists a pedagogical lesson." And a year later, on the anniversary of the "antifascist defensive wall," he wrote in the army journal *Volksarmee:* "If further, more visible proof were needed of the rightness and necessity of the military policy of our party and government, the measures of August 13 have provided it."[44]

The building of the Wall, carried out with a precision worthy of a general staff, strengthened Honecker's position even further. His support of Ulbricht against the Schirdewan group had made him invulnerable in the SED. His part in the building of the "antifascist defensive wall" heightened his prestige in the eyes of the Soviet leadership.

13. The Party Organizer

Economic Tasks in the Foreground

IMMEDIATELY AFTER THE BUILDING of the Wall, the fight against all "enemies of the state" was intensified in the DDR. Dissident high school and college students, "slackers," opponents of the Wall, and others were physically threatened and sometimes even beaten up.[45]

On September 20, 1961, the *Volkskammer* passed the "law for the defense of the DDR" giving the Council of State extraordinary plenary powers in an emergency.[46] This terrorism, however, did not last long, because the Twenty-second Congress of the Russian Communist Party initiated a new phase of de-Stalinization. This confronted the SED leadership with a difficult situation. On the one hand, it wanted to eliminate all its opponents now that the Wall prevented their escape; on the other hand, it had to go along —at least formally—with the official repudiation of Stalin and his personality cult. The leaders tried to mitigate the consequences of the Twenty-second Congress for the SED by stressing that they had always observed "the Leninist norms of party life."

Nevertheless, strong criticism was voiced in the SED, and some of it was directed against Ulbricht. Again Honecker stood firm beside the head of the party. At the fourteenth session of the Central Committee (November 23–26, 1961), when Ulbricht reported on the results of the Twenty-second Congress of the CPSU, Honecker made an impassioned speech in his defense. He sharply attacked "all the nonsense about the alleged Ulbricht cult" (to which, like every Marxist-Leninist, he was firmly opposed) but issued the warning: "In future anyone who dares to smear our leader, who has proved himself in the revolutionary struggle, will get his knuckles rapped, just as he has in the past."

The climax of Honecker's speech was a quotation from a letter from "a comrade who has proved himself in many battles":

Anyone fortunate enough to get to know Comrades Wilhelm Pieck and Walter Ulbricht personally, as I do, realizes how fortunate it is for our party and our state, how fortunate it is for the German nation and the German labor movement, that, in the present crucial struggle in Germany, an outstanding Leninist stands at the head of the Central Committee and the government.[47]

As Ulbricht himself had done in 1953 and 1956, Honecker tried to denounce the SED leader's opponents as dogmatists and enemies of the party. "History long ago gave its verdict on antiparty groups like those of Herrnstadt and Zaisser or Schirdewan, Wollweber, and Ziller."[48] (Ziller had committed suicide in December, 1957.)

But Honecker did not stop with a defense of Walter Ulbricht. As the functionary responsible for party organizations and cadre policy, it was his task cautiously to adapt SED leadership methods to the new situation created by the Twenty-second Congress. Here his period of study in the Soviet Union, which had been influenced by the Twentieth Congress, was very helpful. He realized that at this point it was of vital importance to avoid ideological conflict and instead to orient the party toward the solution of economic problems and to strengthen its unity. For this reason he followed his defense of Ulbricht at the fourteenth session of the Central Committee by some criticism of the activities of "our comrades in the organizations and institutions" who had so far failed "to concentrate solely on the solution of economic tasks, on the realistic direction of the national economy." Top party agencies, he said, were still not paying enough attention to the role of the basic organizations "as the chief cell of the party." (Here Honecker was deliberately using a term from the vocabulary of the 1920s, when Ulbricht—or "Comrade Cell"—had been responsible for building up the party cells.) The top party directorates still relied far too little on the basic organizations.[49]

Honecker came aggressively to Ulbricht's defense in public,

too, because even outside the SED, discussion of the resolutions of the Twenty-second Congress were continually causing controversy about the Ulbricht personality cult. At a mass meeting in Suhl he spoke the words that have so often been quoted: "Ulbricht will win—never Strauss. Ulbricht—that means all of us!"[50]

As far as Honecker was concerned, the liberalization that resulted from the Twenty-second Congress stopped with his efforts to increase the efficiency of the SED agencies. He took no definite stand on the ideological questions. At the sixteenth conference of the Central Committee, eight months after its fourteenth plenary session, he again emphasized the necessity of introducing a new working style for the party.

He condemned what he called "administration," the bureaucratic way of working, and contrasted it with persuasive methods. In both professional and ideological matters, the comrades should rely on the force of example. The party must devote particular attention to the new cadre generation, which "takes a very critical though optimistic attitude to the questions under discussion." The new quality of political work with the masses demanded a higher level of leadership. It was the duty of the leading party and government organizations "not to evade the complex, difficult problems posed by the further strengthening of our political and economic power but to tackle them courageously and, with the combined help of the party and all workers, to solve them." He called for more consultation with nonparty scientists and with the directors and staff of research institutions, and cited examples of SED district and county delegates' conferences where nonparty scientists and technologists had helped to deal with problems.[51]

Honecker spoke often on this theme right up to the Sixth SED Congress. During this period he seemed to be concentrating on fighting "tendencies to authoritarianism, paternalism, and sectarian isolation from the masses"[52] as his contribution toward bringing the SED into line with Khrushchev's de-Stalinization policy. He studiously avoided taking any stand on the changed social situation, especially in the field of cultural politics.

The Sixth Congress

The Sixth Congress (January 15–21, 1963) focused on economic reform. Ulbricht gave a preview of the principles of the New Economic System, which the presidium of the Council of Ministers adopted in June as the "New Economic System of Planning and Management." Its purpose was to increase "people's material incentive," rigorously to enforce the principle of economic accounting, and to make the "people-owned industries" (*Volkseigener Betriebe* or VEBs) more self-responsible.

In his report on the party statute, Honecker dealt with the party's role in the production process. He outlined the "production principle," by which the SED's organizational structure was keyed to production requirements and which would in future regulate the work of the party units. "The development of productivity requires that the leading party organizations concentrate their effort on the solution of economic problems. For this reason the statute states that the party will organize its leadership activities essentially in accordance with the production principle."

Honecker took no position on the second major question that came up at the Sixth Congress: the repudiation of the Chinese Communists. He confined himself to explaining the new party statute and left ideological questions aside. The main body of his speech dealt almost exclusively with the SED's new leadership methods. His chief points were these:

1. The leading party organizations must radically improve their work "with people"; perfect their system of drawing up, supervising, and implementing resolutions; eliminate "old, outdated bureaucratic working methods"; and concentrate on solving the major problems.

2. According to the new statute, the members of the party must "take the lead in planning the most advanced production techniques" and show "respect and consideration" for their co-workers.

3. The battle "on the Western front of the European socialist world system makes it essential to devote special attention to ideological work."

4. No one should believe "that socialist consciousness can be promoted by authoritarianism, paternalism, and the callous treatment of others. On the contrary, it is necessary to eliminate inflexible routine, impersonal, bureaucratic administration, dogmatism, and the habit of talking over people's heads." What is needed is "intelligent, patient work to convince others" and responsiveness to "suggestions from the people."

5. The evolutionary law of criticism and self-criticism must be applied more rigorously and "the suppression of criticism in any form must be vigorously opposed."

Honecker went into the criticism and self-criticism complex very thoroughly, giving many examples of suppressed criticism and censuring functionaries by name. He made another attack on the cult of personality, but did not omit the accompanying tribute to Ulbricht: "The cult of personality and the authority of the leader of the revolutionary working-class movement have nothing—nothing whatsoever—in common."[53]

Signs of Liberalization

After the Sixth Congress the SED permitted a certain liberalization in the field of social politics, paralleling the adoption of the New Economic System in the economic sphere. In the mass media —television, films, and radio—and in cultural life as a whole, there was a feeling of relative freedom. Movies such as *Der Geteilte Himmel* (Divided Heaven) based on Christa Wolf's novel, attracted international attention. Many books by Western authors, including Peter Weiss, Max Frisch, Ingeborg Bachmann, and Carl Zuckmayer, were published in authorized editions. The SED seemed particularly interested in revising its youth policy. The young generation's critical attitude toward the regime was treated with unusual frankness. Passive resistance to regimented recreational activity, Western cultural influences, complaints about the treatment of young people in factories and at school were subjects of open discussion. In September, 1963, the SED published a communiqué on youth questions (of which Ulbricht is believed to have been the originator), giving the young generation greater independence and responsibility. In crowded halls in East Berlin, Potsdam, and Magdeburg, young poets read from their critical works, among them Wolf Biermann, whose poems also appeared from time to time in the FDJ's official magazine *Junge Welt*.[54]

The initiation of reform in agriculture, justice, and especially industry clearly reflected the efforts the SED leadership was making to modernize its mode of government and evoke a more positive reaction from the people. This trend was closely associated with the name of Walter Ulbricht. During the Sixth Congress Ulbricht is also believed to have nominated Erich Apel, one of the originators of the New Economic System, as a candidate for the Politburo.

Honecker, by contrast, was obviously maintaining a certain reserve at this time. At the fourth session of the Central Committee, which dealt principally with relations between the party and the people and with economic questions, he made the concluding address—a privilege usually reserved for Ulbricht. Apart from calling for closer relations between the party and all citizens, he did not discuss the social-political changes that were evident all over the DDR. Instead he again stressed improvement in the leadership activities of the party organizations, especially in industry, and called for a more scientific spirit in party work. He devoted much more time than usual to problems of science and technology, vocational training, fulfillment of quotas, and realistic cost accounting. Obviously Honecker wanted the new direction the SED had taken with the New Economic System to be confined essentially to the industrial sphere.[55]

By early 1964 the SED was already tightening up again. At the fifth session of the Central Committee (February 3–7, 1964) Professor Robert Havemann was sharply attacked by Horst Sindermann, reporting for the Politburo, on the grounds that his philosophy lectures at Humboldt University in East Berlin had "gone beyond productive discussion to the point of radical divergence from the party line and Marxist-Leninist theory." Sindermann assumed a connection between Havemann's views and revisionist tendencies "forcing themselves upon us from Prague." He also accused the Austrian Communist Ernst Fischer of wanting to "efface and eliminate the fundamental opposition between bourgeois and socialist society."

Honecker, who gave a report on preparations for the 1964 party elections, again confined himself mainly to problems in the party's educational work and the introduction of the new working style, especially in factory groups. He refrained from taking any stand on ideological problems of revisionism or on the Chinese Communist Party's attacks on the CPSU, which Sindermann had also denounced in his Politburo report. On the other hand, he sharply criticized the arrogance and complacency of many functionaries in industry: "The party organizations have not yet learned how to make a critical evaluation and tackle existing deficiencies and weaknesses in a manner befitting the party."

The SED was still struggling to reestablish its authority over subordinate party units, which had been diminished since the

Twenty-second Congress. For this reason Honecker criticized the prevalent practice of "improving" the Central Committee's resolutions. Again he stressed the necessity for "working with people" and criticized the activities of local directorates "which still spend too much time writing things down on paper."[56] In this transitional period Honecker concentrated entirely on the radical reorganization of the SED, consistently trying to adapt the party organizations, with their traditional methods of work and leadership, to the new context of a complex technology.

Honecker is still pursuing his goal of a new style of leadership, greater contact between the party and the people, and collaboration with nonparty specialists. His success, however, seems to have been slight. More than ten years ago he frequently criticized the same shortcomings to the FDJ Central Council but never achieved any radical changes. While he is clearly aware of the deficiencies and difficulties in leadership work, he does not or will not recognize the causes implicit in the system, because the only possible solution would then be a radical structural reorganization of the system, including the demolition of the central bureaucratic apparatuses, the reduction of centralized planning, and ultimately a limitation of the party's dominant role. This kind of solution, however, is beyond Honecker's imagination; it conflicts with his training, his ideology, and probably also his ambition. Even the modern techniques for ascertaining public opinion, which he has regularly used since 1964 to determine the effectiveness of party work, cannot change this situation.[57] One of the contradictions in Honecker's personality is that he is by nature an antibureaucrat trying to fight bureaucracy with antibureaucratic methods.

Honecker Slows Down the Liberalization Trend

At the seventh session of the Central Committee (December 2–5, 1964)—the first since the fall of Khrushchev in October, 1964—ideological work since the Sixth SED Congress was critically analyzed. This led to what is believed to have been the first overt difference of opinion between Walter Ulbricht and Erich Honecker before the Central Committee forum. Ulbricht criticized the application of the "production principle," which Honecker had described at the Sixth Congress as the guiding leadership principle and had been stressing ever since. But at the seventh session of the Central Committee Ulbricht complained that the production principle had resulted in departmentalization and a one-sided orientation toward economic questions. Although the production principle had been widely adopted in the Soviet Union, he condemned the view that the party was "an economic party in the narrow sense" and said that it was necessary "to use the right combination of the regional and the production principles."[58]

Honecker, however, championed the production principle:

> By introducing the production principle we have preserved unified leadership and unified expansion of the party organizations. It may be objected that we have failed to do so in one field or another, but the district conferences have clearly shown that to conduct party work according to the regional and production principles works out in practice and is proving increasingly effective on the county and district levels.[59]

Khrushchev's fall also produced varying reactions at this session of the Central Committee. Honecker spoke of the probable reasons for it, mentioning Khrushchev's "tendency toward permanent reorganization." Ulbricht, however, treated the power shake-up as an internal Soviet affair. He even underlined the significance of the June, 1964, agreement with Khrushchev on "friendship, mutual aid, and cooperation" and refused to repudiate any of the party reforms the SED had adopted from Khrushchev, which had been extensively revised by his successors.

But the most conspicuous divergence of views between Ulbricht and Honecker concerned policy for Germany. In connection with Willy Brandt's candidacy for the chancellorship, Ulbricht urged that they investigate what effects West Germany's possible orientation on the Swedish model might have on the prospects for closer understanding between the two Germanys. "I think this might in fact produce some interesting starting points, which would be worth serious consideration and discussion."

Honecker, for his part, complained about the inadequate political and ideological work of the party, governmental, and economic organizations and warned that it was not being conducted "on a scale commensurate with the demands of our struggle." It must never be forgotten that:

> Our struggle for the extensive development of socialism and the solution of the national question in Germany is being waged under

the complicated conditions produced by the existence of two Germanys and by West Berlin as a specific political entity. We should also never forget for a minute that in the interests of securing peace and safeguarding the extensive development of socialism we are often compelled to use complicated measures.

Honecker backed up these warnings by citing the results of a poll showing that the people were confused about "the character of the two Germanys and the relationship between them."[60]

The Eleventh Session of the Central Committee (December 15–18, 1965)

In many respects 1965 was a year of fierce ideological controversy, which can only be outlined here. In late autumn (September 17–28, 1965) a party delegation led by Ulbricht and including Honecker went to the USSR for important conferences. These talks, which included the details of a long-term trade agreement, seem to have introduced a significant new phase in the SED policy. Conspicuous items on the agenda were problems in the New Economic System arising out of the DDR's stronger economic tie to the Soviet Union, agreement on a common front against the People's Republic of China, and the parade route for the Twenty-third Congress of the CPSU. The Soviet government openly criticized the efforts of East Berlin economic experts to orient themselves toward Western technology rather than Russian experience. At the eleventh session Honecker therefore recalled that during his visit to the DDR from November 27–29, 1965, Party Chairman Brezhnev had emphasized that "industry in the Soviet Union did not work badly."[61]

During 1965 the SED also speeded up the deliberalization in the cultural sphere that had provoked famous writers and poets such as Stefan Heym, Werner Bräunig, Christa Wolf, and Wolf Biermann to open criticism. Stefan Heym attacked the SED's monopoly of truth and called for general disregard of its taboos. Christa Wolf protested against increased paternalism on the part of the party. But the SED had learned from the events in Hungary to nip resistance in the bud and answered the writers' challenges with a strong reprimand.[62]

The more liberal youth policy introduced in 1963 had not produced the results the SED had expected. A basic article in the party's theoretical journal *Einheit* expressed dissatisfaction with young people's lack of engagement in social politics:

So far as education in socially responsible thought, feelings, and actions is concerned, we have inalienable goals, which are materially solid, tested in political conflict and grounded in ideological positions. We will not let them become vague. We will tolerate no diminution of substance or meaning, but this does not mean that we reject new developments.[63]

The New Economic System was not working as the SED would have liked either. Making the associations of nationalized enterprises (VEBs) more self-responsible had led to selfish departmentalism, lack of planning, and the overtaxing of executives who had been accustomed to receiving orders from higher up. The long-term trade agreement between the USSR and the DDR defeated the technocrats' attempts to look to the West rather than to the Soviet Union in science, research, and technology. A symptom of this was the suicide of Dr. Erich Apel, generally regarded as one of the originators of the New Economic System, on December 3, 1965, the day the long-term trade pact was signed.

Such is the background—sketched in its barest outlines— against which Honecker's speech at the eleventh session must be read. He began with a demonstrative declaration of faith in the Soviet Union. His report centered on ideological and cultural-political problems.[64] He emphasized that no one was in a position "to destroy the firm alliance between our parties and our peoples" and went on to criticize those scientists, technologists, and government leaders who had not yet overcome their "tendency" to adopt Western standards in all matters concerning the new technology, without trying to find out how things stood in the Soviet Union. He called for stronger cooperation between factories in the DDR and the USSR, and characterized the 1966–70 pact between Moscow and East Berlin as "unprecedented in history."

All in all, Honecker's speech was marked by an overemphasis of the Soviet Union's role such as had not been put forward by an SED leader for a long time. In an almost servile tone he thanked the new party chairman, Leonid Brezhnev, for his great economic aid. He repeatedly stressed the DDR's complete agreement with the Soviet Union on foreign policy. In discussing cooperation in the Council for Mutual Economic Aid (Comecon), and particularly with reference to the denunciation of China, he underlined their identical viewpoints.

If we compare this speech of Honecker's with earlier ones, we note that it is distinctly sharper in tone and content. There is no more mention of criticism and self-criticism, nor of the necessity for patient work to convince others, no more censure of arrogant and dictatorial party functionaries. At the eleventh plenary session all tendencies to liberalize or even democratize social politics, as a parallel to the New Economic System, were effectively nipped in the bud because they threatened the autocracy of the party.

This was particularly obvious in the portion of Honecker's speech devoted to cultural-political questions. He condemned "antihumanistic presentations," "injurious tendencies," and "propaganda for immorality" in films, television, and literature and said this led to "hooliganism and decadence." He asserted that films such as DEFA's *Das Kaninchen Bin Ich* and *Denk Bloss Nicht, Ich Heule,* plays such as *Der Bau,* and certain television productions "show injurious tendencies and viewpoints alien to socialism." He attacked Wolf Biermann particularly sharply, saying that his poetry reflected his "petty bourgeois, anarchist attitude, his arrogance, skepticism, and cynicism." In recent years, he said, a new kind of literature had developed "which consists essentially of a mixture of sex and brutality. Is it surprising, after this wave in literature, films, television, and magazines, that many young people do not know whether they are right or wrong in taking these for their models?" The DDR, he said, is a "decent country" with unshakable standards of ethics and morality, decency and good behavior.

Naturally he also discussed youth problems and criticized the FDJ. The danger of German imperialism must be more strongly brought home to young people. Two primary tasks confronted them: "the struggle against the ideology of doubt and against anarchistic tendencies." Honecker sharply attacked the prevalence among young people of "unfounded doubt in the superiority and ascendancy of the German social order as compared to the capitalist one." As he summed it up, the characteristic feature of all negative phenomena is that "objectively they pursue the same line as our enemies: contaminating our intelligentsia and youth through the dissemination of immorality and skepticism and weakening the DDR from within through so-called liberalization."

All-German Activity and the Seventh Party Congress (1966–67)

The answer (dated March 18, 1966) that the SED received from the executive committee of the West German Social Democratic Party to the letter it had addressed to the SPD congress in Dortmund on February 11, 1966, seemed to confuse the party leadership. Apparently it had not expected a reply. Now it had to reexamine its German policy.

During the conflict with Schirdewan in 1958, Honecker had said unequivocally that "the tensions in Germany can never be relaxed unless the German Democratic Republic is secured and strengthened on all sides."[65] At the eleventh session of the Central Committee in 1965 it had become clear that the SED did not regard the situation in the DDR as stable in its sense of the word. Here we may refer back to Honecker's discussion speech at the seventh session of the Central Committee on December 25, 1964, when he spoke relatively openly about the mood of the people, citing the first results of a scientific poll.[66] The people's behavior when Chancellor Brandt visited Erfurt four years later confirmed a certain continuity of mood in the DDR.

It is quite understandable that after his return from the Twenty-third Congress of the CPSU (March 29–April 8, 1966) and the twelfth plenary session of the Central Committee (April 27–28, 1966), Honecker, who was responsible for the security of the DDR at home and abroad, should have been asked by the Politburo to set forth the SED's standpoint in a keynote address to party activists in Berlin. The importance attached to his statement can be seen from the fact that the text of his report was printed in full in the three major newspapers of the DDR, the official *Neues Deutschland,* the *Berliner Zeitung,* and the *Leipziger Volkszeitung.*[67]

In brief he stated that the SED took a positive attitude toward a dialogue with the SPD. The SED's main goal was to strengthen its influence on "the peace-loving people in West Germany." At the same time he imposed conditions for these talks, still to be

begun, and demanded a change in Bonn's policy: "The alternative is clear: either the workers—the working people of the two
Germanys—reach an understanding, or the solution of the German question is impossible." He also made a veiled attack on the
SPD leadership and (with an eye to the population of the DDR)
assumed a threatening, militant tone:

The DDR stands on a firm basis, is making good progress and is
militarily secure. Any idea—any intention—of bringing back the
days of blood-letting before August 13, 1961, of turning our fortified
frontiers into unfortified ones, is built on sand. Any kind of infiltration into the German workers' and peasants' state is over forever. We
protect and defend humanity against the inhuman, blood-stained imperialist system.[68]

As we know, the SED declined the dialogue, using the law of
safe conduct as a pretext—which must have made its decision
easier. It is impossible to say whether Honecker was one of those
who had been against the exchange of speakers from the outset.
It is, however, undeniable that the day after the SPD and SED
representatives set the date for the exchange, the SED's official
paper *Neues Deutschland* published its first sharp attack on Herbert Wehner, followed during the next few days by many more
attacks on SPD leaders.[69]

14. The Great Test (1967-68)

DDR—Self-Confident Partner

FOR THE SED and for Honecker, 1967 and 1968 were testing years. The SED saw the new *Ostpolitik* of the West German "Grand Coalition" government as an attempt to isolate the DDR from its allies. Bonn's establishment of diplomatic relations with Bucharest and Belgrade was taken as an alarm signal. Events in Prague in the spring of 1968 and the fear that they might spread to the DDR forced the party to increase its vigilance. The occupation of Czechoslovakia confronted Honecker with his greatest military challenge since the erection of the "protective wall."

During this period Honecker was steadily assuming the role of all-round party leader and deputy to Walter Ulbricht. He was equally active as foreign politician, party organizer and functionary in charge of military and security matters. The Seventh SED Congress notably strengthened his position. He made the second report (after Ulbricht) on "The Party's Role during the Period of the Completion of Socialism." His speech centered on questions of party organization. More strongly than ever before he emphasized the leading role of the party, because skepticism on this subject was already becoming noticeable in neighboring Czechoslovakia. He pointed to "radical changes in the structure of the working class and the social behavior of the workers" as new elements in the evolution of society and said that here the most important and most difficult task was "to develop socialist man's personality and sense of community." For this it was important to be able to count on long-term planning of party work and above all on better-trained cadres. In this context he made the interesting observation that the party must "take a creative approach to problems," because "the unity of the world communist movement is not based on a formal organizational principle. Today no one demands that we adopt organizational principles and forms from earlier evolutionary phases of the world communist movement that were valid and necessary in different historical contexts."[70]

Honecker's modified declaration of faith in the Soviet Union reflected the DDR's growing self-confidence, which was a factor in Ulbricht's official policy at this time. "In the communist movement we recognize neither leading nor led parties. But communists all over the world know that history has awarded the role of pioneer in human progress and vanguard of the international movement to the party of Lenin, the Communist Party of the Soviet Union."[71]

After underlining the significance of the Soviet Union in the international communist and socialist movement, he emphasized the SED's position of equality, speaking of a "militant partnership with the Communist Party of the Soviet Union." We can say with satisfaction and pride that there is complete agreement between our fraternally allied parties on all political and ideological questions." Then came a pledge of allegiance to their alliance, which again recalled Comintern terminology, because he referred to the SED as a "division of the international communist movement."[72] Instead of closing with the usual stereotyped tribute to the Soviet Union, he ended with the words, "Long live our German Democratic Republic!"[73]

The fiftieth anniversary of the October Revolution in 1967 gave Honecker several more opportunities of singing the praises of the USSR and its Communist Party. But he never did so without at the same time pointing out the successes of the DDR and the SED, which he ascribed to "fraternal socialist cooperation between the German Democratic Republic and the Union of Soviet Socialist Republics."[74] During the celebration of the anniversary, he said at the Novovoronezh atomic plant: "Although until August 13, 1961, we were forced to pursue our socialist development under the conditions dictated by an open frontier, we succeeded, with the fraternal support of the Soviet Union, in making the

DDR a stable, socialist state in which the ideas of Lenin are triumphant." *Neues Deutschland* published this speech under the banner headline "Our Cooperation Represents International Relations of a New Type."[75]

Honecker and the Czech Crisis

Because of the crisis in Czechoslovakia, the year 1968 was dominated for Honecker by problems of foreign policy and ideology. In February and March he was chief SED delegate to the Budapest consultative conference of communist and labor parties. Here he suffered a severe setback. The Russian and Romanian viewpoints on the function of the Budapest meeting were irreconcilable, and compromise seemed impossible. The Romanians faced the alternative of being outvoted by the pro-Soviet bloc and thus isolated or of withdrawing from the meeting. If they were to take the latter course, they needed a plausible pretext. Honecker supplied it. True to his belief that the leading role in world communism belonged to the CPSU, but not demonstrating much tactical finesse, he sharply attacked not only the Chinese Communists but "narrow nationalism" in general and called loyalty to the Soviet Union the touchstone of true Marxist-Leninism and proletarian internationalism. When the Syrian delegate Khaled Bagdash made a direct attack on Romania for its stand on the Near East conflict, the Romanian delegation withdrew from the conference, describing the behavior of Honecker and Bagdash as a violation of the spirit of constructive fraternalism.

He attacked the reform movement in Prague even more violently. At the sixth session of the Central Committee in June, 1968, he discussed the Czech revisionists' views on the role of the party, their relationship to the Soviet Union, and their social-political attitudes, especially with regard to social democracy, freedom of opinion, and civil rights. Here he took an extremely conservative and dogmatic position. He emphasized the party's role as the guiding force in social progress and firmly opposed letting "the scientific, technological revolution weaken the party's leading role or invalidate the former necessity for centralized direction of social processes by the socialist state." Without naming the Czech leaders, he condemned all attempts to make the dictatorship of the proletariat appear outdated "on the grounds

that class antagonism no longer exists in the socialist countries."
While indirectly admitting erroneous leadership methods, he refused to hold the system responsible for them:

> The dictatorship of the proletariat has been equated with erroneous
> leadership methods, with violations of democracy and legality, and
> with other subjectively grounded errors. But this is turning
> things completely upside down. . . . We will not permit the central
> principle of our ideology to be watered down. We know very well that
> Marxists and revisionists have differed on the question of power since
> time immemorial.[76]

After the occupation of Czechoslovakia, in which the National
People's Army participated (with Honecker assuming the responsibility for this vis-à-vis the Politburo), he became even more outspoken. In his discussion speech to the ninth plenary session of
the Central Committee, he spoke of "the antisocialist development in the Czechoslovakian Soviet of Socialist Republics" and
defended the entry of Warsaw Pact troops into that country.
"Once the revisionist, counterrevolutionary trend in the USSR
reached a point where political measures no longer sufficed to
protect the country from the clutches of the imperialists, international socialist solidarity had to be maintained through military
assistance, too."[77]

In the same speech Honecker rejected the theories of "building
bridges," "change through *rapprochement*," "the seduction of
Eastern Europe," the "new *Ostpolitik*," and the "so-called convergence theory." These theories, he said, disregarded the questions
of who owns the means of production, who owns governmental
power, in whose interest the economy produces, and whose interests politics serve. The upholders of these ideologies denied the
polarity of the systems and hence not only ignored the objective
laws governing the development of society but "also betrayed
their supporters in a primitive manner."

Honecker's talent for simplistic yet highly persuasive argument
is effective, especially with citizens of the DDR, who are dominated by the party and the state from kindergarten to the university and even beyond, at all levels of the educational system. On
the other hand, this example also shows clearly that he has no
interest in analyzing Western social theories in any subtle or
meaningful way. He does not distinguish between scholars who

use the methodology of sociology, economics, and the social sciences to establish the existence of formal similarities in advanced industrial societies under both systems and political cold-war strategists improvising tactics to isolate the DDR from its allies. For him they are all alike. For him it can all be very simply reduced to terms of "who gets whom?" and "who benefits?" Hence this conclusion:

The enemy, supported by all varieties of revisionism, attacks the leading role of the party because he is aiming at the very heart of socialism's principle of leadership. In attacking the party he is attacking the bearers of the Marxist-Leninist ideology without which there can be no socialism. In attacking the party he is also attacking all progressive forces, because, recognizing the historic role of the working class, they rally to the party of the working class.

During 1968 and 1969 Honecker built up his position as party strategist, theoretician, politician, and statesman through frequent position papers and trips abroad, especially to the Soviet Union. He made regular attacks—far more numerous than Ulbricht's—on the Chinese Communists, stressing the military aspect of the Peking-Moscow conflict. He condemned "the bloody provocations to which the socialist Soviet Union is being subjected on the Soviet-Chinese frontier by the Mao Tse-tung group." This policy, he said, played directly into the hands of "imperialism." It was not by chance that the Mao Tse-tung group was carrying on its "armed provocation against the Soviet Union" at the very time when "West German imperialism in West Berlin" was organizing a serious provocation and when "the Israeli aggressors" were increasing their military provocations against the Arab states. The Mao Tse-tung group was encouraging "U.S. imperialism to continue its criminal aggression against the Vietnamese people and to persist in blocking the Paris talks."[78]

In July, 1969, Honecker visited the Soviet Union as a member of an East Berlin party and government delegation. He made a speech to a Russian naval staff in Kronstadt on German-Soviet brotherhood in arms, affirming the DDR's loyalty to its ally. We have no proof of any direct connection between his attacks on the People's Republic of China at the tenth session of the Central Committee in April, 1969, and this Kronstadt speech three months later. Reports that Honecker had full authority from the Politburo at that time to use NVA troops to support the USSR on the Asiatic front are also purely speculative. It is more likely that he stressed loyalty to the Russian alliance in the matter of China in order to remind the USSR of its own obligations to the DDR. This move proved useful in the dispute between Moscow and East Berlin over the Brandt-Scheel government's new Eastern policy of détente, which began at the end of 1969.

Erfurt and Kassel

On October 28, 1969, Chancellor Willy Brandt stated the basic principles of his government in a speech which included an expression of readiness for dialogue with the East German leadership. He acknowledged the existence of "two states within Germany," but refused to recognize the DDR under international law.

Honecker was the first member of the Politburo—not excluding Ulbricht—to comment on the Chancellor's statement; he outlined the official party standpoint. While he acknowledged that some new accents were certainly discernible in Brandt's remarks —for instance, in his words about "the existence of two German states," he immediately qualified this positive reaction:

There are still influential forces that will not relinquish the cold war or their expansionist ambitions. It was precisely the policy of the former government of the West German Federal Republic under the leadership of the CDU–CSU that caused West Germany to be generally regarded as the major troublemaker where European security is concerned."[79]

Honecker thus went on record as one of the SED leaders who took a reserved, skeptical attitude to the new policy of the West German social-liberal coalition. But the political stance of top DDR functionaries is determined largely by the extent to which their own department is affected by a particular measure and by how much detailed information is available to them. It was no accident that in 1953 and 1956 the functionaries in charge of security and party organizations (Zaisser, Wollweber, Schirdewan, etc.) belonged to the opposition. They had access to the most reliable information, and they were much more aware of the mood of the general public and the party than most other SED decision-makers. Now Honecker held this key position. But circumstances had changed since the building of the Wall, and he drew the opposite conclusion. While the information available to his predecessors had led them to advise concessions, Honecker was afraid that top-level talks between East Berlin and Bonn might give rise to new unrest and illusions and destroy the carefully cultivated image of the Federal Republic as an enemy.

Honecker and most of the SED leaders realized that normalization of relations between the two Germanys could not be achieved without some alleviation of personal hardships. There would have to be some relaxation, at least so far as travel, freedom of movement between West and East Berlin, and the mutual exchange of newspapers were concerned. The SED leadership could hardly accept such concessions, even for the sake of recognition. But it could not admit this officially, because to do so would have meant isolating itself not only from the people of the DDR but also from many of its own office-holders as well. So long as Bonn's proposals fell short of official recognition, as was the case with Brandt's statement of his government's basic principles, and it was just a matter of alleviating hardships, it was easy enough for the East Berlin leadership to decline, because it knew that the majority of the East German people shared its views on the existence of a second German state. But once the Brandt-Scheel government had recognized the existence of two German states and proposed a comprehensive exchange of views, on a nondiscriminatory basis, on the settlement of all questions outstanding between them, including "relations on an equal footing," it was no longer so easy to refuse.

Moreover, morale in the DDR had deteriorated during the winter of 1969–70. Inability to keep pace with the demand for electric power resulting in frequent power cuts, shortages of coal for household use and of food, organizational difficulties in modernizing the economy, especially in capital and consumer goods industries and in the building trade,[80] had aroused a certain amount of unrest. Not for a long time had the authority of the SED apparatus over the people been so low.

For this reason the SED leadership tried to prove that the new West German government was still pursuing the old goals and was using new methods only because the old line had not been successful. It was also speculating on the possibility that the majority of the East German people would reject the Federal Republic's demand to be the "sole representative" of Germany and continue to back the East Berlin government, even if it could not fully accept its social policy.

The guidelines were laid down at the twelfth session of the Central Committee (December 12–13, 1969). This plenary session was in effect the one at which the present policy of sealing off the DDR from the Federal Republic was first clearly articulated in connection with the new West German *Ostpolitik*. Honecker stated with unusual acerbity:

> What they really want is to get a foot in the other fellow's door. . . . One could dictate pages and pages on these gentlemen's ideas on the subject of infiltrating socialist countries according to their notorious "gray plans." . . . First they want to make themselves look open-minded and objective, then they want "contacts" below what they call the threshold of international recognition to lull our political vigilance, and on top of that they want the expertise of our specialists to help them close their own scientific gaps.[81]

Honecker was strongly supported in this attitude by Defense Minister Heinz Hoffmann, who went even further in his discussion speech at the twelfth session of the Central Committee. With unusual outspokenness Hoffmann revealed the tactical disagreements between the DDR, on the one hand, and the Soviet Union and most of the other East European governments, on the other. While Moscow and Warsaw were already preparing for early negotiations with representatives of Bonn, Hoffmann radically opposed all powers in the Eastern bloc, including the USSR, that were taking a cooperative attitude to the new Bonn government. For the first time in the history of the SED, a member of the Central Committee accused—even if only indirectly—a Russian leadership group still in power of the worst crime in the Communist vocabulary: Trotzkyism.[82]

Since Hoffmann is now a member of Honecker's team, it is worth quoting this passage from his speech. Citing the reform movement in Czechoslovakia (a veiled hint of possible internal consequences for the DDR of a revision of its attitude to the Federal Republic), he drew a parallel from the history of the Soviet Union:

> At the Nineteenth All-Russian Congress of 1921, Lenin summed up the international situation after the annihilation of the counter-revolutionaries and interventionists. He passionately opposed all at-

tempts to reduce their defensive potential on the grounds that certain foreign powers were seeking a *rapprochement* with the Soviet state. The Trotzkyites were even ready to disband the Red Army on those grounds. Lenin warned that foreign representatives were making gestures of offering help but that actually those representatives were helping to overthrow the Soviet power. "Important as it is to concentrate on the vital economic reconstruction of the country and to pursue every possibility of economic cooperation with capitalist states," said Lenin in that same speech, "be on your guard. Watch over the defensive potential of our country and the Red Army like the apple of your eye. Remember that we have no right to permit such a weakening, even for a second."[83]

After Chancellor Brandt's answer of January 22, 1970, to Chairman of the Council of Ministers Walter Ulbricht's letter of December 17, 1969, to President Heinemann, Honecker stepped up his campaign—which, however, was directed chiefly toward the East German people, with the idea of nipping incipient illusions in the bud. At an "inspiring celebration" of the twentieth birthday of the Ministry of State Security at the Friedrichstadt Palace in East Berlin, he said:[84]

In the old days the imperialists could scheme and plot behind the scenes. They could talk peace in public while actually preparing for war. Today these security agencies of ours are helping to expose the mystery of what causes wars. Their courageous efforts are making us familiar with West German revanchist plans so that the public may be alerted. Here our comrades in the state security services are making a true contribution to peace.[85]

Minister of State Security Erich Mielke, whom Honecker "put on his team" by nominating him to the Politburo when he himself became First Secretary, wrote in an article on his ministry's twentieth birthday, two weeks after Willy Brandt's letter:

Through the systematic demand for and exploitation of revisionist manifestations, through the spread of social democracy and the unscrupulous misuse of all available opportunities for contact, they are trying to create the requisite conditions for organizing a creeping counterrevolution. The enemy is intensifying the criminal activity of his secret services, agents, and other centers of hostility, always seeking new and more sophisticated means and techniques.[86]

On February 18, 1970, after thorough discussion with his cabinet and consultation with the opposition, Chancellor Brandt informed the DDR, through Minister Horst Ehmke, that he was prepared in principle to meet with Premier Willi Stoph. On February 22, two days after the letter from East Berlin suggesting that the meeting be held on March 2, Honecker arranged for the official *Neues Deutschland* to publish an extract from a speech he had delivered on February 16 at the Karl Marx party training college. This speech contained the most violent attacks Honecker had launched since the West German government announced its new Eastern policy. He accusingly told the SPD leadership that its "integration into the imperialist system" was "the mature fruit of a ten-year ripening process." The aim of the present Bonn government was to strengthen "by somewhat different methods, the hegemony of the West German ruling groups over western, southern and northern Europe" and, with the help of "bridge-building," "convergence," and "economic aid policies," to extend the thrust into the socialist countries. Obviously the bridge-building was designed, if "the general weather picture" permitted, to permit the West German army to march across the bridge when the right moment came. This was also the purpose of the West German army's "big maneuver plan."[87]

The shifting back and forth from irrelevant attacks on the West German government to *de facto* agreement to negotiate is only superficially contradictory. Actually the SED's vituperations are not directed against the Federal Republic so much as against certain circles within the DDR which the party regards as the proponents of revisionist ideas. When Honecker accuses the West German government of using phraseology "to brush aside what divides us" and of "obscuring people's vision of reality and camouflaging its real goals by means of a trick," this is to be read as a warning to elements that have been claiming since 1956 that the development of the DDR into a socialist democracy, plus a West German government led by social democrats, would create a basis for German reunification. Such ideas had been bolstered in 1968, because these elements had visions of a democratization process in the DDR like the one the Czechoslovak Communist Party had instituted under Dubček. Honecker's warnings that it was the task of social democratism at the present time to serve as the advance guard in the fight against socialism in Europe[88] were directed against ideas of this kind and against people's hopes that an understanding between the two governments might soon lead to an easing of travel and other restrictions.

Because the SED leadership considered students especially vulnerable to "social democratism," Honecker instituted opinion polls. Students were asked what they understood by "the solution of the present national problem" and what form it should take In conjunction with these problem-complexes, they were also asked to evaluate the various thought models. This was an indirect way of ascertaining their views on the convergence theory, the SPD's concept of the German problem, and the ideas of the SED. The questionnaire was thirty pages long and contained ninety-four questions, many of which dealt with the problem of the German nation. From the way they were phrased it is evident that student opinion was not only being polled but also manipulated.[89]

When Bonn's negotiations with Moscow and Warsaw reached a concrete stage and Soviet Foreign Minister Andrei Gromyko spent several days in East Berlin (February 23–27, 1970) for talks intended to eliminate disagreements with the SED leadership, Honecker kept quiet. And during the conversations between Brandt and Stoph in Erfurt and Kassel he made no public statements on basic issues. The mass welcome the citizens of Erfurt gave Brandt, which obviously could only have occurred because the local party and security organizations misjudged the situation, must have strengthened his conviction that it was essential to force a policy of radical separation.

During this phase, disagreement between Ulbricht and Honecker is said to have increased. At the thirteenth session of the Central Committee (June 9–10, 1970) and especially during "Baltic Sea Week" in Rostock a month later, Ulbricht indicated that recognition under international law was no longer a prerequisite for talks between East and West German experts. Premier Stoph is said to have been bound by a Politburo resolution when he suggested a "pause for reflection" in Kassel, saying: "The government of the DDR is prepared to continue the conversations of its premier as soon as the government of the Federal Republic gives evidence of a realistic attitude on this basic question [recognition under international law]."[90] Ulbricht, however, disregarded this resolution. In Rostock he said that the length of the pause for reflection "depends only on the time the West German government needs to sign the treaty with the Soviet Union outlawing the use of force."[91] Apparently he was trying to regain the initiative, since his allies were becoming increasingly annoyed by East Berlin's persistently defensive position.

According to unverifiable sources, Honecker is supposed to have tried to prevent the publication of Ulbricht's Rostock speech on the grounds of the Politburo resolution, but Ulbricht overrode him. Observers of the Eastern bloc say that in Moscow in mid-1970 Honecker was already pressing for Ulbricht's resignation. However, no decision was reached at that time.

The Change of Leadership

At the fifteenth session of the Central Committee Ulbricht presented his ideas (later revised at the sixteenth session) on preparations for the Eighth Party Congress. He said that "in the process of establishing the fully developed social system of socialism," the DDR had created "certain elements of the transition to communism."[92] Honecker, on the other hand, reporting on preparations for and conduct of the party elections, confined himself to problems of ideological work and leadership methods. After repeating his familiar theme that the basic organizations were the essential foundation of the SED and that the art of political leadership must be further perfected, he strongly emphasized the principle of democracy within the party. Every member had the right freely to express his opinion of the party statute at the forthcoming election meetings, to criticize members and functionaries without regard for person, and to submit suggestions for improving the party's work and leadership and increasing its closeness to the people. This would decisively help to increase "the activism and militancy of our party" and to unify and close its ranks.

While Honecker renewed his attack on the SPD leadership and called on the party for more vigorous ideological work, he ignored the problem of "the fully developed social system of socialism." It is impossible to say whether he already knew by this time that the subject Ulbricht had taken up at this session of the Central Committee would be dropped at the next one, but it is certainly striking that he should have abandoned the practice he had followed for the last few years of devoting his speech to basic subjects of this kind.

Be that as it may, events proved him right. From March 30 to April 9, 1971, he attended the Twenty-fourth Congress of the Communist Party of the Soviet Union, along with Walter Ulbricht, Willi Stoph, Hermann Axen, and Paul Verner. The final decision as to the time and method of the change of leadership must have been made in Moscow. Between April 3 and April 4 there was a change of protocol. Ulbricht remained in Moscow while the rest of the delegation went to the provinces. On April 3 the delegation's order of precedence in press reports was Stoph, Honecker, Axen, Verner; but from April 4 on it was changed to Honecker, Stoph, Verner, Axen. So the decision was presumably made about April 3.

On April 12 Honecker and Ulbricht met with the Secretary-General of the Central Committee of the CPSU, Leonid Brezhnev. In "complete unanimity between the CPSU and the SED," they set their seal on what later became a resolution of the sixteenth session of the SED Central Committee, passed on May 3, 1971. According to the communiqué of the plenary session:

> Comrade Walter Ulbricht made a statement on Point 1 of the agenda. For reasons of age he asked the Central Committee to relieve him of his functions as first secretary of the SED Central Committee so that they might be entrusted to younger hands.
> The Central Committee unanimously accepted Comrade Walter Ulbricht's statement and on a motion proposed by the Politburo resolved to accede to his request. In recognition of his meritorious service, Comrade Ulbricht was elected chairman of the SED and will continue to serve as chairman of the Council of State.
> The Central Committee unanimously elected Comrade Erich Honecker first secretary of the SED Central Committee.[93]

The first effects were seen even before the session was over. A change of speakers (Honecker for Ulbricht) was announced for the keynote address at the Eighth SED Congress, and the themes were to a great extent de-ideologized. The agenda for the Eighth SED Congress drawn up at the fifteenth session of the Central Committee provided for the following major reports:

> 1. The Fully Developed Social System of Socialism in the 1970s (basic problems of the Five-Year Plan, 1971–75). Speaker: Walter Ulbricht.

2. The Future Development of the Socialist State. Speaker: Willi Stoph.

3. The Role and Tasks of the SED in the Fully Developed Social System of Socialism. Speaker: Erich Honecker.

The Central Committee's report of activities and the report of the Central Review Commission were to be presented to the Eighth Congress in written form only.

Ulbricht's speech on "The Fully Developed Social System of Socialism," approved by the Seventh Congress in 1967, was dropped from the agenda adopted by the sixteenth plenary session of the Central Committee and replaced by the Central Committee report as the principal item. This report was to be delivered by Erich Honecker. The second speaker was to be Kurt Seibt, with the report of the Review Commission. Only after that would Willi Stoph discuss "the Directives of the Eighth SED Congress concerning the Five-Year Plan for the Development of the National Economy of the DDR in the Years 1971 to 1975." An agenda which had originally consisted of ideological position papers was thus reduced to a mere report of activities on the model of the Twenty-fourth Congress of the CPSU.

There was one more interesting point. In his report on the Twenty-fourth Congress of the CPSU, Honecker attacked the People's Republic of China, whereas Ulbricht had not mentioned this subject in his address to the Soviet Congress. There are many indications that the change of leadership was not accomplished without friction. For Honecker, at all events, it was the beginning of a new phase at the summit.

15. Leader of the Party

Why Honecker Became Ulbricht's Successor

THAT HONECKER SHOULD succeed Ulbricht as leader of the party was the logical sequel of the developments we have described. Since the Sixth SED Congress it had been clear that Ulbricht had selected him and was systematically grooming him for this position. Nevertheless we may legitimately ask why Ulbricht's choice fell on Honecker and why the Soviet Union agreed to it—because there is no doubt that, however independent the DDR may be, the Russian Communist Party had a voice in a decision of this magnitude.

When Honecker was sent to the party training college in Moscow in 1955, no decision had been made on this matter, and after his return, even as Ulbricht's protégé, he had to work hard to build up and secure his position in the party leadership. Ulbricht's gratitude for Honecker's unconditional loyalty is not enough to explain the choice, although it certainly must have played a part. Probably the decisive factor was Ulbricht's conviction that Honecker was the only Politburo functionary who offered a reasonable guarantee that his own policy would be continued. Ulbricht certainly did not make his decision overnight; it is unquestionably the result of long observation and mature reflection and of Honecker's own achievements in accordance with Ulbricht's policies. And indeed Honecker met every test that Ulbricht submitted him to: helping to overcome the Schirdewan opposition; reorganizing the armed services and linking them more closely with the party; rejuvenating and modernizing the party apparatus and the mass organizations; directing military operations during the building of the Wall and the occupation of Czechoslovakia in 1968, to name only the most important.

Above all, Erich Honecker had succeeded in gaining the confidence of the aging Walter Ulbricht and in relieving him of more and more of his load. Ulbricht wanted to maintain his strong grip on everything and merely delegate specific jobs to his younger assistants. Honecker never let him down. He never exceeded his authority, cleared everything with Ulbricht, and stayed strictly within his assigned role as the party leader's right-hand man. Recently, however, differences are said to have arisen, some of which have already been mentioned. It is difficult to determine how serious they are. After all, differences of opinion within party leaderships exist in the West, too, without necessarily causing a break, so a similar situation within the Eastern governmental system should not be dramatized. Functionaries close to Ulbricht say that he has recently shown increasing signs of the inflexibility of age—which would not be surprising in a man approaching eighty. In all political systems old politicians accustomed to power have difficulty in recognizing that their time is past. Adenauer was an example. This inevitable tendency, combined with the problems of Berlin and Germany and relations with the DDR's allies, must certainly have had a negative influence on the atmosphere within the party leadership, and that in turn must have affected the relationship between Ulbricht and Honecker. Yet it was too late for Ulbricht to reorient himself radically to his successor's views.

The crucial characteristic that predestined Honecker to be Ulbricht's heir, so far as the Russians are concerned, is his unconditional loyalty to the CPSU and the USSR, demonstrated times without number. The Russian Communist Party had long been mistrustful of Ulbricht's attempts to hold up the DDR as a model to other parties in the Eastern bloc and in Western Europe and to claim a measure of ideological leadership on the strength of its strong economic position. In Lenin's day it was accepted that Russia would have to relinquish its leading role as soon as the revolution had succeeded in a highly developed industrial country. Lenin himself wrote in 1920:

It would likewise be a mistake to ignore the fact that after the victory of the proletarian revolution, even if it is confined to one single developed country, there will probably be a sudden reversal as a result of which Russia will again become a backward country instead of an exemplary one (in the sense of socialism and the Soviet system).[94]

This idea must haunt the Soviet leaders of today. Ulbricht's attempts to appoint himself schoolmaster of the socialist camp touched an exposed nerve in Moscow. Even though the SED's assertive attitude was at first confined to economic affairs—and it began almost simultaneously with the New Economic System of 1963–64—it has recently been noticeable in the ideological and political sphere, too. A basic article in the East Berlin journal *Deutsche Aussenpolitik* of February, 1970, on problems of the DDR's international position said with regard to the East German role:

> The fully developed socialist society will be established in a European country which even under capitalist conditions ranked among the highly industrialized nations. This again is certainly an objective reason for the increasingly dynamic influence the DDR exerts over progressive forces in the capitalist countries of Western Europe.[95]

Two pages further on the writer stresses that the DDR "with its resources and potentialities, is making a growing contribution to the building of communism in the USSR" and states bluntly that the DDR has proved for the first time that the building of socialism is feasible even in highly industrialized countries.

At the reception for the participants in the international conference commemorating the 150th birthday of Friedrich Engels, held in East Berlin in mid-November, 1970, Ulbricht openly criticized what he considered insufficient cooperation in ideological matters between the various communist parties. Brezhnev immediately assumed that the criticism was directed at him. At the Hungarian Communist Party congress, which took place soon afterward, he said, without mentioning Ulbricht's name, that consultations on theoretical and other matters had made good progress.[96]

At the Twenty-fourth Congress of the CPSU Ulbricht resumed his didactic tone. He underlined the SED's special position in the alliance and stressed its specific ideological insights—which must have aroused great ill-feeling in the CPSU and other communist parties of the Eastern bloc.[97] The Russians are also said to have been offended at the way Ulbricht boasted at the Congress that he was one of the few surviving party leaders from the time of Lenin's struggle, apparently assuming that this gave him the right to play the schoolmaster.[98]

Ideological differences emerged most clearly during the preparations for the Eighth SED Congress, particularly in connection with the already mentioned changes in the agenda. They are also suggested in a leading article in *Neues Deutschland* on the sixteenth session of the Central Committee. This article clearly defines the line the party leadership was to follow after Ulbricht's retirement, without even mentioning the fifteenth session of January 28, 1971, which had voted to call the party congress:

> When we speak of our "road," we know that the next milestone is the Eighth Congress. That is where we are heading—armed with the resolutions of the fourteenth and sixteenth sessions. When we say "armed by the sixteenth session," we are referring to the depth and thoroughness with which our brotherhood in arms assimilates our Soviet comrades' experience as summed up in the resolutions of the Twenty-fourth Congress of the CPSU.
>
> The report of the delegation that was present in Moscow shows what an invaluable help and support the analyses, ideas, and long-range plans of the CPSU, and its Leninist style, have been to our party's work.[99]

The indications are quite clear. The fifteenth plenary session was deliberately ignored not only because the sixteenth adopted a new agenda for the party congress but also because the central event at the fifteenth session had been a position paper by Walter Ulbricht on "Political Preparation for the Eighth Party Congress," which dealt exhaustively with the problems of "the fully developed social system of socialism" and proposed the thesis that "in the process of establishing the fully developed social system of socialism, certain elements of the transition to communism are already being created."[100]

There was no more talk of this at either the sixteenth session of the Central Committee or the Eighth Congress. By this time the focus had clearly been switched to the leading role of the CPSU. Erich Honecker, not Walter Ulbricht, reported to the Central Committee plenum on the Twenty-fourth Congress. His report consisted entirely of a declaration of loyalty to and solidarity with the Soviet Union. He did not self-confidently bring up the subject of the DDR's special position, as Ulbricht had done at the fifteenth session, either in connection with the international situation or with the economic or social-political development of Soviet society. Honecker urged modesty. It was not the DDR but "the joint efforts of the socialist states" that had made it possible "to achieve significant progress in solving a problem so crucial to the stabilization of the European situation as the strengthening of the international position of the German Democratic Republic."

As if to console the members of the Central Committee for the loss of their country's special position, he continued:

"The DDR," added Comrade Brezhnev, paying tribute to the achievements of the workers of our socialist state under the leadership of the SED, "has already been recognized by twenty-seven states, and there is no doubt that this process will continue." How right Comrade Brezhnev was is shown by the fact that in the few weeks since the Twenty-fourth Congress, two more states, Chile and Equatorial Guinea, have established diplomatic relations with the DDR.[101]

The Timing of the Change of Leadership

The Soviet Union's pressure for a change of leadership even before the Eighth Congress was probably not due primarily to the ideological differences we have described nor to conflicts of interest in the policy for Germany. The ideological conflict finally culminated in the SED's acknowledging the major role the USSR had played as midwife of the DDR and guarantor of its security and expecting in return an acknowledgment of the exemplary function the DDR exercises today both within the Eastern bloc and for developed industrialized countries of the West. While this must have annoyed the CPSU, it can scarcely have alarmed it. And so far as policy for Germany was concerned, the idea of the complete sealing off of the DDR from the Federal Republic had been sanctioned in principle at the Twenty-fourth Congress of the CPSU.

In his report at the sixteenth session of the Central Committee Honecker said:

In decisively corroborating the basic course of socialist policy for Europe, the Twenty-fourth Congress confirmed the rightness and necessity of the process of completely sealing off the socialist German

Democratic Republic from the imperialist Federal Republic of Germany advocated by the fourteenth session of the Central Committee of our party. This is completely in line with the necessity of establishing relations of friendly coexistence between the DDR and the Federal Republic—that is, between states with different social systems.[102]

This seems to prove that the reason why the Soviet Union supports the DDR at all levels in its policy of radical separation from West Germany is that such support is what induced the DDR to make concessions on the Berlin question. Moscow's eagerness for a Berlin settlement was also the CPSU's main reason for insisting on Ulbricht's speedy retirement.

There is considerable evidence for this. At the ambassadors' talks in March and April (specifically the seventeenth meeting on March 26 and the eighteenth on April 16) the Russians are said still to have been maintaining their inflexible attitude. At the seventeenth meeting Soviet Ambassador Abrassimov submitted to the ambassadors of the Western powers a Russian position paper which, according to government spokesman Conrad Ahlers, reflected the familiar Soviet standpoint.[103] On the day of the eighteenth meeting, *Neues Deutschland* reprinted an article from the Polish newspaper *Zycie Warszawy* on April 15 quoting significant extracts from the Soviet position paper on Berlin. Ulbricht is said to have been responsible for this. Whether he was or not, the publication of the extracts was obviously intended to pin down the Soviet Union and provoke the Western opponents of the Berlin negotiations.

The effect was exactly as foreseen, because this position paper provided for the Federal Republic to relinquish all political presence in Berlin and left traffic arrangements to "competent agencies," i.e., to separate negotiations between the DDR and the West Berlin Senate.[104] One day later, in another leading article, *Neues Deutschland* welcomed this draft treaty and said that "in complete accordance with it" the DDR was prepared "to conduct negotiations with the interested parties on the question of traffic through its sovereign territory from and to West Berlin and to agree on contractual arrangements which would take into account the legitimate interests of all parties."[105]

But the nineteenth meeting of the ambassadors, on May 7, four days after the change of leadership in the SED, took a quite different course. Ambassador Abrassimov said optimistically that it had carried them a good step forward, and from then on progress was slow but sure. At the twentieth talk, on May 25, they began to discuss concrete questions. After this three-hour meeting, the French ambassador said they had reached "a concrete phase in the conversations," and Ambassador Abrassimov, who was in an excellent mood, said that "good work had been accomplished."[106] The connection between Ulbricht's resignation and progress in the ambassadorial talks seems beyond dispute.

Another indication was the conspicuous tension between Ulbricht and Abrassimov. The Soviet ambassador gave open expression to his displeasure when he sent a long and extremely friendly message of congratulation to Erich Honecker on his election as first secretary of the SED,[107] but no message of appreciation to Walter Ulbricht. The CPSU's congratulatory message to the Central Committee of the SED on the occasion of the party's twenty-fifth anniversary on April 21, 1971, also indicated differences with Ulbricht. The salutation confined itself to "Loyal Comrades!"[108] although the congratulatory message on the twentieth anniversary of the SED in 1966 had been addressed to "The First Secretary of the Central Committee, Walter Ulbricht."[109]

If any further proof is needed, the leader of the SED, who, before the ambassadors reached their agreement, had frequently voiced his ideas on a Berlin settlement, for whom West Berlin was located "in the middle of" or "on" the territory of the DDR, and who had once described West Berlin as "the Western suburbs of the capital of the DDR," remained silent on the results of the ambassadorial talks for a remarkably long time. Not until September 6 did he make a positive statement,[110] although Ambassador Abrassimov had informed him fully on August 24.[111]

The Soviet Union was prepared to pay a price for a settlement of the Berlin problem because it knew that this was the condition for further success in realizing its concept of Europe. Apparently, as the Soviet Union sees it, the Berlin Agreement is to become a model for further East-West agreements on a coexistence basis. For if agreement can be reached on such an explosive issue, the prospects of a conference on European security—the next objective in the Soviet policy for Europe—look much more optimistic. The Russians hope that this conference will bring them a big step nearer their ultimate goal of establishing a solid economic and political footing in Western Europe.

The motives seem clear. If Moscow succeeds in establishing cooperation of this kind, backed by official agreements, with Western Europe, then the United States will in the long run lose a major base of influence, while the Soviet Union will be able to link up with contemporary developments. The USSR is coming to realize that cooperation with the industrial countries of Europe is of prime importance.

The reduction of expenditure on armaments in favor of an urgently necessary improvement in the living standard of the Russian people is another major reason for removing all obstacles in the way of a détente in Europe. And finally, the political and diplomatic offensive of the People's Repubic of China is also strengthening the Soviet Union's determination to create a clearly defined situation in Europe.

If the Soviet Union is thinking in such global terms, it is understandable that it should not allow one of its allies—even a major partner of the status of the DDR—to put a crimp in its plans. Ulbricht fell victim to this global-scale thinking when the Soviet Union had to put its cards on the table over Berlin. It would have been very difficult for Moscow to make such a change of course seem credible—for instance in the matter of access for traffic—so long as the exponent of the old Berlin policy remained at the helm in the DDR.

Unlike Ulbricht, Honecker apparently understood that through the treaty with the West German government the Soviet leadership had annulled the so-called Ulbricht Doctrine (according to which West German recognition of the DDR was the condition for the normalization of Bonn's relations with the Eastern bloc) and thus regained the initiative in policy for Germany. Ilse Spittmann says in a note on the background of Ulbricht's fall:

> Communist policy for the West has to be a bloc policy under Soviet leadership. Through flexibility toward Bonn, Ulbricht tried to preserve the DDR's right to be consulted and its freedom to maneuver in the new phase of East-West relations and thus obstructed Soviet intentions, despite their apparent unanimity.[112]

There is no more to be added. The USSR wanted to embark on the next phase of its German and European policy with a new man at the helm in the DDR—a partner more agreeable to it than Walter Ulbricht.

The Team

It is now, at the time of this writing, five months since Erich Honecker became head of the SED—too early to come to any conclusion as to how the policy and style of the party have developed and will develop under its new first secretary. But his own statements, his political appointments, and his working style provide a number of pointers. Walter Ulbricht reigned with the authority of a party member from the pioneer days. He personified the evolution of the Soviet Zone of Occupation into the German Democratic Republic and the first twenty years of its history. He was omnipresent and directly in touch with the pillars of power. He did not possess—and did not need—a personal empire. Honecker, on the contrary, relies heavily on his, and the following survey will show that he has already established himself on a firm personal foundation.

Of the 135 members of the SED Central Committee, well over half are probably his supporters. More than fifty are either former FDJ functionaries or ex-colleagues of many years' standing. In the control center, the Politburo of the Central Committee, the situation is less transparent. It is difficult to determine which of the sixteen members and seven candidate-members of this committee sympathize with the new first secretary. There are indications, for instance, that Albert Norden, Kurt Hager, and possibly Horst Sindermann (who is said to be slated to succeed Stoph when he replaces Ulbricht as chairman of the Council of State) stand somewhat aloof from him. Paul Verner's attitude to Honecker can probably be safely described as ambivalent. On the one hand, they have worked together for twenty-five years without any radical differences of opinion; on the other, they have both been in the running for the same position and every time it was Honecker who won out.

Particular attention should be paid to the two members of the Politburo elected since the change of leadership: Werner Krolikowski and Werner Lamberz. Both belong to the young generation and are said to be intelligent, tactically skillful functionaries. Krolikowski had been first secretary of the Dresden branch of the SED since 1960. As secretary of the Central Council of the FDJ, Lamberz was in close contact with Honecker in the 1950s; Honecker took him into the Central Committee apparatus in 1963.

Every party leadership relies heavily on the loyalty of the first secretaries of the county directorates (*Bezirkssekretäre*), who, with the help of their organizations, direct and control the whole political and administrative apparatus of the fifteen county or regional divisions of the DDR. Honecker has worked closely with them since he first became head of the division of leading party organizations in the Politburo. Six of these fifteen first secretaries have recently been replaced—with Honecker's approval, of course. At least five of the new appointees came up through the ranks of the FDJ while Honecker was its president. Four of them held high positions and were among Honecker's close associates. Konrad Naumann (now first secretary of the SED county directorate for East Berlin) was a member of the FDJ Central Council from 1962 to 1964 and its second secretary from 1957 to 1967. In the 1950s Honecker sent him to the Komsomol training college in Moscow for a year. Horst Schumann (first SED secretary in Leipzig) had been an FDJ functionary since 1947; he was president of the FDJ for several years and had also directed the youth division of the SED Central Committee. Werner Felfe (first SED secretary in Halle) was second secretary of the FDJ Central Council from January, 1954 to March, 1957, and as such was Honecker's deputy for more than a year. Hans-Joachim Hertwig had previously been secretary of the central directorate of the Ernst Thälmann Pioneer organization.

No less important than the first secretaries are the cadres that direct the party organizations within important mass organizations or are responsible for the political work in great institutions. Here we need mention only the Ministry for State Security and the State National Railways. The first secretary for party organizations in the Ministry for State Security, holding the rank of a first *Bezirkssekretär*, is Gerhard Heidenreich, for many years a top FDJ functionary in Saxony and second secretary of the Central Council. Head of the political division of the German National Railways and deputy Minister of Transport, controlling the whole political apparatus of the vitally important East German transportation system, is Robert Menzel, a friend of Honecker's since they were imprisoned together in Brandenburg-Görden. Menzel was first FDJ secretary in Halle and East Berlin in the 1950s.

Honecker has strong backing in the Central Committee apparatus too. The key departments—leading party organizations, cadre and security affairs—are still headed by the functionaries he selected when he was in charge of those divisions himself. The heads of at least four more departments are close associates from his FDJ days:

Agitation: Hans Modrow, first secretary of the FDJ county directorate for East Berlin during the 1950s. Modrow has held his present position only since the Eighth SED Congress, when Werner Lamberz became a full member of the Politburo. Modrow was already a protégé of Honecker when he was in the youth organization.

Women's Affairs: Inge Lange, also a former secretary of the Central Council.

Youth Affairs: Siegfried Lorenz, a divisional director in the Central Council.

Agriculture: Bruno Kiesler, a member of the Central Council.

Honecker's brother-in-law, Manfred Feist, was made director of the division of foreign information in 1971.

Honecker's nominees to the cadre division demonstrate the undoctrinaire approach to political appointments for which he was known even in his FDJ days. Its director, Fritz Müller, is a wholesale merchant who did not join the SED until he was twenty-eight.[113] He is therefore not one of the proletarian elite of "Old Communists" for whom these key positions were for many years reserved. Neither did he rise through the ranks in practical party work; two years after joining the SED he was already working for the Central Committee in the division of planning and finance.

In the governmental apparatus, too, Honecker can count on the support of several top functionaries—though not as many as in the party. They include Alfred Neumann, first deputy chairman of the Council of State, with whom Honecker worked when they were fellow prisoners in Brandenburg-Görden; Heinz Kessler; and his wife Margot Feist-Honecker, Minister of Education. He has been a friend of Minister of the Interior Friedrich Dickel for many years.

Honecker's relationship with Chairman of the Council of Ministers Willi Stoph is not clear. When Honecker was president of the FDJ and Stoph was Minister of the Interior, there was a noticeable coolness between them. Honecker considered Stoph a dry, unenterprising bureaucrat who sought Ulbricht's backing even on decisions that fell within his own competence. At least, that was what Honecker used to say when the FDJ leader had to wait for a decision from the Ministry of the Interior until Stoph had checked with Ulbricht. A former member of Stoph's planning staff even claims that Ulbricht often had to use his own influence to smooth things over between Honecker and Stoph.

Honecker is on excellent terms with the directors of some of the mass organizations; for example, Major-General Günther Teller, head of the Society for Sport and Technology and a former FDJ official; Dr. Günther Jahn, head of the FDJ; and Gerald Götting and Manfred Gerlach, chairmen of the Eastern Division of the Christian Democratic Union and the Liberal Democratic Party respectively. Both Götting and Gerlach worked closely with Honecker in the FDJ; Gerlach in particular feels bound to him by ties of friendship. In the Free German Trade Union Federation a change of leadership is said to be imminent. Sixty-nine-year-old Herbert Warnke is supposed to be replaced by the new Politburo candidate, Harry Tisch, who is counted among Honecker's followers.

Honecker has always regarded the party press as an important instrument of power. Soon after he became first secretary of the party, he therefore made his old friend Joachim Hermann, former chief editor of the FDJ magazine *Junge Welt*, chief editor of the SED's official paper *Neues Deutschland*, succeeding Rudi Singer, who became chairman of the Government Radio Committee.

But we must not leap to conclusions. We cannot assume that former service as an FDJ functionary, followed by a rise through the SED hierarchy, automatically implies close contact with Honecker. Other angles have to be considered too. After all, inescapable objective factors affect political appointments in the DDR as much as anywhere else.

Working Style and New Departures

The most striking innovation in the SED since Honecker took office is a conspicuous change in working style in the widest sense, including a refocusing of domestic policy. The new style is characterized by a more objective attitude and stronger emphasis on the practical aspect. There is more sober analysis and less formulation of permanent long-term projections than there was in the

last few years under Walter Ulbricht. One of Honecker's first official actions as first secretary is said to have been to commission
a group of economists and other experts to analyze certain economic miscalculations objectively, openly, and quickly. Immediately after the Eighth Congress, the party organizations, especially in the government institutions and mass and cultural
organizations, took their stance on questions of the new working
style, utilizing the resolutions of the Eighth Congress.

What are the essential characteristics of this new attitude?
More attention than before is to be paid to the needs of the civilian
population. Honecker said at the Eighth Congress: "For our society, the economy is the means to an end—the means of satisfying the growing material and cultural needs of the working
people."[114] To dispel any impression that this was meant as criticism of Ulbricht, he added reassuringly: "Of course this was our
party's guiding principle in the past too." However, he immediately resumed: "But with the fuller development of socialist
society and its economic potential, this law connecting man's
production and his needs can and must become more immediately effective. This is what our primary obligation seeks to
achieve."[115]

Another characteristic is that economic targets are more modest and are dictated by realistic rather than wishful thinking. In
indirect criticism of former long-range planning (and hence of
Walter Ulbricht), Honecker said at the Eighth Congress that the
economic system of socialism was developing well, "only it can't
stand too many unplanned miracles. It needs the well-balanced
plan as a secure foundation." In another passage he became even
more explicit, saying with a candor he had rarely displayed in
congressional speeches:

We go soberly forward, evaluating our possibilities realistically.
Thanks to our systematic, successful work, our means of improving
the conditions of work and life are steadily growing, but they do not
grow by sudden spurts. So we must carefully consider where such im-
provements are most urgent and where, with the means at our disposal, we can achieve advances of particular importance to our workers.[116]

This was certainly a reaction to widespread criticism within
the SED. The dissatisfaction is said to have come to a head at the
SED county delegates' conferences that preceded the Eighth

Congress. It was known that Ulbricht had protested against "personal disparagement" and "lack of respect" at the East Berlin delegates' conference. His pet ideas in the field of political economics, "prognosis" and "cybernetics," had been violently attacked by some delegates. Honecker is said to have dissolved several central task groups working on projections for the 1970s and 1980s even before the Congress, and *Effekt,* the journal of theoretical economics, was abolished.[117]

Honecker's remarks at the Congress on problems of housing construction and the protection of the environment illustrate his advocacy of more modest goals and more candor about the real situation, even at the risk of embarrassment. He openly admitted that "we need more apartments" and that the possibility of building them was limited. "Together with our colleagues in the building trades we have checked and rechecked the possibilities of achieving a bigger increase than ever before. Between 1971 and 1975 half a million apartments are to be made available to workers." These results would not be achieved by new construction alone but by "modernizing, remodeling, and expanding existing units."

This concern for the needs of daily life was also expressed in connection with the service occupations. In his congressional speech Honecker said that business must help the general public to save time by making shopping easier through customer service and service in general. The people, he said, "must be well served and competently advised." Indifference toward service or "disdain for it" as an "inferior occupation" was no longer to be tolerated anywhere. "More and better products which people like and which meet their needs, ideas for mass-producing them on the required scale, initiative in the field of service—these are what our society considers important governmental concerns."[118]

The simplification of language is striking. If we compare Ulbricht's speech at the Seventh Congress of April, 1967, with Honecker's speech on similar themes at the Eighth, we are immediately aware of Honecker's effort to express complicated problems in simple, understandable words. This is what Ulbricht had to say about the economic system of socialism:

The economic system of socialism involves the proportional development of our national economy with a highly effective economic structure based on systematic, prognostic work, the attainment of the highest possible scientific and technological standard for the vitally important products, for technology and the organization of output, as well as a modern system of planning and management.[119]

Honecker, on the other hand, never attempts "complex" definitions. For him everything is much simpler:

One of the most important things our nation learns from life is that our society can never consume more than is produced. To come closer to satisfying people's needs is a high challenge to the hard work, expertise, and sense of responsibility of every citizen, no matter where in our great community he carries out his duties.[120]

Honecker apparently takes this so seriously that he has begun a regular campaign for simple language. When Harry Tisch, first secretary of the Rostock branch of the SED, was elected a candidate for the Politburo at the Eighth Congress, he said in his discussion speech:

We are sure the whole country will understand Comrade Honecker's formulation of our tasks and the language of his speech. . . . Why do I say that? Not long ago I read a doctoral dissertation on maritime shipping, which stated that nowadays a ship is no longer a means of transportation but has developed into a social system. So in future when you stand on the jetty at Warnemünde, please don't say: "Here comes the S.S. Brandenburg." Say: "Here comes the Social System Brandenburg."[121]

That this is not just a matter of style but a new mode of leadership, a new way of tackling problems, was shown when Tisch went on to express his pleasure in the fact that the Central Committee's report did not call for "food supply models" but set up plans "for supplying the people with food." The campaign was continued after the Congress. In a leading article on the revised directives of the Eighth Congress for the Five-Year Plan of 1971–75, *Neues Deutschland* made fun of the abstract language of the draft, with the result that in the final version the simple word "ash" replaced the original phrase "residues from the production of electrical energy based on coal combustion."[122]

Language everyone can understand is of course no proof of a change of system—especially since Honecker's speeches still contain plenty of linguistic monstrosities. All the same, there is an attempt to make the style of leadership more objective, and to create closer contact between the people and the party.

The reformulation of the DDR's social political position, on the other hand, is of fundamental importance. Honecker made no mention of Ulbricht's invention, "the fully developed social system of socialism," and spoke only of the development of the socialist society within the DDR. During the conferences we have already referred to at which the various ministries analyzed Honecker's speech, it was apparently stressed even more frankly that the DDR was still only on the way to socialism. A "socialist human community" could never be created so long as there were private entrepreneurs.

A new trend is discernible in cultural and educational policy too, though it is still too early to evaluate it. At the Eighth Congress Honecker underlined the importance of the press and other mass media, whose function, he said, was to make it possible for workers "to exchange their most advanced experience." The first effects of this were seen immediately after the Congress. Out of twenty leading articles in *Neues Deutschland* during the month of August, 1971, fifteen dealt with practical questions in the field of industry and agriculture, with "the needs of people" or with problems of management and working style.[123]

The collective-leadership style is creating a new situation within the control center. At the Eighth Congress and afterward, Honecker laid the utmost stress on the unconditional necessity of collective leadership, together with a strengthening of criticism and self-criticism. He had harsh things to say about self-righteousness, subjectivism, window-dressing, claims to be beyond criticism, and so on:

> Whenever tendencies of this kind crop up, they must be ruthlessly fought. . . . There are a few comrades here and there who can no longer appreciate the value of criticism and self-criticism. They think themselves smarter than the collective group. They do not like constructive opposition. They think themselves infallible and beyond criticism. An attitude of this kind must be corrected with all the force of the collective group.[124]

Whether Honecker really intends to introduce fundamental changes in the working style of the leadership is actually not particularly important. What is far more significant is that the new distribution of authority is automatically producing a different style of leadership. Since Honecker's authority in the control center of the SED does not approach Ulbricht's, it is quite impossible for him simply to take over his predecessor's style. To stress collective leadership is therefore his only chance. But this means that material discussions will become tougher. Decisions contrary to the First Secretary's views—something unheard of for the last fifteen years under Ulbricht—will become part of the normal way of running things. This makes it easier, at least so far as concrete problems are concerned, for loose groupings to form within the leadership and to be articulated. In a centrally directed system it is almost a law that the directoral style of the leading organizations extends downward to the lower-level bodies—for after all, why should anyone hesitate to vote against a first county secretary if he knows that this happens to him all the time on top party committees? So the effects and scope of this new collective working style under Honecker, as dictated by the redistribution of political power, cannot yet be foreseen.

Honecker's Strengths and Weaknesses as Party Leader

The way Honecker grew up to his responsibilities as leader and his position as Ulbricht's assistant does not explain why he was cast for precisely that role among all others. One decisive factor was that in his capacity as director of party organizations and security matters he succeeded in gaining control of the party apparatus. Here his ten years of activity in the youth organization stood him in good stead. He was able systematically to maneuver a considerable number of top FDJ functionaries whom he knew personally into key positions in the party, the army, and the security agencies. This systematic cadre policy in itself goes a long way toward answering the question of how qualified for leadership Honecker is.

Moreover, his fundamental viewpoint coincides with the main line of the party's overall plan. His power to convince others stems from the credibility he radiates. Honecker's ability to impress the leading strata of the party, the mass organizations, the army, and labor functionaries does not derive from superior intellect, but his firm conviction that he is on the right track produces an impression of integrity and optimism. He speaks in simple language—except when he uses the typical stilted party jargon. But this simplicity of speech is at once a strength and a weakness. It identifies him as a simplifier. Subtlety is not his line. On the contrary, any capacity for sophisticated argument always puts him on his guard for possible revisionism. On the other hand, it is advantageous that he has the knack of issuing clear directives in accordance with dogma and that all those who have been through the same school understand him because they know where they stand and nothing is left for them to puzzle out for themselves.

Honecker has been through a unique school for party leaders in a centralized bureaucratic system—the school of Walter Ulbricht. But he knew how to develop what he learned there and enriched it with his own personal style by increasing the substance of Ulbricht's leadership methodology with the help of his gift for personal contact. (This gift, it must be said, has been hampered by daily confrontation with the bureaucratic system and the necessity of conforming to ready-made stereotypes.)

Who would ever have thought of voluntarily going to Ulbricht with his personal problems or suggesting a private get-together with him—with no ulterior motive—after a meeting? With Honecker it is quite different. For many people it is perfectly normal to confide their personal worries to him, invite him to parties, even sit down to a game of *skat* with him. Of course his present power status reduces the opportunities for this, but the feeling of intimacy alone produces a different atmosphere. The only condition is that you must belong to his set and accept his habits—in short, that he must like you. This, however, could also cause complications. Ulbricht treated nearly everyone in the same reserved, cool manner; no one could call himself his friend. This is not the case with Honecker. As a result there is a feeling of informal cooperation among colleagues but at the same time a danger of cliques. Those who are not in his favor feel slighted; others feel privileged.

There is no question that Honecker uses his openness and simplicity and his uncomplicated working style for tactical purposes. Lower- and medium-level functionaries especially see him as one of their own kind. Most functionaries who were close to Ulbricht were never sure what he really thought. They were always looking for what was behind things and trying to interpret them; they sometimes scented danger where there was none. With Honecker no one looks for schemes or intrigues or imputes cryptic meanings to his statements; everyone knows that he means what he says. This of course applies chiefly to the leadership corps, not necessarily to the general population.

Scientists, artists, and some young technological experts who have not yet fully adjusted, or who are not stuck in a rigorous pattern of thought to the same degree as the apparatus of power itself, find his linguistic repertoire primitive and are sometimes too ready to take his simple way of expressing himself as an indication that he is not qualified to direct the control center of an increasingly complex industrialized society. Such judgments are even more prevalent in the West. We should not be deceived. Honecker's decisive qualification for leadership is his ability to grasp essentials quickly and—now that he has the necessary power—to make and enforce quick decisions. Here he can confidently compete with the managers of big Western concerns. At the same time he attaches great importance to expert opinion.

Honecker has a capacity for self-limitation. He deliberately stays in the background and stresses collective leadership. He did not speak at the Rostock "Baltic Sea Week," for instance, although he might well make use of such opportunities to increase his popularity. He is also said to have had an issue of the old-established magazine *Weltbühne* (No. 24, 1971) withdrawn from circulation because it contained an article by Professor Jürgen Kuczynski, the economist, entitled "My Comrade Honecker," which showed unmistakable symptoms of the personality cult.[125]

Honecker is more successful than many who share his proletarian social background in turning it to account politically. It is not that he deliberately exploits it—that is why his credibility is so high with minor labor functionaries—but somehow his upbringing, fundamental beliefs, and sense of mission interact to his advantage. Even today it is easier for him than for other functionaries to understand the problems of the working class. Of course he has made his adjustments and long ago learned to take advantage of the privileges high rank confers. People close to him say that when his daughter Sonya was attending an institute in Halle which prepares students for study abroad he would send an official Central Committee car to bring her home

to Berlin every weekend, although the other girls were allowed to
visit their parents only once a month. Honecker now has his
clothes custom made and lives in a fairly luxurious villa rather
than a four-room apartment. Nevertheless, much that other functionaries seem to have forgotten is still very much part of his life.
It is said he still insists on his housekeeper sitting down to table
with him, and his chauffeurs and bodyguards still speak highly
of his kindness and consideration.

Another of Honecker's strengths is his age. He does not belong
to the generation of Ulbricht, Dahlem, Ebert, and Matern, never
took part in their factional fights to the death, never retired into
self-isolation. But he is not one of the "New Communists" either
—those who espoused communism only after World War II under the protection of Russian bayonets. Nevertheless Honecker
is recognized by both groups. The "Old Communists" consider
him one of themselves because he fought with them before 1933,
when it was still dangerous, and because he later had to suffer
for his convictions. The middle generation—those over thirty—
know him from his FDJ days. He grew up with them into adult-
hood and advancing age. Only the very young regard Honecker
as one of the oldtimers who are always talking of things that mean
nothing to them.

We may conclude with a short analysis of the various inconsistencies and contradictions in Honecker's behavior that this
portrait has revealed. First a brief résumé. Honecker's party discipline seems to be unconditional, yet occasionally he overrides
it. For decades he has been inveighing against bureaucracy, yet
he fights it with bureaucratic means. For a long time he ignored
the importance of theoretical studies; today he considers scientific or scholarly qualifications mandatory for any successful leadership activity. He always upholds the collective style of work but
used to become authoritarian when he could not get his own way.
He constantly spoke of the primacy of internationalism, although
he treated the various communist and labor parties in widely dif-
fering ways.

Most of these apparently irreconcilable views and ways of be-
having are to be explained by the basic contradiction between
the theory of Marxism-Leninism and the practice of the bureaucratic system. It is easier to establish norms than to create the
conditions for meeting them. If the cult of personality is to be
condemned, then the party must be democratized from bottom

to top. It is no use demanding more democracy within the party and at the same time maintaining the principle that the high-level bodies must approve all candidates the subordinate organizations propose to elect. It is meaningless to denounce bureaucracy without saying a word about all-pervasive centralized planning and control. The demand for criticism and self-criticism is nonsense if there are rules about what may and may not be criticized. Willingness to give the parliamentary bodies more responsibility is lip service so long as the leading role of the party may not be questioned. How can the authority of the trade unions be strengthened so long as it is not acknowledged that conflicts of interest and inconsistencies exist even in a socialist society?

In addition to these fundamental contradictions, which can only be suggested here, there is the fact that it is often impossible to put the leadership's abstract directives into practice. How can you meet a quota which was too high from the start? How can you execute cadre plans that bear no relation to the actual personnel situation? While the director of a VEB may have to engage in illegal barter to fulfill his quota, the president of the FDJ sometimes had to ignore the resolutions of the party in order to meet its demands.

To repeat, many of the discrepancies in Erich Honecker's behavior can be explained by contradictions inherent in the system, some of which have now been reduced. Others still exist. Perhaps they can be gradually eliminated as the new leadership introduces the more objective working style and the sober approach to planning that are its aims. But it still remains to be seen whether these measures are really based on a new concept. The more heed the new leadership pays to reality, the less will it need to govern by decree.

Other inconsistencies are explained by the generation gap within the SED leadership. There is also the fear—latent ever since June 17, 1953—that the power that has been gained could be lost again. Throughout thirty years of experience Honecker confronted a "class enemy" who was always materially stronger than himself. From 1945 up to the most recent past, he was never free of a feeling of inferiority vis-à-vis an economically stronger "enemy"—particularly as far as the Federal Republic of Germany was concerned. This is reflected in his extreme insistence on recognition under international law.

However, not only communism but also its representatives are capable of change. The only people who still doubt this are those whose fear of the future and opposition to reform prevent them from changing their way of thinking.

Rarely is it possible to trace the development of a human character so clearly as in the case of Honecker, who grew with and through the tasks he performed. He is living proof that a worker who had little opportunity for education in his youth is quite capable of carrying great responsibility, even in a completely industrialized society. As the Dresden nuclear physicist Manfred von Ardenne once said: "The mere fact that this state is the practical achievement of a handful of carpenters, joiners, and laborers who, when they began, hadn't the vaguest inkling of government, economics, or administration is remarkable in itself."[126]

Great tasks lie ahead of Honecker. The four-power Berlin Agreement and the supplementary contractual arrangements between Bonn and East Berlin have made the admittance of both Germanys to the United Nations and the worldwide recognition of the DDR under international law purely a matter of time. This will inevitably create a new situation in Central Europe and between the two Germanys. It might be the beginning of a period of active coexistence: that is, of a real contest between the two systems, without discrimination, and starting from more or less equal positions. In this crucial phase the DDR will be represented by Honecker. The Federal Republic of Germany is not the only power that will have to reckon with him.

Appendix

Extracts from the Verdict of the People's Court against Erich Honecker

A photocopy of the verdict reached by the People's Court on August 6, 1937, against Erich Honecker was obtained for my publishers by the Anti-Fascist Resistance Committee in the DDR. The summing up conflicts to some extent with the official biographies of Honecker on which I have relied. The contradictions are explained by the fact that the court included statements made by the accused in his own defense. The following extracts are taken from the court's summation.

I. In the Name of the German People

Copy

17 J 28/36

2 H 24/37

In the criminal proceedings against:

1. Bruno Baum, electrician, 19 Usedomer Strasse, Berlin, born February 13, 1910, in Berlin, single, previously convicted;

2. Erich Honecker, roofer, 26 Brüsseler Strasse, Berlin, born August 25, 1912, in Neunkirchen, Saar, single, no previous convictions;

3. Sarah Fodorovà (born Libun), medical student, Doudova 23, Prague-Podoli, born June 21, 1912, in Spola, Ukraine, married, Czech citizen, no previous convictions;

4. Edwin Lautenbach, skilled mechanic, 12 Herschelstrasse, Berlin-Charlottenburg, born April 18, 1909, in Berlin-Neukölln, single, no previous convictions,

all at present imprisoned on remand, on a charge of conspiracy for high treason, with aggravating factors and gross forgery of documents, the Second Division of the People's Court, in the public session of June 8, 1937, based on the oral hearings of June 7 and 8, 1937, in which the following participated:

As judges:
    Volksgerichtsrat Hartmann, presiding,
    Landgerichtsrat Waller,
    Gauamtsleiter Fischer,
    SA Brigadeführer Bunge,
    Bezirksstadtrat Friedlein,
Representing the Office of the Public Prosecutor:
    Staatsanwalt Dr. Drullmann,
Representing the Registrar's Office:
    Secretary Sonnenschein,
has reached the following findings according to the law:

I. The defendant Fodorovà is acquitted.

II. The defendants Baum, Honecker, and Lautenbach are convicted of conspiring to commit an act of high treason with aggravating factors. Baum and Honecker in coincidence with a crime of gross forgery of documents, and are sentenced as follows:
    Baum to 13 (thirteen) years penal servitude;
    Honecker to 10 (ten) years penal servitude;
    Lautenbach to 2 (two) years and 6 (six) months penal servitude.

III. They are deprived of their civil rights as follows:
    Baum and Honecker for a period of 10 (ten) years;
    Lautenbach for a period of 3 (three) years.

IV. The 18 (eighteen) months Baum, Honecker, and Lautenbach have already served on remand are to be deducted from the above terms.

V. Objects 2, 3, 4, 6, and 7 listed under Exhibits III on p. 47 of the indictment are to be confiscated.

VI. Costs are to be paid by the convicted defendants. In the case of the acquitted, the Reich Treasury is to pay the costs.

According to the law.

II.

...

2. After attending elementary school in his native Wiebelskirchen, Saar, and completing the highest grade, Defendant Honecker worked for a farmer in Neudorf near Neustettin, Pomerania, for two years. In 1928 he returned to Wiebelskirchen to learn the roofing trade. He did not complete his apprenticeship but gave it up in 1930 to devote himself to full-time political work. Since then he has not worked at his trade.

Defendant Honecker became familiar with communist thinking at an early age. His father was a member of the KPD, then the strongest political party in Wiebelskirchen. In 1923 or 1924 the accused was already a member of the communist children's organization that later became the Pioneers, in which he held minor official positions. In

1928 he joined the Communist League of German Youth. As treasurer of the local branch, he was soon responsible for its business affairs. Shortly afterward he became leader of the Wiebelskirchen branch, which at the time had about eighty members. In December, 1928, he attended a training course for functionaries arranged by the Saar branch of the KJVD.

From November, 1930, to March, 1931, he traveled in the Soviet Union as a member of a German delegation to which he had been elected at the suggestion of the Saar headquarters of the KJVD. The delegates visited industrial plants in the Moscow area and in the Urals and attended special lectures on socialist reconstruction and communist economic methods. They did not attend special courses at party training schools, specifically the Lenin School in Moscow. On his return to Wiebelskirchen, the accused gave accounts of his trip at youth discussion evenings arranged for this purpose by the KJVD.

In 1931 he was appointed to the Neunkirchen district committee of the KJVD and in the summer of 1931 was made *Agitprop* director of its Saar branch. In the autumn of 1931 he was promoted to political director for the Saar and held this position until February, 1934. During this time he was paid a monthly salary of 250 francs. After retiring as political director, he remained a member of the leadership of the Saar branch of the KJVD and worked in the secretariat until February 27, 1935, immediately before the Saar was reunited with Germany, when he left for Forbach en route for Paris.

III. The Events

. . .

Toward the end of August, "Erwin" informed Defendant Baum of the arrival of Defendant Honecker. They agreed to use Honecker as a courier and as their personal contact man. On August 28, 1955, on orders from "Erwin," Defendant Baum met Defendant Honecker at the Putlitzstrasse subway station and immediately instructed him in his duties. He gave him an account of the status of underground KJVD work in Berlin and of morale in the factories, stressing that while labor approved the measures taken by the national government to regain its freedom to rearm, it was very critical as regards social problems. In order to promote the work of the KJVD it was essential to establish contact with members of the former Socialist Working-Class Youth, with the Socialist Youth League, the free-trade union groups, the Hitler Youth, and the *Arbeitsdank*. It has not been possible to ascertain whether such contacts already existed in Defendant Baum's district. On this point Defendant Honecker qualified the statements he made in his preliminary interrogation and stated without contradiction that reports from other districts that had passed through his hands as a courier mentioned already existing contacts of this kind. Following this original conversation, Defendant Baum put Defendant Honecker in touch with a man who arranged for him to rent a furnished room.

A few days later, Defendant Baum introduced Defendant Honecker to "Erwin." From then on, alternating meetings took place between Defendants Baum and Honecker, Honecker and "Erwin," and Honecker and a courier substituting for "Erwin," at which Honecker would deliver Baum's reports on his district to "Erwin" and be given "Erwin's" new instructions for Baum. At these meetings Defendant Honecker would also receive from "Erwin" illegal printed material and envelopes containing written communications for Defendant Baum. Reports from other districts of Berlin also passed through Defendant Honecker's hands to be forwarded to Defendant Baum for his information. Meetings between Defendants Baum and Honecker usually took place several times a week. The only interruption was between November 9 and 20, 1935, when, as previously arranged, Defendant Honecker went to Prague on orders from "Erwin."

In September, 1935, with the object of creating special distribution channels for printed material intended for the subdistricts and establishing the direct communication between the subdistricts and "Erwin" that might be needed in an emergency, Defendant Baum introduced Defendant Honecker to the courier "Hans." From then on Honecker passed printed material intended for the subdistricts to "Hans."

C and D. Honecker and Fodorovà

I. *Defendant Honecker's Activity before the Return of the Saar to Germany*

In February, 1934, Defendant Honecker went to Essen from the Saar with the approval of the leadership of the Saar branch of the KVJD in Saarbrücken. His instructions were to make a personal investigation of the young comrades' attitude toward the Labor Corps (*Arbeitsdienst*), conditions in the Ruhr mining industry, and unemployment in the Ruhr. He was given no specific orders of an organizational nature. For this trip Defendant Honecker received an allowance of 180 francs from the Saar branch of the KJVD, and a member of the KJVD Central Committee known as "Julius" arranged a safe house for him in Essen.

In Essen he made contact, according to instructions, with a member of the KJVD underground, who put him in touch with other comrades from the youth organization. He was also introduced to members of the Labor Corps and learned that they had joined it (although they disliked the military drill) because they could find no other jobs. His conversations with young comrades also gave him the impression that the people were "by no means unanimously pro-Hitler" and that unemployment had not decreased to any significant extent. He thought wages and working conditions in the Ruhr were comparable to those in the Saar: that is, wages were insufficient and the "pressure system" was being widely used. Ways and means of requiring and obtaining increased output were described in a leaflet made available to him from a pit in the Ruhr, which sharply attacked the "pressure system."

On February 15, 1935, Defendant Honecker, who had been under police surveillance since his arrival in Essen because it was known that a KPD functionary from the Saar wanted to visit the Ruhr, was arrested on the pretext of suspected larceny outside the Lichtburg movie theater, after a meeting with the KJVD functionaries Weinand and Mark, who have since disappeared. Shortly afterward he was released, after a check of his identification papers. Disturbed by this, Honecker left Essen the same day and returned to the Saar. After his return, he made a report on his findings to the Saar branch of the KJVD.

II. *Defendant Honecker's Stay in France, Switzerland, and Czechoslovakia before Entering Germany (August 27, 1925)*

After the Saar plebiscite, Defendant Honecker left the Saar immediately before it was reincorporated in the Reich and went to Forbach on February 27, 1935. There he received the money for his fare to Paris, where he reported to the *Rote Hilfe* office as a "refugee from the Saar." He had to undertake to obey any orders the organization there might give him, but was not told what the nature of his assignments might be. He was then given room and board in a hotel and approximately five to ten francs a week for expenses.

At a meeting in the Place de l'Opéra with a KJVD functionary in mid-June, Honecker was asked whether he was willing to work underground in Germany. He agreed and some time later was ordered by the comrade from the youth organization to go by way of Zurich to Prague. He was given five hundred francs for travel expenses. In late July or early August, 1935, Defendant Honecker left for Zurich, going first to Mülhausen and crossing the Swiss frontier at an unguarded point. In Zurich he reported to the address given to him. To facilitate his future underground activity, he was there provided with a forged or doctored Dutch passport in the name of "Marten Tjaden of Amsterdam" to which his only contribution was his photograph. Using this passport, Defendant Honecker then left for Prague by way of Austria on August 20, 1935, arriving in Prague on August 22, 1935.

The young comrade who met him there took him to a representative of the Central Committee of the KJVD called "Franz" or "Ernst," who told him that he was to work in the Berlin headquarters of the KJVD. He instructed him to enter Germany at Eger, using the Dutch passport, and return to Prague a few weeks later to report on his activity in Berlin and the status of the KJVD's underground work there. During his stay in Prague, new underground publications such as *Rote*

Fahne and *Junge Garde* were available to him. Defendant Honecker was given a railway ticket to Nürnberg, money for his fare to Berlin and an additional hundred marks in German bank notes to cover his expenses for the next few weeks. On August 27, 1935, he went via Eger to Berlin, as he had been instructed.

III. *Defendant Honecker's Activity in Berlin up to November 9, 1935*

On August 28, 1935, Defendant Honecker met Defendant Baum at the rendezvous at the Putlitzstrasse subway station previously agreed upon in Prague. The latter told him that he was to serve as a courier between the leading functionaries of the Berlin KJVD, especially between himself and "Erwin." At the same time he (Baum) gave him more detailed instructions and introduced him to a fellow traveler who arranged for him to board with a Frau Semiller in the Brüsseler Strasse, where he introduced himself as "Herbert Jung, commercial traveler." He filled out a registration form in that name and had it signed by his landlady but never filed it at the police registry office.

During the period of his Berlin activity Defendant Honecker used the cover name "Franz."

Soon after Defendant Honecker's arrival in Berlin, Defendant Baum introduced him to "Erwin," with whom he worked until his arrest under the circumstances described in paragraph A of the proceedings against Defendant Baum.

Through Defendant Baum he was introduced to other comrades from the youth organization in addition to "Erwin." On special instructions from Defendant Baum, he would meet them to pick up reports and other material which he would pass on to Defendant Baum or, if so instructed, directly to "Erwin." Through "Erwin" Defendant Honecker also made the acquaintance of a comrade from the youth organization who in September or October passed him a small suitcase with a false bottom containing illegal printed material such as issues of *Rundschau, Junge Garde*, and *Jugend-Pressekorrespondenz*. On instructions from Defendant Baum, Defendant Honecker passed these publications to the courier "Hans" at two meetings, returning the suitcase, with the jacket packed in it for camouflage purposes, to the comrade from the youth organization from whom he had received it.

IV. *Defendant Honecker's Second Trip to Prague*

Early in November, 1935, Defendant Honecker was ordered by "Erwin" to go to Prague and to be on Wenceslaus Square at a certain time on November 10 or 11. He was given his fare and ten marks for expenses. He was to report to Prague that the last courier had failed to arrive and that the Berlin organization urgently needed money.

In accordance with instructions, Defendant Honecker went to Prague via Dresden on November 9, 1935, and after waiting in vain in Wenceslaus Square on November 10, met his contact, whom he already knew, on November 11, 1935. His contact put him in touch again with "Franz" or "Ernst" and Defendant Honecker informed him of the special requests of the KJVD leadership in Berlin and particularly of the shortage of money. "Franz" or "Ernst" told him that no funds were currently available but that money had been sent to Berlin in the meantime and the next courier would bring more. Defendant Honecker was not able to report on his own activity in Berlin because, according to "Franz" or "Ernst," the comrade who had requested this report was not in Prague at the time. He learned, however, that organizational changes were planned for the near future. Functionaries who were not regularly registered with the police were to be withdrawn from the Reich. Defendant Honecker was also given a Prague address to which he was to send certain National Socialist papers such as *HJ, Das junge Deutschland,* and *Arbeitsmann.* Lastly, he was instructed to continue his activity as a courier in the Berlin district as before, with the special duty of meeting the couriers arriving in Berlin from Prague and arranging the distribution of the material they brought. He was also to tell "Erwin" to come to Prague as soon as possible.

Defendant Honecker was to meet the next Prague-Berlin courier at 3 P.M. on December 3, 1935, in the Solinger Strasse or, failing that, an hour later in the Joachimsthaler Strasse. For identification he was to wear a red carnation in his buttonhole; the courier would conspicuously carry a magazine and would say: "Are you Herr Meier?" Because Defendant Honecker wanted to wait for the Prague comrade from the youth organization and make his report to him, and also because he had misgivings about leaving Czechoslovakia on his Dutch passport (which identified him as a seaman) after such a brief stay, he remained in Prague until November 19, 1935, with the approval of "Franz" or "Erwin." During this time the Prague KJVD housed him first in a hotel and then in a private apartment, and he received twenty crowns a day for expenses.

Without having spoken to the comrade from the youth organization, Defendant Honecker left Prague on the night of November 20, 1935, and returned to Berlin. Before leaving he was given his fare and 120 marks as salary for the month of December, 1935. Defendant Honecker used the false Dutch passport to leave Czechoslovakia, as he had when entering.

V. *Defendant Honecker's Further Activity in Berlin. Collaboration with Defendant Fodorovà.*

1. After his return to Berlin, Defendant Honecker met Defendant Baum and "Erwin" at a joint meeting at which he reported to them on the results of his Prague trip and relayed the order for "Erwin" to go to Prague.

From then until his arrest, Defendant Honecker continued his former activity as a courier between Defendant Baum and the subdistricts he was in charge of. From this time on, he was only in indirect contact with "Erwin," through a contact designated by "Erwin" himself. From this man, who in September, 1935, had already delivered to him a small suitcase containing illegal material, he received toward the end of November, again on "Erwin's" instructions, two envelopes of material to be delivered to Defendant Baum. He was not able to effect delivery of this material, which was confiscated in his apartment after his arrest.

2. In accordance with instructions, Defendant Honecker went to the Solinger Strasse at 3 P.M. on December 3, 1935, to keep the rendezvous with the courier due to arrive from Prague, having been there a few days earlier to familiarize himself with the locality. As arranged, he wore a red carnation in his buttonhole. At the appointed time Defendant Fodorovà arrived, conspicuously carrying a magazine, and said to Defendant Honecker: "Are you Herr Meier?" Defendant Honecker gave the prearranged answer. Defendant Fodorovà told Defendant Honecker that she had brought a suitcase from Prague and it was at her hotel. Defendants Honecker and Fodorovà then went to an Aschinger Restaurant at the Zoo subway station in the Joachimsthaler Strasse. Here Defendant Fodorovà handed Defendant Honecker a sealed envelope containing 350 marks in German currency and a scratchpad on which were written the address of a safe house in Prague and the recognition signals and passwords for the next courier's rendezvous. Defendant Honecker copied these into a smaller notebook he carried with him and then destroyed the notes on the scratchpad Defendant Fodorovà had given him.

Before leaving the restaurant, where they had spent about half an hour, Defendants Honecker and Fodorovà arranged to meet at 6:30 P.M. outside the Vaterland House on the Potsdamer Platz to make arrangements for transferring the suitcase. Defendant Honecker was late for this appointment, and when he arrived, Defendant Fodorovà had already left. Concluding that Defendant Fodorovà would probably go to her hotel, the Habsburger Hof, Defendant Honecker walked down the Saarland Strasse and caught up with her. She asked him to pick up the suitcase at her hotel. Honecker hesitated to do this and told her that the suitcase contained illegal printed matter and it was too dangerous for him to pick it up from the hotel himself. When Defendant Fodorovà asked in some consternation what was to be done, Defendant Honecker told her to leave the suitcase in the baggage checkroom at the Anhalter Bahnhof and give him the check outside the Columbus House on the Potsdamer Platz at 8 P.M. To make the contents of the suitcase look innocent, Defendant Fodorovà was to pack in it some of her own clothing, which he would return to her the day after he collected it.

In accordance with instructions, Defendant Fodorovà checked the suitcase at the Anhalter Bahnhof and went at the appointed time to the Columbus House, where Defendant Honecker was waiting for her. She handed him the baggage check and the key to the suitcase, and then both went by taxi to an Aschinger Restaurant in the Bahnhof Friedrich Strasse, where they had dinner. Defendant Fodorovà told Defendant Honecker that she had brought the suitcase to Berlin as a favor to a friend named "Ruth," who had been prevented by illness from coming herself. She was upset, as she had been a few hours earlier at the meeting in the Saarland Strasse, about the contents of the suitcase, of which she had known nothing, and said she was afraid the affair might get her into trouble. Defendant Honecker did not hide his astonishment that she had not been told what the suitcase contained but reassured Defendant Fodorovà that nothing would happen to her. He then left.

While Defendant Fodorovà went to a movie theater and then returned to her hotel, Defendant Honecker claimed the suitcase at the Anhalter Bahnhof and took a taxi to the Zoo subway station. From the odd behavior of the railway official at the baggage counter and from the fact that a car was obviously following his taxi, he concluded that he was being followed. He therefore hurriedly left the taxi at the Zoo station, abandoning the suitcase, and fled into the zoo, where he succeeded in escaping. He was arrested the next day on leaving his apartment.

The suitcase found in the taxi after Defendant Honecker had fled contained the following publications concealed under a false bottom:

Deutsche Zentralzeitung, Moscow, issue of Nov. 22, 1935	1 copy
Neuer Vorwärts, issue of Dec. 1, 1935	1 copy
Der Gegenangriff, issue of Nov. 30, 1935	1 copy
Inprekorr, Vol. XV, No. 41	2 copies
Inprekorr, Vol. XV, No. 42	1 copy
Inprekorr, Vol. XV, No. 43	1 copy
Inprekorr, Vol. XV, No. 44	4 copies
Jugend-Information, issue of mid-Nov., 1935	6 copies
Co-Report of Comrade Guyot at the Sixth Congress of the Communist Youth International	6 copies
Informationsdienst of the Free German Trade Unions, No. 4, Nov.–Dec., 1935	5 copies
Rote Fahne, special edition on the release of Thälmann	2 copies
Rundschau über Politik, Wirtschaft und Arbeiterbewegung, Nos. 62–68	1 copy each
Michel: "Closing Address"	7 copies

After the arrest of Defendant Honecker, the following material was confiscated in his apartment:

1. *Jugend-Pressedienst*, No. 1, late Aug., 1935	1 copy
2. *KJ*, No. 9	1 copy

3. Brochures with fake title pages: "The Happiness
   of Sister Ellen Smith" and "Uncle Bräse's Will"   1 copy each
4. Copy of clipping from *Neue Zürcher Zeitung* of
   June 18, 1935   1 copy
5. *Inprekorr*, Vol. XV, Nos. 24, 25, 26   1 copy each
6. Leaflet: "Against Hitler for Peace"   1 copy
7. *Internationale   Gewerkschafts-Pressekonferenz,*
   Vol. V, No. 11   1 copy
8. Copy of clipping from *Wille und Macht* of Aug.
   15, 1935   1 copy
9. Report on second negotiation with the Activist
   Association for German Worker Sports   1 copy
10. Proclamation of the International Youth Confer-
    ence for Peace, Freedom, and Progress   1 copy
11. Typewritten leaflets: "Workers in Overalls and
    Uniforms,"   "Conscription   and   Proletarian
    Youth," "How We Young Anti-Fascists Fight in
    the Hitler Youth," "Dear Friends"   1 copy each
12. Several clippings from legal journals
13. Handwritten notes by Defendant Honecker from
    the youth magazine *Das Junge Deutschland* or
    Wille und Macht
14. Two unused stencils
15. Leaflet: "To the Working People of Greater Ber-
    lin:"   3 copies
16. Pamphlets: "Youth in Distress," "To Young Work-
    ers," and "News, Third Week of September"   1 copy each
17. *Die Junge Garde,* KJVD, Charlottenburg, late
    Sept., 1935   1 copy
18. *Die Junge Garde,* KJVD, Sub-District South-East,
    Oct., 1935   1 copy
19. *Freie Jugend,* Nov., 1935   2 copies
20. *Die Wasserratte,* No. I (May, 1935) and special
    edition (late May, 1935)   1 copy
21. *Mobilmachung,* antiwar newspaper of the KJVD,
    Sub-District South-East (mid-Nov., 1935)   1 copy
22. *The Young Bolshevik* (early Oct., 1935)   1 copy
23. Pamphlets: "Report from a Friend from WW,"
    "Report on my Work in the *Arbeitsdank* to Date,"
    "Report from a Membership Meeting in Ul. Be-
    trieb Te.," "Athletic Club," "Factory Meeting at
    O's," and "Dear Friends"   1 copy each
24. Handwritten factory reports: "Steady Develop-
    ment at AEG Turbine and Osram"   1 copy each
25. Photographic prints: "Waiting Lines Outside
    Stores! In Berlin—Not Moscow!" and "Monu-
    ment to Nazi National Heroes Torn Down"   1 copy each

Defendant Honecker continued his work for the illegal KJVD even while he was in prison awaiting trial. In late August, 1936, he passed to a Czech citizen, also imprisoned on remand, who was shortly to be released, the following note, with instructions to forward it to the Prague KJVD office:

> Dr. Frds, Let's hope this sign of life reaches you. Greetings from Walter and myself. We are all quite well. We were 8; now we are 5, and we are to be brought before the People's Court. But we're not letting that shake our convictions, and we're in good shape. They've got proof of my courier work between Walter and E. St. They've also proved that Walter tried to recruit several young people in our area for our cause and that he was in charge of two subdistricts, with a staff of at least 25. I don't know any of the people who've been arrested. No one I've been in contact with is among them. I hope E. St. is back with you now. The reason is surveillance from outside. Probably Erw. or I on arrival on October 20. The only thing that surprises me is that only friends close to Walter were arrested. A member (former) of the Socialist Working-Class Youth, a girl from Siemens and one from Osram, and two more.
>
> They probably had two people following Fodorovà. She took her suitcase with her to the hotel and later took it back to the station. The scratchpad and money were later found on me, together with passport and some drawings and reports. I testified that I didn't know whether she knew what those things contained. If she sticks to that, she can get off. They're trying to pin something on me in connection with the Ruhr. A certain Albert Mauermann testified against me. Of course I deny anything of the sort. We were all arrested on December 4, I myself outside my apartment, Walter at a rendezvous and Fodorovà at her hotel. Klinger has offered to cooperate with the Gestapo. I've read his letter. They tried to hire me too, ha ha ha! If you want to send anything, my prison number is 4534. All the best,
>
> Your Friend
> Case may come up in December. Everything else, my parents.

The fellow-prisoner turned this note over to the police.

IV. *Defense of the Accused and Its Evaluation*

. . .

3. Defendant Honecker:

Inasmuch as the indictment of Defendant Honecker charges him with illegal activity on behalf of the KPD and the KJVD in the year 1933 in Oberkirchen, consisting of oral and written attempts to recruit Scheer for illegal work, Defendant Honecker has denied this. On the basis of the testimony of the witness Scheer, this charge has not been sustained. Otherwise Defendant Honecker has admitted in their entirety the facts as presented with respect to him under III C and D. He denies only having used the name "Herbert" during his stay in Essen in February, 1935, and having carried out certain orders pertaining to the organization of the KJVD in the Ruhr. It is true that at approximately the same time a KJVD functionary who called himself "Herbert" appeared in the Ruhr and spent some time there on organizational business. However, such activity on the part of Defendant Honecker could not be proved, because none of the witnesses testifying in the trial who had known "Herbert" in Essen (Weichert, Titze, and Kappe) was able to identify Defendant Honecker as "Herbert." Neither could the sworn testimony of the witness Schröder confirm the suspicion to which Defendant Honecker was subject, because the witness, as a police officer, had merely directed the surveillance and observation of Defendant Honecker. As regards motive, Defendant Honecker stated at the trial that he had been a communist for a long time before taking this action and had not changed his convictions; neither did he intend to change them. His illegal work in Germany was devoted exclusively to the revolutionary aims of the KPD.

Notes

PART I

1 Karl Marx and Friedrich Engels, *Communist Manifesto*, Part II.
2 A. von Limberg, *Geschichte des Saarlandes* (Saarlouis, 1948), pp. 295–297.
3 Ibid.
4 W. Langenbach, *Die Frage der landsässigen Lohnarbeiter* (diss. Bonn, 1939), p. 33.
5 P. Kiefer, *Die Organisationsbestregungen der Saarbergleute, ihre Ursachen und Wirkungen auf dem Bereich des Saarbrücker Bergbaues und ihre Berechtigung* (diss. Strassburg, Sulzbach, 1912), p. 130.
6 Kiefer, p. 131.
7 W. Lehmann, *Abriss der Wirtschaftsgeschichte des Saargebietes* (Saarbrücken, 1925), p. 49.
8 Information furnished by the Anti-Fascist Resistance Committee in the DDR, August 27, 1971, in response to a query addressed to Erich Honecker.
9 Ibid.
10 Ibid.
11 Letters from City Registrar, Neunkirchen, Saar, June 2 and 14, 1971.
12 Information from Anti-Fascist Resistance Committee.
13 M. Zenner, *Parteien und Politik im Saargebiet unter dem Völkerbundregime, 1920–1935* (diss. Cologne, Saarbrücken, 1966), p. 26.
14 Dechant J. Backes, *Memorandum zur Bergarbeiterstreikbewegung im Saarrevier 1912–1913* (Neunkirchen, 1913), pp. 23–51.
15 Ibid., p. 5.
16 E. Walsch, "Ein Arbeiter aus Wiebelskirchen" in *Unsere Zeit* (Düsseldorf), February 22, 1971.
17 B. Krajewski, "Aus dem Industrieraum Neunkirchen" in *Unsere Heimat an der Saar*, Series II (Neunkirchen, 1954), p. 20.
18 F. Osterroth and D. Schuster, *Chronik der deutschen Sozialdemokratie* (Hanover, 1963), p. 158.
19 Information from Anti-Fascist Resistance Committee.
20 Zenner, p. 29.
21 Zenner, p. 28.

22 Zenner, p. 29.
23 Ibid.
24 *Weissbuch über das Saargebiet, 1921*, p. 46f.
25 *Weissbuch*, p. 47.
26 Information from Anti-Fascist Resistance Committee.
27 Zenner, p. 150f.
28 Zenner, p. 351.
29 "Erich Honecker—Kandidat der Jugend" in *Junge Welt* (East Berlin), September 23, 1954.
30 Zenner, p. 345ff.
31 "Der Ausschluss von Max Waltz bestätigt" in *Arbeiterzeitung* (Saarbrücken), June 7, 1922.
32 Zenner, p. 197.
33 Zenner, p. 73ff.
34 "Erich Honecker—Kandidat der Jugend."
35 "Erich Honecker—Vorbild der Pioniere" in *Die Trommel* (East Berlin), August 16, 1962.
36 M. Karius, "Zur Sozialpolitik im Saargebiet" in *Das Saargebiet, seine Struktur, seine Probleme*, ed. Kloevekorn (Saarbrücken, 1929), p. 362.
37 Zenner, p. 73f.
38 "Erich Honecker—Vorbild der Pioniere."
39 Ibid.
40 E. Honecker, "Für das Glück der Jugend," letter to young voters published by the Volkswahlausschuss der Nationalen Front des Demokratischen Deutschland (East Berlin, 1954), p. 6f.
41 All official biographies of Erich Honecker either pass over this period or deal very vaguely with it. The biography in *Neues Deutschland* of May 4, 1971 simply says: "After leaving school, he became an apprentice roofer and joined the woodworkers' union." The official biography furnished by the Anti-Fascist Resistance Committee also says simply: "After leaving grammar school, he worked for a time on the land until he found a position as an apprentice roofer." On the other hand, the findings of the People's Court state that Erich Honecker worked "for two years for a farmer in Neudorf near Neu-Stettin, Pomerania. In 1928 he returned to Wiebelskirchen to learn the roofing trade," (*see* Appendix). It is possible of course that this statement is based on Honecker's testimony in his own defense.
42 Information from Anti-Fascist Resistance Committee; "Erich Honecker—Kandidat der Jugend"; Honecker, "Für das Glück der Jugend," p. 6f.
43 J. W. Stalin, *Werke*, vol. VII (East Berlin, 1952), p. 34.
44 H. Weber, "Von Rosa Luxemburg zu Walter Ulbricht, Wandlungen des deutschen Kommunismus" supplement to *Das Parlament* (Bonn), July 29, 1959, p. 402f.
45 R. Chitarow, "Der Kampf um die Massen, vom II. bis zum V. Weltkongress der KJI" in *Geschichte der Kommunistischen Jugendinternationale*, Vol. III (Munich), first published by Verlag der Jugendinternationale (Berlin, 1929/31), p. 191.
46 H. Weber, *Die Wandlung des deutschen Kommunismus, die Stalinisierung der KPD in der Weimarer Republik*, vol. I (Frankfurt on the Main, 1969), p. 124ff.
47 *Zur Geschichte der Arbeiter jugendbewegung in Deutschland*, pub-

lished by the Wilhelm Pieck Youth Training College under the Central Council of the FDJ in cooperation with the Institute for Marxism-Leninism under the Central Committee of the SED (East Berlin, 1956), p. 172f.

48 Ibid., p. 172.
49 Ibid., p. 175.
50 From a speech by Ernst Thälmann to the Central Committee of the KJVD in autumn, 1932, as printed in *Junge Generation,* the FDJ Central Council's publication for its organizational leadership, vol. XV, 2nd issue of March, 1961, p. 28.
51 "Zur Geschichte der Arbeiterjugendbewegung," p. 173f.
52 "Aus dem Leben des Genossen Erich Honecker" in *Junge Welt* (East Berlin), May 4, 1971.
53 Official biography of Honecker supplied by the Anti-Fascist Resistance Committee in the DDR.
54 W. Küchenmeister, "Erich Honecker" in *Die erste Stunde,* ed. F. Selbmann (East Berlin, 1969), p. 204.
55 Ibid.
56 Ibid.
57 Ibid.; also G. Friedrich, *Die Freie Deutsche Jugend* (Rote Weissbücher, Cologne, 1953), p. 13.
58 Erich Honecker, "50 Jahre Arbeiterjugendbewegung in Deutschland" in *Junge Welt* (East Berlin), September 22, 1954.
59 "Zur Geschichte der Arbeiterbewegung," p. 219ff.
60 Ibid., p. 221f.
61 Ibid., p. 226.
62 "Zur Geschichte der Arbeiterjugend," p. 224.
63 "Aus dem Leben des Genossen Erich Honecker."
64 Weber, vol. I, p. 378f.
65 Zenner, p. 335.
66 Zenner, p. 197.
67 "Er war immer der Beste seiner Klasse" in *Der Spiegel* (Hamburg), no. 1/2, 1967, p. 36.
68 Zenner, p. 335.
69 J. Zimmermann and F. Böhm, "Sag's grad heraus, wie's unter Arbeiternüblich ist . . . , Gedanken und Notizen über den Besuch Erich Honeckers in Grossbetrieben Karl Marx-Stadt" in *Neues Deutschland* (East Berlin), May 18, 1971.
70 Information from Anti-Fascist Resistance Committee; Küchenmeister, p. 205.
71 "Aus dem Leben des Genossen Erich Honecker."
72 Speech to workers in Magnitogorsk published in *Neues Deutschland* (East Berlin), April 4, 1971.
73 Küchenmeister, p. 205.
74 E. Voltmer, "Begegnung vor 40 Jahren" in *Saarbrücker Zeitung,* May 5, 1971.
75 Küchenmeister, p. 206.
76 Zenner, p. 186.
77 Zenner, p. 205, p. 335.
78 Zenner, p. 335.
79 Erich Honecker, "Für das Glück der Jugend," p. 7.
80 Zenner, p. 260f.

81 Zenner, p. 280.
82 E. Honecker, "50 Jahre Arbeiterbewegung in Deutschland" in *Junge Welt* (East Berlin), September 22, 1954.
83 Zenner, p. 280.
84 E. Honecker, "Für das Glück der Jugend," p. 7.
85 C. Stern, *Ulbricht, eine politische Biographie* (Cologne, 1963), p. 77.
86 E. Kaiser, "Junge Kommunisten und Katholiken—eine Front" in *Junge Welt* (East Berlin), June 15 and 16, 1963.
87 Küchenmeister, p. 204.
88 Küchenmeister, p. 207.
89 E. Honecker, "Für das Glück der Jugend," p. 7f.
90 Zenner, p. 260f.
91 Zenner, p. 281.
92 Zenner, p. 316.
93 Küchenmeister, p. 208.
94 Ibid.; see also *Neues Deutschland*, August 26, 1971.
95 Here there are two conflicting accounts. Küchenmeister's biography, which was certainly authorized by Honecker, says: "The comrades in Paris said what was to be done now in Germany, in Berlin. And Herbert Jung, member of the Central Committee of the KJVD, traveled through Switzerland and saw Prague. And as Marten Tjaden of Amsterdam he crossed the frontier." (p. 208) Honecker himself, however, writing about this period in the already cited letter to young voters, says: "In Essen I was arrested for the first time. But I managed to put one over on the police and got away. Then I worked in southern Germany for the united front of working-class youth under the Central Committee of the KJVD, of which I was a member. In summer, 1935 I became KJVD secretary for Greater Berlin," ("Für das Glück der Jugend," p. 8).
96 Küchenmeister, p. 210 and "Für das Glück der Jugend," p. 8f.
97 Küchenmeister, p. 210.
98 Interview with former prisoners and members of the illegal KPD organization in the Brandenburg-Görden Prison Schwertfeger, Edu Wald and Uhlmann.
99 "Vom einfachen Arbeiterjungen zum Stellvertretenden Minister" in *Junge Generation*, vol. X, no. 3 (East Berlin, March, 1956).
100 "Er war immer der Beste seiner Klasse," p. 36.
101 R. Havemann, *Fragen—Antworten—Fragen, aus der Biographie eines deutschen Marxisten* (Munich, 1970), pp. 89–97.
102 Küchenmeister, p. 202.
103 Havemann, p. 94.
104 "Für das Glück der Jugend," p. 8f.
105 Küchenmeister, p. 203. Here again there are two conflicting accounts. According to Küchenmeister: "He escaped on March 6, 1945 at about 11 A.M. from the Berlin-Lichtenberg girls' prison. After March 6 bombs continued to fall; later the battle raged around Berlin. Could a fugitive experience the quiet of May 9 without uneasiness? He experienced it at our house." However, the official biography published in *Neues Deutschland* (May 4, 1971) after Honecker's election as First Secretary of the Central Committee of the SED stated: "After his liberation by the Soviet Army, Erich Honecker became one of the pioneer activists." See also the interview of the USSR Gov-

ernment Committee for Television and Radio with the First Secretary of the Socialist Unity Party of Germany, Comrade Erich Honecker in *Neues Deutschland*, August 26, 1971.

106 Information from the Anti-Fascist Resistance Committee.

107 Küchenmeister, p. 203.

108 W. Leonhard, *Die Revolution entlässt ihre Kinder* (Cologne, 1955), p. 348.

109 Küchenmeister, p. 203.

110 Leonhard, p. 353. Walter Ulbricht openly acknowledged this later with reference to the formation of the Greater Berlin Municipal Council in May, 1945. "Our advantage lay in being well prepared. When the Soviet troops crossed the Vistula, a commission had already been set up within our party leadership to plan the first essential measures in the struggle against Hitlerist fascism. . . . We worked out every detail, including the organization of cultural life. We also had a list of anti-Hitler people we assumed to be in Berlin, with names of communist and social democratic members of the Reichstag and other opponents of Hitler from bourgeois groups. So we arrived in Germany on April 30, 1945 well prepared. We reached Berlin on May 1, and then our work began." (Speech by Walter Ulbricht at a reception for pioneer activists at the Berlin Rathaus, May 12, 1960. Evidently because of its outspoken language, this speech was not published until five years later, when extracts from it appeared in *Neues Deutschland*, April 17, 1965.)

111 Leonhard, p. 351f.

112 Leonhard, p. 370.

113 Leonhard, p. 369.

114 H. Kessler, "Wir vertrauen der Jugend" in *Neues Deutschland*, July 31, 1965.

115 *Neues Deutschland*, April 17, 1965.

116 *Neues Deutschland*, May 5, 1960.

117 *Neues Deutschland*, April 11, 1965.

PART II

1 Leonhard, p. 406.

2 "Jugend geht neuen Weg" in *Neues Deutschland*, June 20, 1965.

3 Kessler, "Wir vertrauen der Jugend."

4 W. Ulbricht, *Zur Geschichte der deutschen Arbeiterbewegung*, vol. II (East Berlin, 1953), p. 446.

5 A. Kaden, *Einheit oder Freiheit, die Wiedergründung der SED 1945/46* (Hanover, 1964), p. 32.

6 *Der deutsche Kommunismus, Dokumente*, ed. H. Weber (Cologne/ Berlin, 1963), p. 555.

7 On a joint conference on December 20 and December 21, 1945 of the central committees of the SPD and the KPD with representatives of both parties from districts in the Soviet Zone of Occupation, see *Wir schaffen die Einheit*, Resolutions of the joint conference (East Berlin, 1946); see also E. W. Gniffke, *Jahre mit Ulbricht* (Cologne, 1966), p. 119ff.

8 *SBZ-Biographie*, published by the West German Ministry of All-German Affairs (Bonn/Berlin, 1964), p. 26f.

9 Ibid., p. 363.

10 M. Klein, *Jugend zwischen den Diktaturen, 1945/56* (Mainz, 1968), p. 21f.

11 *Geschichtliche Zeittafeln, Deutsche Demokratische Republic* (East Berlin, 1954), p. 10.

12 Ibid., p. 13. Also Gerd Friedrich, *Die Freie Deutsche Jugend* (Rote Weissbücher, Cologne, 1953), p. 21.

13 *Geschichtliche Zeittafeln*, p. 13.

14 Robert Bialek, unpublished manuscript in the possession of Frau Inge Bialek, Cologne, p. 96ff.

15 Ibid.

16 Ibid., p. 100.

17 Ibid., p. 102.

18 Robert Bialek was expelled from the SED in 1952 after prolonged conflict with the leadership over his allegations of corruption, hypocrisy, and errors of political judgment. In 1953, having been unemployed for a year and being threatened with arrest, he fled to West Germany. He became a free-lance journalist in West Berlin and worked for the BBC German-language service. In 1956 he was drugged in his West Berlin apartment and taken to the Eastern sector, where he is said to have died from an overdose of narcotics. (Bialek had a heart defect.)

19 *Dokumente der SED*, vol. IV (East Berlin, 1954), p. 407f.

20 *Die Volkskammer der DDR, 4. Wahlperiode* (East Berlin, 1964), p. 174.

21 Bialek, unpublished manuscript, p. 68f.

22 Ibid., p. 67f.

23 Ibid., p. 75.

24 Klein, p. 42f.

25 Ibid.,

26 Friedrich, p. 22.

27 *Dokumente und Beschlüsse der Freien Deutschen Jugend*, vol. I (East Berlin, 1951), p. 3.

28 Ibid.

29 *Zur Geschichte der Arbeiterjugendbewegung in Deutschland—Eine Auswahl von Materialien und Dokumente* (East Berlin, 1956), p. 366.

30 H. Weber, *Ulbricht fälscht Geschichte* (Cologne, 1964), appendix.

31 *Wir sind die junge Garde*, ed. H. Thur, published by the Central Council of the FDJ (East Berlin, 1971), p. 43.

32 Friedrich, p. 22f.

33 *Protokoll des Vereinigungsparteitages* (East Berlin, 1946), p. 204.

34 Klein, p. 51.

35 *Erstes Parlament der Freien Deutschen Jugend, Brandenburg an der Havel, Pfingsten 1946* (East Berlin, 1946), p. 45.

36 Ibid., p. 46.

37 Bialek, unpublished manuscript, p. 133.

38 *Erstes Parlament der FDJ*, p. 203.

39 Bialek, unpublished manuscript, p. 137.

40 Klein, p. 59.

41 Ibid., p. 61f.

42 Bialek, unpublished manuscript, p. 141f.

43 Ibid., p. 143.

44 Ibid., p. 144.
45 Ibid., p. 162ff.
46 *Dokumente zur Geschichte der Freien Deutschen Jugend,* vol. I (East Berlin, 1960), pp. 61–63.
47 Friedrich, p. 32.
48 Ibid., p. 36f.
49 E. W. Gniffke, "Leserbrief" in *Der Spiegel* (Hamburg), March 3, 1958.
50 The motion "that the FDJ resolve that to use force in any way in political life, or to advocate its use, automatically result in expulsion from the FDJ." Adapted from Klein, p. 80.
51 *Dokumente zur Geschichte der FDJ,* vol. I, p. 78.
52 Ibid.
53 *Protokoll des II. Parlamentes der Freien Deutschen Jugend* (East Berlin, 1947), p. 111f.
54 Ibid., p. 113.
55 Ibid.
56 Ibid., p. 126.
57 Ibid., p. 127f.
58 Ibid., p. 129.
59 Ibid., p. 124.
60 Ibid., p. 124f.
61 Ibid., p. 124ff.
62 Ibid., p. 49.
63 E. Honecker, *Friedensflug nach Osten,* in collaboration with Herbert Geissler (East Berlin, 1947), p. 45.
64 Ibid.
65 "Historisches Ereignis: Vor 20 Jahren flog die erste FDJ-Delegation nach Moskau" in *Junge Welt* (East Berlin), July 21, 1967.
66 *Friedensflug nach Osten,* p. 31.
67 Ibid., p. 49.
68 Ibid., p. 71.
69 Friedrich, p. 48f.
70 Horst Brasch, born Dec. 23, 1922 in Berlin, son of a Jewish merchant but brought up as a Catholic, attended the *Realgymnasium.* For "racial reasons" had to become a toolmaker's apprentice. Emigrated to England in 1939, where he became a metalworker. During World War II joined the refugee KPD group and worked with the pro-Communist cultural league in England. In 1939, on its instructions, founded the FDJ, which resolved at its seventh congress in April, 1946 "to become part of the Free German Youth."

In 1945 Brasch was the only German participant in the London world youth meeting. In 1946 he attended the executive meeting of the WBDJ in Paris. From there he returned to Berlin, where he joined the SED and became the official FDJ representative in Berlin. Honecker had appointed him to this position, assuming that because of his refugee years in England he would have a good knowledge of languages and because of his Jewish background would have a better chance of persuading the Western authorities in Berlin to recognize the FDJ.

Brasch was also on the editorial staff of *Junge Generation* and was a co-editor of *Neues Leben.* In October, 1948, he became first chairman of the Brandenburg branch of the FDJ and in May, 1949, a

member of the Third People's Congress. At the third FDJ congress
he was elected to the Central Council and the secretariat, in charge
of agitation and propaganda. In 1951 he became minister of education
for Brandenburg, and also served as chairman of the Cottbus County
Council for several years. From 1957 to 1959 he was first chairman
of the Neubrandenburg County Council and a member of the SED
county leadership. In April, 1959, he became first chairman of the
office of the Presidium of the National Council of the National Front
and vice-president of the National Council.

From 1960 to 1964 he was chairman of the Committee for Solidarity
with the Peoples of Africa and since the Sixth Congress of January,
1963, has been a member of the Central Committee of the SED. Since
July, 1963, he has been vice-president of the German-British Society
of the DDR. That same year he became a member of the *Volkskammer*
of the DDR. In the late 1960s he was made second secretary of the
Karl Marx Stadt branch of the SED. He was reelected to the Central
Committee at the Eighth Congress.

One of Brasch's two sons was imprisoned for a short time for
public protest against the occupation of Czechoslovakia in 1968.

71 *Dokumente und Beschlüsse der FDJ,* vol. I, p. 32f.
72 Ibid., p. 28f.
73 Friedrich, p. 51.
74 W. Weiskirch, "Spalteraktivist" in *Rheinischer Merkur,* May 14, 1971.
75 *Protokoll des II. Parlaments der FDJ,* p. 118.
76 Statement of the FDJ delegation at the interzonal meeting of German
   youth organizations at Haus Altenberg near Cologne, published in
   Junge Generation, no. 3, 1948 (East Berlin), p. 68.
77 Weiskirch.
78 Friedrich, p. 52.
79 *Friedensflug nach Osten,* pp. 116 and 130.
80 Personal statement of Horst Brasch to the author.
81 Ibid.
82 *Dokumente zur Geschichte der FDJ,* vol. I, p. 176f.
83 Ibid., p. 177ff.
84 Ibid., p. 176.
85 Ibid., pp. 62–65.
86 Friedrich, p. 60.
87 *Protokoll des III. Parlamentes der FDJ* (East Berlin, 1949), p. 22.
88 Ibid.
89 *Dokumente zur Geschichte der FDJ,* vol. I, p. 176.
90 Ibid., p. 43f.
91 Bialek, unpublished manuscript, p. 253.
92 *Protokoll des III. Parlamentes der FDJ,* p. 23.
93 Ibid., p. 31.
94 *Die sowjetische Besatzungszone Deutschlands in den Jahren 1945
   bis 1954, eine chronologische Übersicht* (Bonn, 1955), p. 106.
95 Friedrich, p. 86f.
96 Ibid., p. 87.
97 "Gelöbnis der deutschen Jugend anlässlich der Gründung der DDR"
   in *Dokumente und Beschlüsse der Freien Deutschen Jugend,* vol. II
   (East Berlin, 1951), p. 482f.
98 E. Honecker, "Schritt in die Freiheit" in *Junge Generation,* no. 11,

November, 1949 (East Berlin), p. 482f.

99 E. Kaiser, "Junge Kommunisten und Katholiken—eine Front" in *Junge Welt* (East Berlin), June 15 and 16, 1963.

100 Friedrich, p. 109.

101 However, in the *Liederbuch der deutschen Jugend* (East Berlin, 1954, p. 42f) the title has been changed back to "The Free German Youth Storms Berlin."

102 Friedrich, p. 110.

103 "Adenauers Polizei muss kaptiulieren!" in *Junge Welt* (East Berlin) June 2, 1950.

104 *Geschichtliche Zeittafeln*, p. 41.

105 E. Honecker, "Offener Brief an alle Mitglieder und Funktionäre der FDJ" in *Junge Generation*, no. 5/6, 1950 (East Berlin), p. 194f.

106 H. Weber, *Die Sozialistische Einheitspartei Deutschlands, 1946/71* (Hanover, 1971), p. 205.

107 *Dokumente zur Geschichte der FDJ*, vol. II, pp. 109–112.

108 *SBZ von 1945 bis 1954*, published by the West German Ministry of All-German Affairs (Bonn, 1955), p. 140.

109 Friedrich, p. 97.

110 *SBZ von 1945 bis 1954*, p. 142.

111 E. Honecker, "Die Freie Deutsche Jugend verkörpert die grosse Zukunft unseres Volkes" in *Neues Deutschland*, March 9, 1951.

112 Bialek, unpublished manuscript, pp. 415–418.

113 *Dokumente zur Geschichte der Freien Deutschen Jugend*, vol. II, p. 247f.

114 E. Honecker, "Die Freie Deutsche Jugend verkörpert die grosse Zukunft unseres Volkes."

115 E. Honecker, "Stalinbanner weht über Sachsen-Anhalt," speech at the concluding ceremony of the Mobilization for Stalin on August 12, 1951, published in *Junge Welt* (East Berlin), August 13, 1951.

116 *Dokumente zur Geschichte der FDJ*, vol. II, p. 224ff.

117 Ibid., p. 397f.

118 Ibid., p. 400f.

119 Ibid., p. 339f.

120 *SBZ von 1945 bis 1954*, p. 174.

121 *Protokoll des IV. Parlaments der Freien Deutschen Jugend*, published by the Central Council of the FDJ (East Berlin, 1952), p. 17.

122 Ibid., pp. 18, 72.

123 Ibid., pp. 28f., 31f., 71.

124 Ibid., p. 58.

125 Ibid., p. 71.

126 Ibid., p. 43.

127 Ibid., p. 240.

128 Ibid., pp. 19, 23f.

129 Ibid., p. 71.

130 Ibid., p. 438f.

131 E. Honecker, "Aufgaben der Jugend im Kampf für Frieden, Einheit, Demokratie und Sozialismus," speech at the second session of the FDJ Central Council, August 14, 1952, in Halle, published in *Tägliche Rundschau* (East Berlin), August 16, 1952.

132 Ibid.

133 Ibid.

134 Material taken from *SBZ-Biographie,* a biographical reference work on the Soviet Zone of Occupation, published by the West German Ministry of All-German Affairs (Bonn/Berlin, 1965), p. 155.

135 *SBZ von 1945 bis 1954,* p. 245f.

136 E. Honecker, "Über das Leben der Jugend in unserer Republik und in Westdeutschland," speech to the sixth session of the Central Council of the FDJ, published in *Junge Welt* (East Berlin), August 22, 1953.

137 *Geschichtliche Zeittafeln,* p. 69.

138 E. Honecker, "Über die Verwirklichung der Beschlüsse der 6. Tagung des Zentralrates und die nächsten Aufgaben der FDJ" in *Junge Welt* (East Berlin), January 14, 1954.

139 Ibid.

140 Ibid.

141 E. Honecker, "Pflichten und Aufgaben der Partei gegenüber der Jugend, in *Neues Deutschland,* March 21, 1954.

142 E. Honecker, "Der Marxismus-Leninismus ist unbesiegbar" in *Neues Deutschland,* January 22, 1954.

143 Ibid.

144 "Die Funktionäre der FDJ sind wenig unter der Jugend" in *Neues Deutschland,* September 7, 1954.

145 "Treffen Deutscher Bundesjugendring—Zentralrat der FDJ" in *Junge Welt* (East Berlin), March 11, 1955.

146 *SBZ von 1955 bis 1958, Taschenbuchausgabe,* published by the West German Ministry of All-German Affairs (Bonn/Berlin, 1961), p. 30f.

147 E. Honecker, "Vereint für den Frieden und das Glück der Heimat," report of the Central Council to the fifth FDJ congress, published in *Tägliche Rundschau* (East Berlin), May 26, 1955.

148 *SBZ von 1955 bis 1958,* p. 52f.

149 A. Norden, speech to the 25th plenary session of the Central Committee of the SED in October, 1955, as quoted in H. P. Herz, *Freie Deutsche Jugend* (Munich, 1965), p. 146.

PART III

1 Other biographies state that Honecker took a two-year course in the Soviet Union. This is incorrect. In May, 1955, he was the main speaker at the fifth FDJ congress, and in October, 1956, he was already appearing again in public in the DDR. See "Erich Honecker im Berliner VEB Elektro-Kohle. Wir sehen mit den Augen des Arbeiters" in *Neues Deutschland,* October 30, 1956 and "Aus dem Leben des Genossen Erich Honecker" in *Neues Deutschland,* May 4, 1971.

2 W. Leonhard, *Kreml ohne Stalin* (Cologne/Berlin, 1962), pp. 97f, 101–113ff.

3 "Die FDJ verkörpert die grosse Zukunft unseres Volkes" in *Neues Deutschland,* March 9, 1951.

4 *Neues Deutschland,* February 14, 1956, as quoted in Weber, *Die Sozialistische Einheitspartei,* p. 18.

5 "Erich Honecker im Berliner VEB Elektro-Kohle. Wir sehen mit den Augen des Arbeiters" in *Neues Deutschland,* October 30, 1956.

6 H. Weber, *Von der SBZ zur DDR, 1945–1968* (Hanover, 1968), p. 118.

7 Ibid.
8 Politburo report at the 30th session of the Central Committee, publ. in *Volkswacht* (Gera), February 4, 1957.
9 Ibid.
10 Ibid.
11 Ibid.
12 Ibid.
13 "Die Staatsmacht der Arbeiter und Bauern stärken" in *Neues Deutschland*, March 14, 1957.
14 H. Brandt, *Ein Traum, der nicht entführbar ist. Mein Weg zwischen Ost und West* (Munich, 1967), pp. 326–330.
15 Ibid.
16 Weber, *Von der SBZ zur DDR*, p. 121.
17 Ibid.
18 Ibid.
19 Ibid.
20 M. Jänicke, *Der dritte Weg* (Cologne), pp. 53–90.
21 Ibid., p. 93f.
22 Ibid.
23 E. Honecker, "Aus dem Bericht des Politbüros an das 35. Plenum des Zentralkomitees der SED" in *Neues Deutschland*, February 8, 1958.
24 Weber, *Die Sozialistische Einheitspartei*, p. 21.
25 H. Brandt, *Ein Traum* . . . , pp. 326–330.
26 E. Honecker, "Aus dem Bericht des Politbüros an das 35. Plenum des Zentralkomitees der SED."
27 Ibid.
28 Ibid.
29 Weber, *Die Sozialistische Einheitspartei*, p. 20.
30 *Protokoll der Verhandlungen des V. Parteitages der Sozialistischen Einheitspartei Deutschlands, 10 bis 16.7.1958 in der Werner-Seelenbinder-Halle zu Berlin*, vol. I (East Berlin, 1959), p. 70.
31 "Erich Honecker bei Kali-Kumpeln" in *Neues Deutschland*, October 11, 1958; "Lieber auf die Stimme der Arbeiter hören" in *Neues Deutschland*, October 18, 1958; "Erich Honecker in Illmenau" in *Thüringer Volkszeitung* (Weimar), November 8, 1958.
32 E. Honecker, "Es geht um die straffe Führung durch Partei- und Staatsapparat" in *Volkswacht* (Gera), June 10, 1959.
33 E. Honecker, "Schutz der friedlichen Aufbauarbeit," documentary supplement to *Die Volksarmee* (East Berlin), July 18, 1958, p. 4.
34 Ibid., p. 2.
35 H. Hoffmann, "Lenins militärisches Erbe und die Landesverteidigung der DDR" in *Einheit*, no. 11, 1969 (East Berlin), pp. 1323–1335.
36 Ibid., p. 1326.
37 E. Honecker, "Schutz der friedlichen Aufbauarbeit," p. 2.
38 A. Mallinckrodt-Dasbach, *Propaganda hinter der Mauer* (Stuttgart, 1971), pp. 73–83.
39 Ibid., p. 81.
40 Ibid.
41 H. Hoffmann, "Der 13. August 1961" in *Neues Deutschland*, August 13, 1971.
42 E. Honecker, "Das Leben selbst hat entschieden: Der Sozialismus repräsentiert die Zukunft der Menschheit," speech to "fighters and

officers," published in *Der Kämpfer,* no. 3, March, 1961 (East Berlin), p. 3.

43 "Unsere Stimme, ein Faustschlag gegen Bonner Ultras, Genosse Erich Honecker bei den Werktätigen und bei unserer Grenzpolizei des Kreises Bad Salzungen" in *Freies Wort* (Erfurt), September 16, 1961.

44 E. Honecker, "Waffenträger der Nation" in *Volksarmee,* no. 9, 1962 (East Berlin).

45 "Bitte schön, kommt hervor, wenn ihr tanzen wollt" in *Leipziger Volkszeitung,* August 19, 1961.

46 Defense Law of the DDR (Sept. 20, 1961) as published in *Neues Deutschland,* September 21, 1961.

47 E. Honecker, "Inden Grundorganisationen werden bewusste aktive Kämpfer erzogen," discussion speech at the 14th session of the Central Committee of the SED, published in *Neues Deutschland,* December 1, 1961.

48 Ibid.

49 Ibid.

50 "Erich Honecker in Suhl, Ulbricht—das sind wir alle" in *Neues Deutschland,* September 17, 1961.

51 E. Honecker, "Parteiwahlen—Beweis höherer Kampfkraft," discussion speech at the 16th session of the Central Committee of the SED, published in *Neues Deutschland,* July 1, 1962.

52 E. Honecker, "Ehrenamtliche Tätigkeit, Massstab für neue Qualität der Parteiarbeit" in *Neues Deutschland,* October 19, 1962.

53 "Das Parteistatut der Sozialistischen Einheitspartei Deutschlands," E. Honecker's report to the Sixth SED Congress, published in *Neues Deutschland,* January 20, 1963.

54 *Junge Welt* (East Berlin), January 10 and February 20, 1963. See also Weber, *Von der SBZ zur DDR,* p. 172f.

55 "Wissenschaftlichkeit in der Parteiarbeit, enges Vertrauensverhältnis zu allen Bürgern," E. Honecker's closing speech to the 4th session of the Central Committee, published in *Neues Deutschland,* November 6, 1963.

56 H. Sindermann, "Aus dem Bericht des Politbüros an das 5. Plenum des Zentralkomitees" in *Neues Deutschland,* February 13, 1964. Also "Die Vorbereitung der Parteiwahlen 1964," E. Honecker's report to the 5th session of the Central Committee of the SED, in *Neues Deutschland,* February 12, 1964.

57 "Anforderungen an führende Rolle der Partei wachsen," discussion speech by E. Honecker, published in *Neues Deutschland,* December 5, 1964.

58 From Walter Ulbricht's speech to the 7th session of the Central Committee of the SED, published in *Neues Deutschland,* December 6, 1964.

59 "Anforderungen an führende Rolle der Partei wachsen."

60 Ibid.

61 E. Honecker, Politbüro report to the 11th session of the SED Central Committee, published in *Neues Deutschland,* December 16, 1965.

62 M. Lange, "Wissenschaftlichkeit und Kontinuität unserer Kulturpolitik" in *Einheit,* no. 11, 1965 (East Berlin).

63 W. Dorst, "Erziehung zur gesellschaftlichen Verantwortung" in *Einheit*, no. 11, 1965 (East Berlin).

64 E. Honecker, Politbüro report to the 11th session of the SED Central Committee, published in *Neues Deutschland*, December 16, 1965.

65 E. Honecker, report to the 35th plenary session of the SED Central Committee, February 8, 1958.

66 "Anforderungen an führende Rolle der Partei wachsen."

67 E. Honecker, "Die deutsche Frage kann nur durch Verständigung der Arbeiter gelöst werden" in *Neues Deutschland*, May 13, 1966. E. Honecker, "Weg ebnen für das künftige Vaterland der Deutschen" in *Berliner Zeitung* (East Berlin), May 13, 1966. E. Honecker, "Zur gegenwärtigen Situation und zum Meinungsaustausch SED/SPD" in *Leipziger Volkszeitung*, May 13, 1966.

68 "Die deutsche Frage kann nur durch Verständigung der Arbeiter gelöst werden," E. Honecker's speech to the Berlin SED executive, published in *Neues Deutschland*, May 13, 1966.

69 H. Weber and F. Oldenburg, *25 Jahre SED*, p. 164.

70 "Die Rolle der Partei in der Periode der Vollendung des Sozialismus," E. Honecker's speech to the Seventh Congress of the SED, April 17–22, 1967 (East Berlin, 1967), p. 55.

71 Ibid., p. 58.

72 Ibid., p. 59.

73 Ibid., p. 60.

74 E. Honecker, "Bruderbund, SED und KPdSU" in *Neues Deutschland*, October 26, 1967.

75 "Unsere Zusammenarbeit verkörpert internationale Beziehungen neuen Typs," E. Honecker's speech at the Novovoronezh atomic plant, published in *Neues Deutschland*, November 10, 1967.

76 "Führende Rolle der Partei, Wesensmerkmal unserer sozialistischen Ordnung," E. Honecker's discussion speech at the 4th session of the SED Central Committee, published in *Neues Deutschland*, June 8, 1968.

77 "Auf unsere Partei war und wird in allen Situationen immer Verlass sein," E. Honecker's speech at the 9th session of the SED Central Committee, published in *Neues Deutschland*, October 27, 1968.

78 E. Honecker, Politbüro report to the 10th session of the SED Central Committee (East Berlin, 1969), p. 71f.

79 E. Honecker, speech commemorating the Day of Peace, Friendship between Nations and Internationalism, published in *Neues Deutschland*, November 8, 1969.

80 W. Jarowinsky, "Aus dem Bericht des Politbüros an die 12. Tagung des ZK der SED," discussion speech published in *Neues Deutschland*, December 13, 1969.

81 "Eine entscheidende Phase der gesellschaftlichen Entwicklung in der DDR," E. Honecker's discussion speech at the 12th session of the SED Central Committee, published in *Neues Deutschland*, December 16, 1956.

82 Defense Minister Heinz Hoffmann's speech at the 12th session of the Central Committee, published in *Neues Deutschland*, December 16, 1969.

83 Ibid.

84 "20 Jahre zuverlässiger Schutz des Friedens und des Sozialismus,"

E. Honecker's speech on the 20th anniversary of the Ministry of State Security, published in *Neues Deutschland*, February 7, 1970.

85 Ibid.

86 E. Mielke, "Kompromissloser Kampf gegen die Feinde des Friedens und des Sozialismus," speech on the 20th anniversary of the Ministry of State Security, published in *Neues Deutschland*, February 8, 1970.

87 "Mit dem Blick auf das Jahr 2000, Die Aufgaben von heute lösen," E. Honecker's speech at the Karl Marx Party Training College, February 16, 1970, evaluating the 12th session of the SED Central Committee (East Berlin, 1970), pp. 65 and 68.

88 "Zu den Lehren der Geschichte und einigen aktuellen politischen Fragen," E. Honecker's speech at the Karl Marx Party Training College, published in *Neues Deutschland*, February 22, 1970.

89 Questionnaire on problems of socialist historical consciousness, Karl Marx University, Leipzig. Questions 19 and 20 read as follows:
19. What is your idea of a solution to the present national problem?
(a) The formation of a unified national state.
(b) Everybody living in a certain territory acknowledges that he is part of the nation and works for it.
(c) The achievement of national independence or self-determination and national unity on the basis of peace, democracy, and progress, under the leadership of the working class and its Marxist-Leninist party.
20. How can the German national problem be solved?
(a) If both sides in both Germanys give way.
(b) If the technological revolution brings socialism and capitalism so close together that the differences between the two Germanys gradually disappear.
(c) If the working class and the progressive forces in West Germany overcome imperialism and militarism and a unified socialist German national state arises in unison with the DDR.
(d) Do you think that the rapid progress of socialist development in the DDR will prevent reunification and hence the solution of the national problem of Germany?
This questionnaire is thirty pages long and contains 94 questions. The original is in the possession of the author.

90 "DDR—Vertragsentwurf—einzige Grundlage für Übereinkommen," interview with Willi Stoph on entering the DDR, in *Neues Deutschland*, May 22, 1970.

91 W. Ulbricht, "Den Rechtsblock in der Bundesrepublik gemeinsam schlagen!" speech of the First Secretary of the Central Committee and Chairman of the DDR Council of State, in *Neues Deutschland*, July 17, 1970.

92 W. Ulbricht, "Die politische Vorbereitung des VIII Parteitages" in *Neues Deutschland*, January 30, 1971.

93 "Die 16. Tagung des Zentralkomitees der SED" in *Neues Deutschland*, May 4, 1971.

94 V. I. Lenin, "Leftist Radicalism, Communism's Childhood Disease," translated from the German text in *Ausgewählte Schriften*, ed. H. Weber (Munich, 1963), p. 981.

95 W. Hänisch, "Probleme der internationalen Stellung der DDR" in *Deutsche Aussenpolitik*, no. 2, 1970 (East Berlin), p. 187ff.

96 Leonid Brezhnev, "Unsere Völker bauen gemeinsam eine neue Welt auf," speech of the Secretary General of the Central Committee of the CPSU at the 20th congress of the Hungarian Socialist Workers Party, published in *Neues Deutschland*, November 25, 1970.

97 For a complete account see Harald Ludwig (pseudonym of Heinz Lippmann), "Die SED vor dem VIII Parteitag" in *Deutschland Archiv*, no. 6/71 (Cologne), pp. 584–597.

98 W. Ulbricht, "XXIV. Parteitag wird unser Kompass sein," address of the leader of the SED delegation, First Secretary of the Central Committee and President of the DDR Council of State, published in *Neues Deutschland*, April 1, 1971.

99 "Vom hohen Rang der 16. Tagung" in *Neues Deutschland*, May 6, 1971.

100 W. Ulbricht, "Die politische Vorbereitung des VIII Parteitages."

101 E. Honecker, report of the SED Central Committee delegation on the XXIV Congress of the CPSU delivered to the 16th session of the SED Central Committee, May 3, 1971 (East Berlin, 1971), p. 9.

102 Ibid., pp. 16 and 19f.

103 *Neue Zürcher Zeitung*, March 29, 1971.

104 "Zycie Warszawy zu Verhandlungen über Westberlin" in *Neues Deutschland*, April 16, 1971.

105 "Fälscher am Werk" in *Neues Deutschland*, April 17, 1971.

106 "Die Botschafter behandeln konkrete Fragen" in *Frankfurter Allgemeine Zeitung*, May 26, 1971.

107 "Glückwünsche an Genossen Erich Honecker," congratulatory message of Soviet Ambassador Pjotr Abrassimov to E. Honecker, published in *Neues Deutschland*, May 5, 1971.

108 Reported in *Neues Deutschland*, April 21, 1971.

109 "Sowjetunion wird immer an eurer Seite sein," congratulatory message of the CPSU Central Committee, published in *Neues Deutschland*, April 21, 1966.

110 "Ein Erfolg für alle, die den Frieden wünschen. Walter Ulbricht zum Westberlin-Abkommen," ADN interview with the chairman of the Council of State of the DDR, published in *Neues Deutschland*, September 7, 1971.

111 "P. A. Abrassimow bei Walter Ulbricht" in *Neues Deutschland*, August 25, 1971.

112 I. Spittmann, "Warum Ulbricht stürtzte" in *Deutschland Archiv*, no. 6/71 (Cologne), p. 568.

113 *Neues Deutschland*, June 20, 1971, on members of the SED Central Committee.

114 E. Honecker, report of the Central Committee to the Eighth Congress of the SED, published in *Neues Deutschland*, June 16, 1971.

115 Ibid.

116 Ibid.

117 Spittmann, p. 568.

118 E. Honecker, Central Committee report to the Eighth SED Congress.

119 W. Ulbricht, "Die gesellschaftliche Entwicklung in der DDR bis zur Vollendung des Sozialismus," speech to the Seventh SED Congress (East Berlin, 1967), p. 83.

120 E. Honecker, Central Committee report to the Eighth SED Congress.

121 H. Tisch, "Freundschaft zur UdSSR—nie versiegender Kraftquell,"

speech at the Seventh SED Congress, published in *Neues Deutschland*, June 18, 1971.

122 "Die Direktive" in *Neues Deutschland*, June 26, 1971.

123 See *Neues Deutschland*, August 2, 5, 7, 16, 17, 21, 24, and 26, 1971.

124 E. Honecker, Central Committee report to the Eighth SED Congress.

125 J. Kuczinski, "Mein Genosse Erich Honecker" in *Die Weltbühne*, no. 24, 1971 (East Berlin).

126 J. Dornberg, *Deutschlands andere Hälfte, Profil und Charakter der DDR* (Munich, 1970), p. 96.

Index

Abrassimov, Pjotr A., 222–23
Ackermann, Anton, 114, 157
Adenauer, Konrad, 127, 138, 139, 161, 162, 218
Ahlers, Conrad, 222
Amft, Emil, 61–62
Angenforth, Josef (Jupp), 103
Apel, Erich, 194, 199
Ardenne, Manfred von, 238
Asriel, André, 118
Axen, Hermann, 38, 53–55, 59, 77, 101, 110–11, 160, 215
Axen, Rolf, 53–54

Bachmann, Ingeborg, 194
Bagdasch, Khaled, 205
Bartel, Walter, 147
Barthel, Kurt, 118
Bäsel, Fritz, 25
Bauer, Leo, 151
Baum, Bruno, 30, 241–48
Baumann, Edith, 37, 44–45, 59, 61, 65, 69, 80, 82, 86–90, 94–95, 101, 111, 112, 144, 149
Becher, Johannes R., 152, 179
Becker, Emil, 15
Behrens, Friedrich, 179
Benary, Arne, 179
Bialek, Robert, 50–57, 65, 67–72, 95–96, 102, 129–30
Biehl, Reinhard, 114
Biermann, Wolf, 194, 198, 200
Bismarck, Klaus von, 94
Blanck, Theodor, 162
Bodin, Major, 70
Böhm, Rudolf, 61
Borning, Walter, 184
Bouisson, Guy de, 92
Brandt, Willy, 197, 201, 208–13
Brasch, Horst, 81, 91–93, 112–13
Bräunig, Werner, 198
Brezhnev, Leonid, 198–99, 215, 219–21
Bulganin, Nikolai, 172

Clay, Lucius D., 85

Dahlem, Franz, 128, 142, 153, 236
Denis, Jacques, 107
Dibelius, Otto, 72
Dickel, Friedrich, 227
Dölling, Rudolf, 147
Dubček, Alexander, 212
Dyk, Leo, 46

Ebert, Friedrich (Fritz), 142, 157, 236
Ehmke, Horst, 212

Eisler, Gerhard, 151
Ende, Lex, 151
Engels, Friedrich, 126, 164, 173, 219

Fechner, Max, 44
Feist, Manfred, 149, 227
Feist, Margot, 123, 127, 133, 149–50, 157, 227
Felfe, Werner, 164, 226
Fischer, Ernst, 195
Fischer, Lena, 54
Fischer, Ruth, 18–19
Fodorovà, Sarah, 30, 241–42, 244, 247–51
Frisch, Max, 194
Funke, Otto, 91

Geisler, Herbert, 88–90
Gerats, Hans, 69–70
Gerlach, Manfred, 133, 228
Glückauf, Erich, 161
Goebbels, Joseph, 142
Goethe, Johann Wolfgang von, 78
Goldstein, Kurt, 102–03
Gomulka, Vladislav, 176
Götting, Gerald, 133, 228
Gromyko, Andrei, 213
Grosse, Fritz, 55
Grotewohl, Otto, 61, 106, 109, 118, 128, 137, 142, 154–55, 157, 159, 172
Gruber, Dr., 94

Hager, Kurt, 179, 225
Hanisch, Oswald, 37, 46–47, 59, 61, 70, 87
Harich, Wolfgang, 175
Hartwig, Helmut, 123
Havemann, Robert, 32, 34, 195
Heidenreich, Gerhard, 70–71, 110, 112–14, 128, 226
Heilmann, Peter, 110, 115–16
Heinemann, Gustav, 211
Helsgen, 12
Henselmann, Herrmann, 142
Herde, Klaus, 110
Herrmann, Joachim, 105, 114, 228
Herrnstadt, Rudolf, 142, 144, 157, 159, 165, 191
Hertwig, Hans-Joachim, 224
Heym, Stephan, 198
Hitler, Adolf, 28, 42, 56, 84, 244

Hoffmann, Ernst, 101
Hoffmann, Karl-Heinz, 147, 184–87, 210
Honecker, Erika, 95
Honecker, Gertrud, 4
Honecker, Karl-Robert, 4–5
Honecker, Katharina, 4
Honecker, Sonya, 235
Honecker, Wilhelm, Jr., 4–5
Honecker, Wilhelm, Sr., 4–11, 13–16, 23–25, 33, 242
Hönisch, Erich, 112–13
Hoppstädter, Gertrud, 4
Horn, Ernst, 84, 110

Jahn, Günther, 228
Jendretzky, Hans, 128, 132–33, 142, 144, 147, 157
Jordan, Dr., 94
Jung, Herbert (Honecker's pseudonym), 28, 246

Kaiser, Ewald, 28, 116–17
Keilson, Grete, 35
Keller, Gottfried, 78
Kerstholt, Ludgera, 80
Kessler, Heinz, 37, 41–42, 45–46, 50, 59, 61, 64, 81, 88, 94, 110–13, 123, 227
Keusch, Hannes, 164–65
Khrushchev, Nikita S., 172, 176–78, 180, 186, 192, 196–97
Kiesler, Bruno, 227
Klein, Fritz, 61–62
Klein, Manfred, 47, 58, 61, 70, 79
Komin, Hauptmann, 86
Köppler, Heinrich, 165
Krämer, Karl, 15
Kreikemeyer, Willi, 151
Krolikowski, Werner, 225
Küchenmeister, Klaus, 35–36
Küchenmeister, Vera, 35–36
Kuczynski, Jürgen, 235
Kühn, Lotte, 157
Külkens, Hein, 61
Kurella, Alfred, 64
Kurella, Grischa, 64

Lamberz, Werner, 225–27
Lange, Ingeburg (Inge), 227
Lange, Robert, 37, 46, 59, 61, 70, 87
Lautenbach, Edwin, 30, 241–42

Ledwohn, Josef, 117
Lemnitz, Alfred, 150
Lenin, Vladimir I., 7, 13, 19, 126, 163–67, 171–76, 191, 195, 204–11, 218–20, 236
Leonhard, Wolfgang, 114
Libun, Sarah, 241
Liebknecht, Karl, 6–7, 11
Liebknecht, Kurt, 142–43
Lindstädt, Erich, 94
Lorenz, Siegfried, 227
Luxemburg, Rosa, 6–7, 11

Mao Tse-tung, 207
Mark, 245
Marx, Karl, 3, 126, 151, 164, 167, 171, 173, 191, 195, 205 07, 212, 236
Mascher, Hans-Wolfram, 165
Maslow, Arkadi, 18–19
Matern, Hermann, 56, 142, 146–48, 159, 236
Mauermann, Albert, 251
Menzel, Robert, 33, 88, 226
Merkel, Heinz, 106–07
Merker, Paul, 142, 151
Meyer (prison guard), 31
Michailov, Nicolai, 91
Mielke, Erich, 102, 211
Miessner, Rudolf, 61
Mochalski, Herbert, 133
Modrow, Hans, 227
Molotov, Vyacheslav, 178
Morgenstern, Karl, 110, 112–13
Mückenberger, Erich, 142
Müller, Fritz, 227
Müller, Johannes, 32
Müller, Kurt, 33, 115
Müller, Philipp, 134

Namokel, Karl, 103
Naumann, Konrad, 226
Nelken, Peter, 65
Neumann, Alfred, 33, 172, 178–79, 227
Neumann, Franz, 163
Norden, Albert, 167, 225
Noske, Gustav, 11

Oelssner, Fred, 128, 132, 142, 144–45, 157, 177–78
Ollenhauer, Erich, 163

Orlow (party secretary), 154

Perrey, 94
Petri, Herrmann, 7
Pieck, Wilhelm, 27, 44, 56–57, 61, 62, 82, 98, 106, 109, 112, 137, 142, 146–49, 179, 191

Rau, Heinrich, 142–43, 147, 157
Rehan, Arne, 105
Reimann, Max, 109, 115
Reuter, Ernst, 128–30
Ridgway, Matthew B., 138
Röbelen, Gustav, 184
Robertson, Brian H., 85
Röchling, Herrmann, 10
Rollack, Gerhard, 37, 61
Rommerskirchen, Josef, 80, 94
Rosenberg, Hans, 160
Rossaint, Chaplain, 28, 117

Scheel, Walter, 208, 209
Schelepin, 161
Schilling (prison guard), 31–32
Schirdewan, Karl, 172, 176–82, 189, 191, 201, 208, 217
Schmidt, Elli, 142, 147, 157
Schmidt, Waldemar, 33
Schmotz, Dieter, 57
Schön, Otto, 122, 144–46, 149
Schönecker, Hans, 123
Schröder, Gerhard, 162
Schumacher, Kurt, 127
Schumann, Horst, 178, 226
Seibt, Kurt, 216
Selbmann, Fritz, 155, 177–78
Semyonov, Vladimir, 75, 153–54, 158
Sindermann, Horst, 195, 225
Singer, Rudolf (Rudi), 228
Sperling, Fritz, 115
Spillner, Irmgard, 110
Spittmann, Ilse, 224
Stahlmann, Richard, 160
Stalin, Josef W., 18, 42, 75, 120–21, 125–26, 131, 136, 140, 151–52, 163–64, 172–78, 190–92
Stepanov, 64
Stern, Heinz, 114
Stern, Viktor, 114
Stoph, Willi, 212–16, 225, 227–28
Strauss, Franz-Joseph, 192

Stumm, Karl Friedrich von, 3, 4, 5,
    10

Teller, Günther, 228
Thälmann, Ernst, 20, 22
Tisch, Harry, 228, 231
Tito, Josip B., 115
Tjaden, Marten (Honecker's pseu-
    donym), 30, 245
Truman, Harry S, 127
Tscheile, Werner, 57
Tulpanov, Sergei, 64, 75

Uhland, Ludwig, 78
Ulbricht, Walter, 17, 18, 24, 28,
    35–37, 42, 44, 62, 63, 79–84, 98,
    102–12, 121–30, 133, 137–60,
    163–67, 172–98, 203, 208, 211–36

Verner, Paul, 45, 50, 53, 57–65, 70–
    72, 77, 81, 82, 101–02, 111–12,
    127, 215, 225
Vieweg, Kurt, 179
Voltmer, Erich, 25

Waltz, Max, 13
Wandel, Paul, 179
Warnke, Herbert, 228

Weber, Hermann, 62
Wehner, Herbert, 202
Weidenhof, Karoline, 4–10, 12, 14,
    33
Weidenhof, Ludwig, 17
Weinand, 245
Weiskirch, Willi, 94
Weiss, Peter, 194
Wenzel, Heinz, 144
Westphal, Heinz, 94
Wiechert, Theo, 37, 45, 61
Woituczek, Kurt, 70
Wolf, Christa, 194, 198
Wolf, Friedrich, 64
Wolf, Markus Johannes (Mischa),
    64
Wollweber, Ernst, 177, 178, 179,
    182, 191, 208
Wottke, Hannelore, 137

Yerochin, Hauptmann, 70

Zaisser, Wilhelm, 132, 142, 143,
    147–48, 157, 159, 173, 191, 208
Zhukov, Grigori, 56
Ziller, Gerhard, 177, 178, 191
Zuckmayer, Carl, 194